Smart Workflows with

A Step-by-Step Guide for Beginners

Kiet Huynh

Table of Contents

Introduction

1.1 What is Zapier and Why Use It?

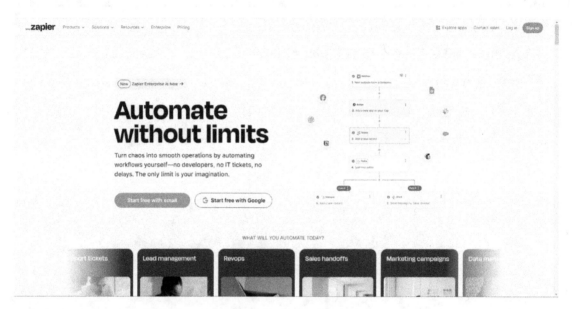

In today's fast-paced digital world, automation has become a key driver of productivity and efficiency. As businesses, freelancers, and professionals juggle multiple tasks across different software platforms, finding a way to streamline workflows is crucial. This is where **Zapier** comes in.

Zapier is a powerful online automation tool that connects your favorite apps and services, allowing them to work together seamlessly. By setting up automated workflows—called **Zaps**—Zapier eliminates repetitive tasks, saving you time and reducing manual effort. Whether you are an entrepreneur, a marketer, a project manager, or just someone looking to optimize personal productivity, Zapier can help you automate everyday workflows with ease.

In this section, we will explore:

- What Zapier is and how it works

- Why Zapier is useful for businesses and individuals

- How automation with Zapier can save time and improve efficiency

What is Zapier?

At its core, Zapier is a **no-code automation tool** that enables users to connect different apps without requiring programming knowledge. It acts as a bridge between applications, allowing them to communicate and perform automated actions based on predefined triggers.

For example, imagine you receive an email with an important attachment. Instead of manually downloading and saving it to Google Drive, Zapier can automatically detect the email, extract the attachment, and upload it to a designated folder—without you lifting a finger.

Key Components of Zapier

To better understand Zapier, let's break down its core components:

1. **Zap** – A workflow automation between two or more apps. Each Zap consists of a trigger and one or more actions.

2. **Trigger** – The event that starts a Zap. For example, receiving a new email in Gmail could be a trigger.

3. **Action** – The event that happens as a result of the trigger. For example, saving an email attachment to Dropbox.

4. **Multi-Step Zap** – A Zap that involves more than one action. For instance, when a new lead is added to your CRM, Zapier can automatically send a Slack message to your team and create a task in Trello.

5. **Filters** – Conditions that ensure a Zap only runs when certain criteria are met.

6. **Paths** – A way to create conditional logic in a Zap, allowing different outcomes based on set conditions.

7. **Webhooks** – A feature that allows you to send or receive data between apps that may not have a direct Zapier integration.

How Zapier Works

Zapier follows a **simple three-step process**:

1. **Choose a Trigger** – Select an app and specify an event that will start the automation.

2. **Define an Action** – Specify what should happen when the trigger event occurs.

3. **Test and Activate** – Run the Zap to ensure it works as expected, then turn it on to automate the workflow.

Zapier operates in the background, continuously monitoring your apps for new triggers and executing actions instantly. This eliminates the need for manual data entry and repetitive tasks.

Why Use Zapier?

Now that we understand what Zapier is and how it works, let's explore why it is a game-changer for businesses and professionals.

1. Saves Time and Reduces Manual Work

One of the biggest benefits of Zapier is automation. Instead of spending hours transferring data between apps or performing routine tasks, you can let Zapier handle it. This allows you to focus on more important work.

Example:
A content marketer might spend hours manually posting blog updates on social media. With Zapier, they can set up a workflow that automatically shares new blog posts on Twitter, LinkedIn, and Facebook, saving time and effort.

2. Increases Productivity

Zapier helps you create efficient workflows that keep tasks moving forward without interruptions. By automating key processes, you eliminate bottlenecks and improve overall productivity.

Example:
A sales team can automate lead management by creating a Zap that sends new customer inquiries from a website form directly to a CRM like HubSpot, while also notifying the sales rep via Slack.

3. Eliminates Human Error

Manual data entry is prone to mistakes. Zapier ensures accuracy and consistency by automating data transfers between applications.

Example:
An HR manager can use Zapier to automatically add new employee details from Google Forms to an Excel spreadsheet, reducing the risk of data entry errors.

4. Connects Thousands of Apps

Zapier supports over **5,000+ applications**, including popular tools like:

- Google Suite (Gmail, Google Drive, Google Sheets)

- Slack, Microsoft Teams, and Zoom

- Trello, Asana, Monday.com

- CRM tools like Salesforce and HubSpot

- E-commerce platforms like Shopify and WooCommerce

- Email marketing tools like Mailchimp and ConvertKit

This flexibility makes Zapier an invaluable tool for businesses of all sizes.

5. No Coding Required

Unlike traditional automation solutions that require coding or IT expertise, Zapier is a no-code platform. Anyone can set up and manage Zaps using its intuitive drag-and-drop interface.

Example:
A freelancer with no programming experience can create a Zap that automatically saves PayPal invoices to Google Drive for record-keeping.

6. Scales with Your Business

As businesses grow, workflows become more complex. Zapier supports multi-step automations, advanced logic (Paths), and integration with Webhooks to scale automation needs without additional resources.

Example:
A fast-growing e-commerce business can automate order processing, inventory updates, and customer follow-ups using Zapier.

7. Affordable for Individuals and Businesses

Zapier offers different pricing plans, including a **free plan** with basic automation capabilities. This makes it accessible to individuals, startups, and large enterprises alike.

Real-World Use Cases of Zapier

Zapier is widely used across various industries. Here are a few real-world examples:

1. Marketing Automation

- Automatically add new email subscribers to Mailchimp or ConvertKit
- Post new WordPress blogs to social media platforms
- Sync leads from Facebook Ads to a CRM like Salesforce

2. Sales and Customer Support

- Send instant Slack notifications when a new customer signs up
- Add Stripe or PayPal transactions to Google Sheets for tracking
- Create automated follow-up emails after a customer inquiry

3. Project Management

- Convert Trello cards into tasks in Asana
- Generate Slack reminders for upcoming deadlines
- Sync Google Calendar events with task management tools

4. Personal Productivity

- Save email attachments to Dropbox automatically
- Get Slack notifications for important emails
- Create automatic reminders based on Google Forms responses

Conclusion

Zapier is a powerful yet user-friendly automation tool that enables businesses and individuals to streamline their workflows. By connecting thousands of apps and automating repetitive tasks, Zapier saves time, reduces errors, and boosts efficiency—all without requiring coding knowledge.

In the next chapter, we will dive into the core concepts of Zapier, helping you build a strong foundation before creating your first automation.

1.2 Who This Book is For

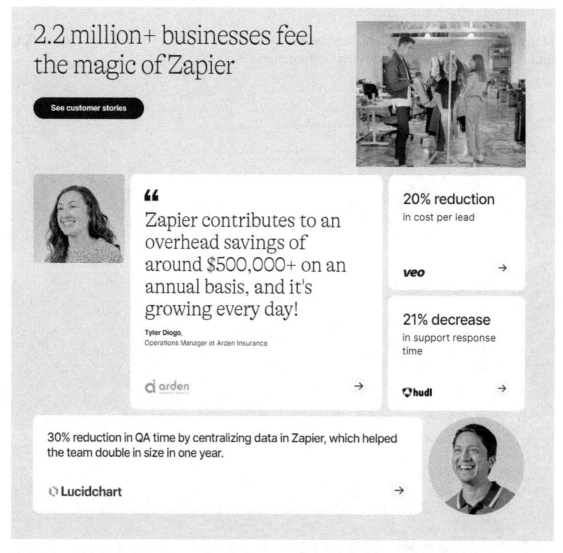

Zapier is a powerful automation tool designed to help individuals and businesses streamline their workflows by connecting different apps and services. However, if you are new to Zapier or automation in general, you might wonder whether this book is right for you.

This book, **"Smart Workflows with Zapier: A Step-by-Step Guide for Beginners,"** is written with a clear focus on helping people of all experience levels—especially beginners—understand and effectively use Zapier to automate their tasks. Whether you are a freelancer, small business owner, marketer, or someone looking to improve productivity, this book will guide you through the essential steps of using Zapier efficiently.

Who Can Benefit from This Book?

This book is structured in a way that makes it accessible to a wide range of users. Below are some of the primary audiences who will benefit from reading this guide.

1. Entrepreneurs and Small Business Owners

Running a business, especially a small one, often requires juggling multiple responsibilities, from managing emails to handling customer service and marketing campaigns. Entrepreneurs and small business owners can use Zapier to:

- Automate email responses to customer inquiries.

- Connect their CRM with email marketing platforms like Mailchimp.

- Auto-generate invoices and send payment reminders.

- Sync sales data between different platforms like Shopify and QuickBooks.

If you are a small business owner looking to save time and reduce manual data entry, this book will help you learn how to set up smart automation workflows that allow you to focus on growing your business rather than handling repetitive tasks.

2. Freelancers and Solopreneurs

Freelancers often work independently, managing everything from project acquisition to invoicing. If you are a freelancer, Zapier can help you:

- Automatically save email attachments to Google Drive or Dropbox.

- Track work hours and send invoices using integration with tools like Toggl and QuickBooks.

- Get notified instantly about new client inquiries from websites or social media.

- Schedule social media posts without manual intervention.

This book will provide you with the necessary knowledge to automate various aspects of your freelancing work, so you can spend more time on high-value tasks and less on administrative work.

3. Digital Marketers and Social Media Managers

Marketing professionals often deal with multiple platforms and data sources, making automation a key factor in staying efficient. With Zapier, marketers can:

- Automate lead capture by integrating contact forms with CRMs.
- Schedule and automate social media posts across platforms.
- Track marketing campaign performance by syncing data with Google Sheets or analytics tools.
- Send automated follow-ups to potential leads and customers.

If you are in digital marketing, this book will teach you how to create smart workflows to eliminate manual tasks and optimize your campaigns more effectively.

4. Customer Support and Sales Teams

For businesses that rely on strong customer relationships, providing quick and efficient responses to inquiries is crucial. Zapier can help customer support and sales teams:

- Automate ticket creation and assignment in helpdesk software.
- Sync new customer inquiries with CRM tools.
- Send personalized responses and follow-ups.
- Create notifications for high-priority customer requests.

By learning how to use Zapier effectively, customer support and sales professionals can spend less time on manual processes and more time building meaningful customer relationships.

5. Project Managers and Team Leaders

Managing multiple projects and coordinating team efforts can be challenging. Zapier can help project managers and team leaders by:

- Syncing tasks between project management tools like Trello, Asana, and ClickUp.
- Automatically updating team members about project status changes.

- Logging team activities in a shared Google Sheet.

- Sending automated reminders for upcoming deadlines.

If you are a project manager looking for ways to improve collaboration and efficiency, this book will help you leverage Zapier to simplify your workflow.

6. Developers and Tech Enthusiasts

Even though Zapier is primarily designed for users with no coding experience, developers and tech-savvy users can still benefit from its advanced features. With Zapier, developers can:

- Use Webhooks to send data between custom applications.

- Automate API calls to fetch or push data.

- Create complex, multi-step automation workflows.

- Reduce redundant development work by integrating tools without writing additional code.

This book will introduce basic and advanced Zapier features, making it useful for tech professionals who want to streamline their workflow.

7. Students and Educators

Students and educators can also use Zapier to enhance their productivity. Some useful applications include:

- Automatically saving class notes and assignments to Google Drive.

- Syncing calendar events with to-do list apps for better task management.

- Sending automatic reminders for deadlines and exams.

- Collecting and organizing survey responses in Google Sheets.

If you are an educator or student looking for ways to manage tasks and information more efficiently, this book will show you how to use Zapier effectively.

Why This Book is Different

There are many guides and tutorials on Zapier, but this book is designed with **step-by-step instructions**, **real-world use cases**, and **practical examples** to ensure that you:

- Gain a **solid understanding** of Zapier's features and functionality.

- Learn **how to set up and manage workflows** effectively.

- Understand **best practices and troubleshooting tips** for optimizing automation.

- Discover **useful Zapier integrations** for different industries and roles.

Whether you are a complete beginner or someone looking to refine your automation skills, this book will provide **a clear roadmap** to help you master Zapier in the most efficient way possible.

What You Will Learn in This Book

By reading this book, you will:

✓ Understand the **core concepts** of Zapier and how automation works.

✓ Learn how to **create and manage Zaps** step by step.

✓ Discover **time-saving integrations** that can optimize your workflow.

✓ Gain insights into **troubleshooting common issues** and improving efficiency.

✓ Explore **real-world case studies** that demonstrate Zapier's capabilities.

If you are ready to **work smarter, save time, and boost productivity**, this book will be your ultimate guide to mastering Zapier.

1.3 How to Use This Book

To get the most out of this book, it's essential to understand its structure, how to approach the content, and how to apply what you learn effectively. In this section, we will outline the organization of the book, the best way to navigate it, and how to integrate the lessons into your daily workflow.

Who Should Read This Book?

This book is for anyone looking to automate repetitive tasks and improve productivity with Zapier. You don't need any coding knowledge or prior experience with automation tools—this book is written specifically for beginners. Here are some types of readers who will benefit the most:

- **Freelancers** who want to streamline invoicing, email responses, and project management.

- **Entrepreneurs and small business owners** looking to automate marketing, sales, and customer support processes.

- **Marketers** who want to integrate social media, email campaigns, and analytics tools effortlessly.

- **Project managers** needing to automate task assignments, notifications, and data tracking.

- **HR professionals** looking to automate recruitment, onboarding, and employee management tasks.

- **Students and professionals** eager to learn no-code automation and improve their workflows.

If you find yourself performing repetitive manual tasks, this book will show you how to automate them efficiently using Zapier.

How This Book is Structured

This book is divided into several chapters, each focusing on a key aspect of using Zapier. It follows a logical progression, starting with the basics and gradually moving toward more advanced features. Here's an overview of how the book is structured:

Introduction

- This section gives you an overview of Zapier, its benefits, and why automation is important.

- It also explains who this book is for and how to get the most out of it.

Chapter 1: Getting Started with Zapier

- This chapter introduces the core concepts of Zapier, including what Zaps are, how Triggers and Actions work, and the possibilities of multi-step Zaps.

- It also guides you through setting up a Zapier account, navigating the dashboard, and connecting your first app.

- You'll learn about Zapier's pricing plans and how to choose the best one for your needs.

Chapter 2: Creating Your First Zap

- This chapter walks you through building your first Zap, from selecting a trigger app to configuring actions.

- You will also learn how to test, modify, and manage Zaps effectively.

Chapter 3: Exploring Popular Zapier Integrations

- This chapter covers real-world use cases and showcases how Zapier integrates with popular tools like Gmail, Slack, Trello, Google Calendar, Shopify, and more.

- You will learn how to automate email workflows, streamline project management, and boost productivity.

Chapter 4: Advanced Zapier Features

- This chapter introduces more advanced concepts, such as multi-step Zaps, conditional logic, and using webhooks.

- It also covers how to use Zapier's Formatter tool to clean and structure data for better automation.

Chapter 5: Troubleshooting and Best Practices

- Here, you'll learn how to troubleshoot common Zapier issues, optimize performance, and ensure your workflows run smoothly.

- This chapter also includes security and privacy considerations when using Zapier.

Chapter 6: Real-World Zapier Use Cases

- This chapter provides real-life case studies of how individuals and businesses use Zapier to automate tasks.

- You'll see examples of how freelancers, small businesses, and remote teams leverage Zapier to improve their efficiency.

Conclusion

- The final chapter recaps key takeaways and provides guidance on what to do next.

- You'll find additional resources and communities where you can continue learning.

Each chapter builds upon the previous one, so it's recommended to read them in order. However, if you already have some experience with Zapier, you can jump to the sections that interest you the most.

How to Apply What You Learn

Learning about Zapier is only valuable if you put it into practice. Here's how you can make the most of this book:

1. **Follow Along with the Examples**

   o Each chapter includes step-by-step tutorials to help you create real Zaps.

   o Try replicating the examples in your own Zapier account as you read.

2. **Experiment with Your Own Workflows**

   o Once you understand the basics, think about the repetitive tasks in your own work.

   o Use Zapier to automate those tasks and customize workflows to fit your needs.

3. **Take Notes and Bookmark Key Sections**

   ○ Highlight important sections and make notes on how certain features apply to your workflow.

   ○ Use bookmarks to quickly revisit tutorials and troubleshooting steps.

4. **Test and Optimize Your Zaps**

   ○ After creating a Zap, monitor its performance in Zapier's task history.

   ○ Make adjustments to improve efficiency and avoid unnecessary task usage.

5. **Join the Zapier Community**

   ○ Connect with other Zapier users through forums, social media groups, and official Zapier resources.

   ○ Learning from other users can provide valuable insights and inspiration.

Additional Resources for Learning Zapier

While this book covers everything you need to get started, learning is an ongoing process. Here are some additional resources to deepen your knowledge:

- **Zapier Help Center** – Official documentation with detailed guides and troubleshooting tips.

- **Zapier Blog** – Regular updates, case studies, and advanced automation ideas.

- **Zapier Community Forum** – A place to ask questions and learn from other users.

- **YouTube Tutorials** – Many creators share step-by-step video guides on using Zapier.

- **Online Courses** – Platforms like Udemy and Coursera offer Zapier courses for deeper learning.

Final Words

Zapier is a powerful tool that can revolutionize the way you work. By automating repetitive tasks, you can save time, reduce errors, and focus on what truly matters. This book will guide you through every step, from setting up your first Zap to mastering advanced automation techniques.

Now that you know how to use this book effectively, it's time to dive into Chapter 1 and start your journey toward automation mastery!

CHAPTER I
Getting Started with Zapier

2.1 Understanding Zapier's Core Concepts

2.1.1 What is a Zap?

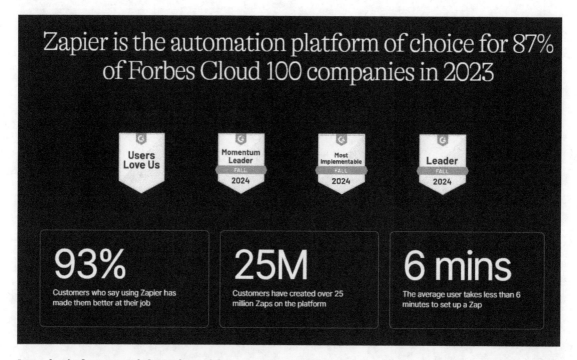

In today's fast-paced digital world, automation has become an essential tool for improving efficiency and productivity. Businesses, entrepreneurs, and individuals are constantly looking for ways to streamline repetitive tasks, reduce manual work, and ensure seamless integration between their favorite apps and services. This is where **Zapier** comes in—a powerful no-code automation tool that allows users to connect different applications and create automated workflows.

At the heart of Zapier's automation system lies the **Zap**—a fundamental unit of workflow automation that enables users to connect two or more applications and execute tasks automatically. In this section, we will explore the concept of a **Zap**, how it works, its components, and why it is a game-changer for workflow automation.

What Exactly is a Zap?

A **Zap** is an automated workflow in Zapier that links two or more apps to perform specific tasks without manual intervention. Each Zap consists of a **Trigger** (an event that starts the workflow) and one or more **Actions** (the tasks that Zapier performs based on the trigger event).

For example, suppose you receive customer inquiries via a Google Form and want them to be automatically added to a Trello board for your support team to follow up. With Zapier, you can create a Zap that:

- **Trigger:** A new response is submitted in Google Forms.
- **Action:** Zapier creates a new Trello card with the details of the form submission.

This means that every time someone submits a response, a new card is automatically created in Trello—saving you the time of doing it manually.

Zaps can be as simple as linking two apps for a single task, or as complex as integrating multiple apps with conditional logic, delays, filters, and formatted data processing.

Key Components of a Zap

A Zap consists of three primary components:

1. Triggers

A **Trigger** is an event that initiates the Zap. Whenever this event occurs in the selected app, Zapier detects it and proceeds to execute the workflow.

How Triggers Work:

- You define a specific action in an app that will serve as the starting point.

- When the event happens, Zapier captures the data from the trigger app.

- The Zap then proceeds to perform the next steps.

Examples of Triggers:

- A new email arrives in Gmail.

- A new row is added to a Google Sheet.

- A new subscriber is added to a Mailchimp list.

- A new sale is recorded in Shopify.

Triggers determine when the Zap will run, making them the foundation of every automated workflow.

2. Actions

An **Action** is the task that Zapier performs after detecting a trigger event. This is the automated response to the trigger and can involve a wide range of activities across various apps.

How Actions Work:

- Once the Zap is triggered, it executes the action(s) based on predefined settings.

- Data from the trigger app is transferred to the action app according to the setup.

- If multiple actions are defined, they are executed in sequence.

Examples of Actions:

- Creating a new contact in HubSpot when a new lead is captured.

- Sending a Slack notification when a Google Calendar event is scheduled.

- Posting a Tweet when a new blog post is published.

- Adding a row to a Google Sheet when a payment is received in PayPal.

Actions allow users to create workflows that eliminate the need for repetitive manual tasks.

3. Task Execution

A **Task** is an individual action performed within a Zap. Each time a Zap runs, it consumes one or more tasks depending on the number of actions it completes.

Task Consumption Examples:

- If your Zap is triggered by a new email in Gmail and the action is to create a new Trello card, this Zap will consume **one task per email received**.

- If your Zap has multiple actions (e.g., sending an email, updating a spreadsheet, and posting to Slack), each action will consume a separate task.

Understanding task usage is important when selecting a Zapier pricing plan, as free plans have a monthly task limit.

Types of Zaps

Zapier provides different types of Zaps to accommodate various automation needs:

1. Single-Step Zaps

A **Single-Step Zap** is the simplest form of automation, consisting of only one trigger and one action. This type of Zap is available for free-tier users and is ideal for basic automation needs.

Example:

- Trigger: A new email arrives in Gmail.

- Action: The email's details are saved to a Google Sheet.

This straightforward automation is great for beginners who want to get started with Zapier without dealing with complex configurations.

2. Multi-Step Zaps

A **Multi-Step Zap** involves multiple actions following a single trigger. This allows for more sophisticated workflows and is available on Zapier's paid plans.

Example:

- Trigger: A new order is placed in Shopify.

- Action 1: An invoice is created in QuickBooks.

- Action 2: A confirmation email is sent via Gmail.

- Action 3: The order details are added to a Google Sheet.

Multi-Step Zaps enable users to automate entire workflows without manual intervention.

3. Zaps with Filters and Paths

Advanced users can create Zaps with **Filters** and **Paths** to add logic-based conditions to their automation.

- **Filters** ensure that a Zap only runs when certain conditions are met.

- **Paths** allow a Zap to take different actions based on input data (similar to IF-THEN logic).

Example with a Path:

- Trigger: A new lead is added to a CRM.

- Path 1 (IF lead is from the US): Send an email via Mailchimp.

- Path 2 (IF lead is from Europe): Add to a different mailing list.

These features allow for customized automation that adapts to different scenarios.

Why Zaps are a Game-Changer for Productivity

Using Zaps in Zapier offers several benefits:

✓ **Time-Saving:** Eliminates repetitive tasks and manual data entry.
✓ **Error Reduction:** Minimizes human errors in workflow processes.
✓ **Scalability:** Allows businesses to automate growing workloads effortlessly.
✓ **No Coding Required:** Enables non-technical users to create complex automations.
✓ **Seamless Integrations:** Connects with thousands of apps to unify workflows.

By leveraging Zaps, individuals and businesses can focus on strategic work rather than spending hours on routine administrative tasks.

Conclusion

A **Zap** is the building block of automation in Zapier, enabling users to connect different apps and automate workflows effortlessly. Understanding its core components—**Triggers, Actions, and Tasks**—is essential for creating effective automations. Whether using simple single-step Zaps or complex multi-step workflows with conditional logic, Zapier empowers users to save time, increase efficiency, and streamline their processes with ease.

2.1.2 Triggers and Actions Explained

Understanding the Foundation of Automation in Zapier

Zapier operates on a simple but powerful principle: automating tasks between different apps. The core of this automation is built on two fundamental components: **Triggers** and **Actions**. These two elements define how information moves between applications and what happens when specific events occur.

To effectively use Zapier, understanding **how Triggers and Actions work** is crucial. In this chapter, we will break down these two components, explore their roles, and provide real-world examples to help you implement them successfully.

What Are Triggers?

A **Trigger** is an event that starts an automation in Zapier. Think of it as a starting point that signals Zapier to take action. When a Trigger event occurs in one app, Zapier automatically initiates a workflow (called a **Zap**) and executes predefined Actions based on the event.

How Triggers Work

1. **A change happens in an app** → Example: A new email arrives in your inbox.

2. **Zapier detects the change** → Zapier continuously monitors the app for new activity.

3. **Zapier starts the automation** → The detected event **triggers** a predefined workflow, executing an Action in another app.

Types of Triggers in Zapier

Triggers can be categorized into different types based on how they detect changes in apps:

1. Polling Triggers

- Zapier periodically checks an app for new data (e.g., every 5 or 15 minutes).

- If new data is found, the Zap starts running.

- **Example:** A Zap that triggers when a new row is added to a Google Sheet.

2. Instant Triggers

- These are real-time Triggers that execute the moment an event occurs.

- They use webhooks, meaning they push data to Zapier instantly.

- **Example:** Receiving a Slack message notification when someone submits a form on your website.

3. Scheduled Triggers

- These run at predefined times rather than responding to real-time events.

- **Example:** Sending a daily summary email with recent sales data.

Examples of Common Triggers

- **Gmail:** "New Email in Inbox" triggers a Zap.

- **Google Drive:** "New File Added" starts an automation.

- **Trello:** "New Card Created" initiates an Action.

- **Calendly:** "New Scheduled Meeting" triggers a follow-up email.

- **WooCommerce:** "New Order Placed" updates a customer database.

What Are Actions?

An **Action** is what Zapier does **after** a Trigger occurs. Once an event activates a Trigger, the Zap performs an **Action** in another app to complete the automation.

How Actions Work

1. **Zapier receives data from the Trigger app** → Example: A new email arrives.

2. **Zapier sends the data to the Action app** → Example: The email details are passed to Trello.

3. **The Action executes a predefined task** → Example: A new Trello card is created from the email content.

Types of Actions in Zapier

Just like Triggers, Actions vary in how they execute tasks:

1. Basic Actions

- Standard actions that occur after a Trigger.
- **Example:** "Create a new row in Google Sheets" after receiving a new email.

2. Search Actions

- These look for specific data in an app before performing the next step.
- **Example:** Searching for an existing contact in HubSpot before adding a new entry.

3. Update Actions

- Modify existing data in an app rather than creating new entries.
- **Example:** Updating an existing lead's status in a CRM.

Examples of Common Actions

- **Google Sheets:** "Add a New Row" in response to a form submission.
- **Slack:** "Send a Message" when a Trello task is updated.
- **Mailchimp:** "Add Subscriber to List" after someone registers for an event.
- **Dropbox:** "Upload a File" from an email attachment.
- **Salesforce:** "Update a Record" when a customer completes a purchase.

Triggers and Actions in Multi-Step Zaps

Basic Zaps consist of **one Trigger and one Action**, but you can create **Multi-Step Zaps** that perform multiple Actions based on a single Trigger.

Example of a Multi-Step Zap:

- ◆ **Trigger:** A new order is placed in Shopify.
- ◆ **Action 1:** Add the customer's details to a Google Sheet.
- ◆ **Action 2:** Send an email confirmation via Gmail.
- ◆ **Action 3:** Notify the sales team on Slack.

Using Multi-Step Zaps, you can build **more complex automations** and eliminate repetitive tasks in your workflow.

Best Practices for Using Triggers and Actions

✅ Choose the Right Trigger for Your Needs

- If you need real-time responses, use **Instant Triggers** (e.g., Webhooks).

- If periodic updates are fine, use **Polling Triggers** (e.g., Google Sheets).

✅ Optimize Your Actions to Reduce Task Usage

- Some Actions consume more tasks (which count toward Zapier's usage limits).

- Example: Instead of sending multiple Slack messages, create a single summary message.

✅ Test Your Triggers and Actions Before Activation

- Always run **test Zaps** to ensure they work correctly before going live.

✅ Use Filters to Fine-Tune Triggers

- Filters allow you to **control when a Zap runs**, avoiding unnecessary automations.

- Example: Only trigger an action **if an email contains a specific keyword**.

✅ Monitor Your Zap History for Errors

- Check the **Zap History** section in Zapier to troubleshoot failed tasks.

- Common issues include incorrect app connections or missing data.

Conclusion

Triggers and Actions are the **building blocks of Zapier automations**. By understanding how they work, you can create **efficient, error-free workflows** that save time and boost productivity.

Key Takeaways:

✔ A **Trigger** is the event that starts an automation.

✔ An **Action** is the task performed after the Trigger occurs.

✔ Zapier supports **Instant, Polling, and Scheduled Triggers**.

✔ Multi-Step Zaps allow for **complex workflows** with multiple Actions.

✔ Best practices include **optimizing Actions, testing Zaps, and using filters**.

2.1.3 Multi-Step Zaps and Paths

Zapier is a powerful automation tool that allows users to connect different apps and services to automate workflows. While single-step Zaps are useful, **multi-step Zaps** and **Paths** take automation to the next level, enabling users to build more complex, dynamic workflows tailored to specific needs.

In this section, we will explore what multi-step Zaps and Paths are, how they work, and how you can use them to create more advanced automations.

1. What Are Multi-Step Zaps?

A **multi-step Zap** is a workflow in Zapier that involves more than one action after a trigger event occurs. While a basic Zap consists of a single trigger and a single action, a multi-step Zap allows for multiple actions to be performed in sequence.

For example, a **single-step Zap** might take a new email in Gmail (trigger) and save the attachment to Google Drive (action).

A **multi-step Zap**, on the other hand, could:

1. Detect a new email in Gmail (trigger).

2. Save the attachment to Google Drive (action 1).

3. Send a Slack notification to your team about the new file (action 2).

4. Log the email details in a Google Sheet (action 3).

1.1 Benefits of Multi-Step Zaps

- **Increased Efficiency** – Automate multiple processes at once, reducing manual work.

- **Better Integration** – Connect more than two apps to create seamless workflows.

- **Customization** – Add filters, conditions, and formatting to refine automation.

- **Scalability** – Create workflows that handle more complex business tasks.

1.2 How to Create a Multi-Step Zap

To create a multi-step Zap in Zapier, follow these steps:

Step 1: Set Up a Trigger

- Choose an app to trigger the Zap (e.g., Gmail).

- Select a trigger event (e.g., "New Email with Attachment").

- Connect your account and configure the trigger details.

Step 2: Add Multiple Actions

- After setting up the trigger, click **"+ Add Action"** to add additional steps.

- Choose the next app (e.g., Google Drive), set up the action (e.g., "Upload File").

- Repeat the process to add more actions as needed.

Step 3: Test and Activate the Zap

- Run tests to ensure each step functions correctly.

- Once verified, turn on the Zap, and it will start running automatically.

2. What Are Paths in Zapier?

While multi-step Zaps follow a linear sequence, **Paths** allow for conditional branching based on specific criteria. This means different actions can be executed depending on the data received from the trigger.

For example, suppose you receive new support tickets from a web form. A Zap with **Paths** could:

- Route **high-priority** tickets to Slack.

- Send **medium-priority** tickets to a Google Sheet.

- Email **low-priority** tickets to a customer support inbox.

Each path acts like an "if/then" rule, enabling more dynamic and tailored workflows.

2.1 When to Use Paths?

Paths are useful when you need different outcomes based on conditions, such as:

- **Lead management** – Route leads based on source (e.g., website vs. referral).

- **Customer service** – Handle support requests differently based on priority.

- **Project management** – Assign tasks based on department or team member.

2.2 How to Set Up Paths in Zapier

Step 1: Create a Zap with a Trigger

- Select a trigger app and event (e.g., form submission).

- Configure the trigger details.

Step 2: Add a Paths Step

- Click **"+ Add a Step"** and select **Paths**.

- Zapier will create **Path A** and **Path B** by default.

Step 3: Define Conditions for Each Path

- Set criteria for each path (e.g., "If priority is high, then notify Slack").

- Add different actions for each path.

Step 4: Test and Activate

- Test to ensure each path follows the expected logic.

- Turn on the Zap once everything is working correctly.

3. Multi-Step Zaps vs. Paths: When to Use Each

Feature	Multi-Step Zaps	Paths
Purpose	Linear automation with multiple actions	Conditional branching based on rules
Use Case	Send an email, update a CRM, and notify Slack	Route high-priority leads to sales and low-priority leads to marketing
Complexity	Simple to medium workflows	Advanced, logic-based workflows
Flexibility	Fixed sequence of actions	Dynamic actions based on conditions

If your workflow requires **a series of actions** that always follow the same order, **multi-step Zaps** are best. If you need **conditional logic** where different conditions trigger different actions, **Paths** are the way to go.

4. Best Practices for Multi-Step Zaps and Paths

Keep Zaps Organized

- Use clear names for each Zap to easily identify its function.

- Use **folders** to group related Zaps.

Optimize for Performance

- Limit unnecessary steps to reduce Zap execution time.

- Use **filters** to prevent triggering unneeded Zaps.

Monitor and Debug Regularly

- Check Zap history to track errors and troubleshoot issues.

- Set up error notifications to stay informed.

Test Before Deployment

- Always test Zaps before activating to ensure accuracy.
- Adjust conditions in Paths to avoid logic conflicts.

5. Real-World Examples

Example 1: Automating Sales Follow-Ups

A **multi-step Zap** could:

1. Capture new leads from Facebook Ads (trigger).
2. Add lead details to a CRM like HubSpot (action 1).
3. Send a welcome email via Gmail (action 2).
4. Assign a task in Asana for the sales team (action 3).

Example 2: Handling Support Tickets with Paths

A **Path-based Zap** could:

- If the ticket is "urgent," send a Slack alert to the support team.
- If the ticket is "medium priority," log it in a Google Sheet.
- If the ticket is "low priority," send a canned email response.

Conclusion

Multi-step Zaps and Paths are essential for creating **advanced, efficient workflows** in Zapier. While **multi-step Zaps** allow you to automate multiple actions in a sequence, **Paths** enable conditional branching, making your automations smarter and more dynamic.

By mastering these features, you can streamline complex business processes, save time, and enhance productivity. In the next chapter, we'll guide you through setting up your Zapier account and connecting your first apps!

2.2 Setting Up Your Zapier Account

2.2.1 Creating an Account and Logging In

Introduction to Creating a Zapier Account

Before you can start automating tasks with Zapier, you need to create an account. Setting up an account is a straightforward process, and in this section, we will walk you through each step in detail. By the end of this section, you will have a fully functional Zapier account and be ready to explore automation possibilities.

Zapier offers both **free and paid plans**, so you can start with a free account and upgrade later if needed. You only need an email address or a Google/Microsoft account to sign up.

Step 1: Navigating to the Zapier Website

To create a Zapier account, follow these steps:

1. **Open your web browser** – You can use Google Chrome, Mozilla Firefox, Microsoft Edge, or Safari.

2. **Go to the Zapier homepage** – Type https://zapier.com in the address bar and press **Enter**.

3. **Click on "Sign Up"** – At the top right corner of the homepage, you will see a "Sign Up" button. Click on it to begin the registration process.

Step 2: Choosing a Sign-Up Method

Zapier provides multiple ways to sign up. You can use:

- **An email address** (requires creating a password)

- **A Google account** (faster login with your existing Google credentials)

- **A Microsoft account** (useful for Outlook and Office 365 users)

- **A Facebook account** (optional but available)

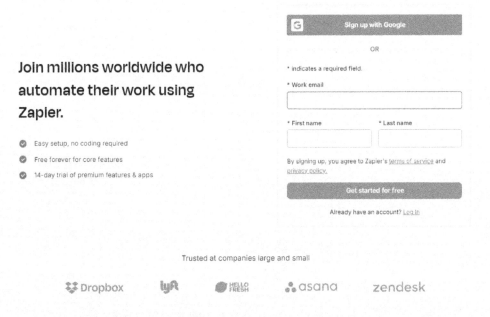

Signing Up with an Email Address

1. On the sign-up page, enter your **email address** in the provided field.

2. Create a **strong password** (at least 8 characters, including uppercase, lowercase, and numbers).

3. Click **"Sign Up"** to proceed.

4. You will receive a **verification email** from Zapier. Open your email inbox and click the verification link.

5. Once verified, you will be redirected to the Zapier dashboard.

Signing Up with Google, Microsoft, or Facebook

1. Click the respective **Google, Microsoft, or Facebook** button.

2. A pop-up window will appear asking for account access permission.

3. Choose the account you want to connect with Zapier.

4. Grant necessary permissions and complete the sign-up process.

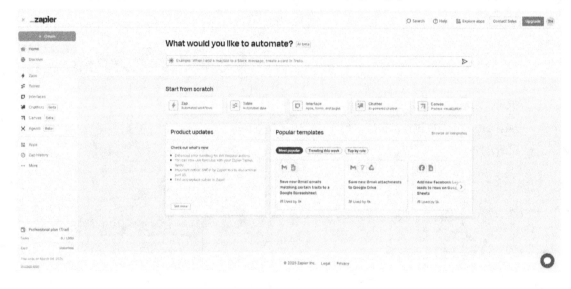

Step 3: Setting Up Your Profile

Once you've signed up, Zapier will guide you through a few initial setup steps:

Providing Basic Information

1. You may be asked to enter your **name** and set a **profile picture** (optional).

2. Zapier may ask what type of automation you are interested in (e.g., Marketing, Sales, Productivity, etc.).

3. Select the category that best describes your needs (you can change this later).

Selecting Your Role and Industry (Optional)

Zapier may ask for additional details such as:

- Your **job role** (e.g., Freelancer, Small Business Owner, IT Manager).
- Your **industry** (e.g., Marketing, Finance, Education).

These details help Zapier suggest relevant automation workflows for you.

Step 4: Logging into Your Zapier Account

Once your account is created, you can **log in** anytime by following these steps:

1. **Go to the Zapier homepage** (https://zapier.com).
2. **Click on "Log In"** at the top right corner of the page.
3. Enter your **email and password**, or log in using **Google/Microsoft/Facebook**.
4. Click **"Log In"**, and you will be redirected to your **Zapier dashboard**.

Step 5: Exploring the Zapier Dashboard

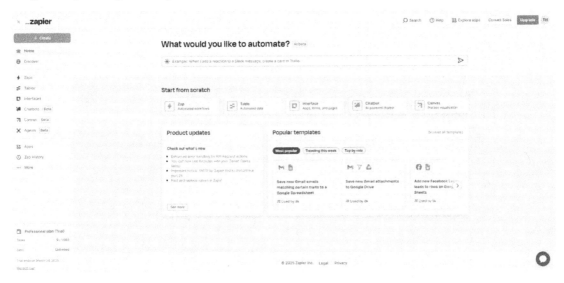

After logging in, you will land on the **Zapier Dashboard**. This is where you will create and manage Zaps.

Main Components of the Dashboard

1. **Home Tab** – Shows recent activities, suggested workflows, and your created Zaps.

2. **Zaps Tab** – A list of all your active and inactive Zaps.

3. **Explore Tab** – Discover pre-made automation templates.

4. **Apps Tab** – View all the apps Zapier can integrate with.

5. **Settings Tab** – Manage your account, billing, and connected apps.

Step 6: Securing Your Zapier Account

Setting Up Two-Factor Authentication (2FA)

For added security, enable **Two-Factor Authentication (2FA)**:

1. Go to **Settings** in the top right corner.

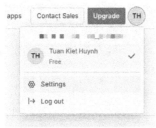

2. Click **Security Settings**.

3. Enable **2FA** and follow the instructions to connect it to your phone.

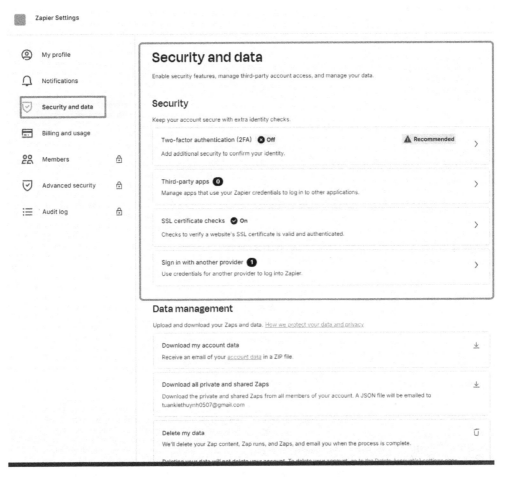

Managing Connected Apps

To review and manage the apps linked to Zapier:

1. Go to **Settings > Third-party apps.**

2. Remove or reauthorize any integrations as needed.

Step 7: Troubleshooting Common Sign-Up Issues

If you encounter issues while signing up or logging in, try these solutions:

1. Didn't Receive Verification Email?

- Check your **Spam/Junk folder**.

- Resend the email from the Zapier sign-up page.

- Ensure you entered the correct email address.

2. Forgot Your Password?

- Click on **"Forgot Password"** on the login page.

- Enter your registered email and follow the reset instructions.

3. Issues with Google/Microsoft/Facebook Login?

- Ensure your third-party account is active.

- Try logging in with an email instead.

Final Thoughts

Congratulations! 🎉 You now have a fully functional Zapier account and can log in anytime. In the next section, we will explore how to **navigate the Zapier dashboard** and **connect your first app** to start automating tasks effortlessly.

2.2.2 Navigating the Zapier Dashboard

Once you've created your Zapier account and logged in, the first thing you'll see is the **Zapier Dashboard**. The dashboard is your central hub for managing automations, connecting apps, and monitoring activity. In this section, we will explore the different components of the Zapier Dashboard, explaining their functions and how you can use them to create and manage your workflows efficiently.

1. Overview of the Zapier Dashboard

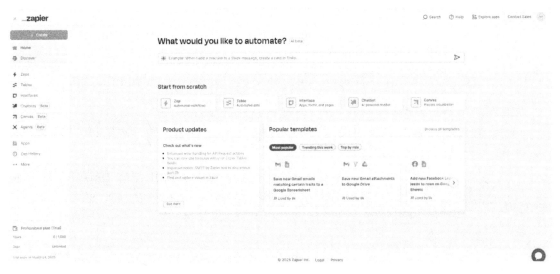

The Zapier Dashboard is designed to be user-friendly and intuitive. The main sections of the dashboard include:

- **Navigation Bar (Left Sidebar)** – Provides access to key features like "Zaps," "Apps," "Explore," and "Settings."

- **Main Workspace (Center Panel)** – Displays recent Zaps, templates, and recommendations.

- **Top Bar (Header)** – Contains search functionality and account settings.

Understanding how these sections work will help you quickly access the tools you need to automate your tasks.

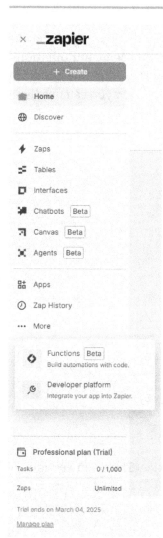

2. Exploring the Navigation Bar

The **Navigation Bar** is located on the left side of the screen and contains the following key options:

2.1 Zaps

This section is where you can create and manage all your Zaps. When you click on "Zaps," you'll see:

- **Your existing Zaps** – A list of all the automated workflows you have created.

- **Search and filter options** – Helps you find specific Zaps based on name, date, or status.

- **Create a new Zap** – A button to start building a new automation.

Each Zap in the list has a **status indicator** (on/off), an **edit button**, and an **activity log** showing recent executions.

2.2 Apps

The "Apps" section is where you manage your app integrations. Here, you can:

- Browse and search for apps that you want to connect to Zapier.

- See a list of all the apps you've connected.

- Remove or update app connections.

If an app requires authentication (such as Google Drive or Slack), you can manage credentials here.

2.3 Explore

The "Explore" section helps you find **pre-made Zap templates** and automation ideas. This is useful if you're not sure where to start or want inspiration for common use cases. You can:

- Search for templates based on the apps you use.

- Browse featured workflows.

- View popular integrations by category (e.g., marketing, sales, finance).

2.4 Transfer

Zapier's **Transfer** feature allows you to move data between apps in bulk. Unlike regular Zaps, which automate ongoing processes, **Transfer** is used for one-time data migrations.

For example, you could use Transfer to:

- Migrate customer data from a spreadsheet into a CRM.

- Move old email contacts into a marketing tool.

- Sync historical records between apps.

2.5 My Apps

"My Apps" is a subsection where you can manage all the apps connected to your account. You can:

- Reauthorize apps if a connection expires.

- Add new integrations.

- Remove unused apps.

Managing app permissions properly is crucial for security and efficiency.

2.6 Settings

The "Settings" section allows you to configure your account preferences. You can:

- Update your **account details** (name, email, password).

- Manage **billing and subscription plans**.

- Configure **security settings** like two-factor authentication (2FA).

It's important to review your settings periodically to ensure everything is optimized.

3. Exploring the Main Workspace

The **Main Workspace** (center panel of the dashboard) is where you interact with your Zaps and find automation suggestions.

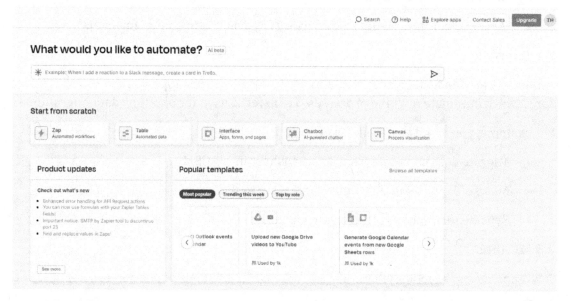

3.1 Recent Zaps

At the top of the workspace, you'll see a list of your **most recently edited Zaps**. This section allows quick access to workflows you frequently modify.

Each Zap card includes:

- **Zap name** – A clickable link to edit the Zap.

- **Last run time** – Shows when the Zap was last triggered.

- **Status toggle** – Allows you to enable or disable the Zap.

3.2 Recommended Workflows

Below your recent Zaps, Zapier suggests **recommended templates** based on the apps you've connected. These are pre-built automations that help you get started faster.

3.3 Search Bar

The search function at the top of the workspace lets you quickly find specific Zaps, apps, or templates by typing keywords.

3.4 Create a Zap Button

The bright "Create a Zap" button allows you to start building a new automation from scratch. Clicking this opens the **Zap Editor**, where you can configure triggers and actions.

4. Exploring the Top Bar (Header Section)

The **Top Bar** is a small but important section that provides quick access to essential tools. It includes:

4.1 Account Menu

Located in the top-right corner, this menu allows you to:

- Access **settings** and **billing details**.
- Switch between different Zapier accounts.
- Log out securely.

4.2 Help & Support

Clicking the "Help" icon provides access to:

- Zapier's **Help Center** (guides, FAQs, troubleshooting tips).
- **Live chat support** (available for paid plans).
- **Community forums** where users share tips and solutions.

4.3 Task Usage & Plan Details

Zapier limits the number of automated tasks you can run per month based on your plan. In the top-right corner, you can view:

- **Your current task usage** (e.g., "1,200 of 2,000 tasks used").

- **Upgrade prompts** if you are approaching your limit.

Monitoring this ensures you don't unexpectedly run out of automation capacity.

5. Customizing Your Dashboard Experience

Zapier allows some customization to improve your user experience:

5.1 Organizing Zaps with Folders

If you have many Zaps, organizing them into **folders** helps maintain a clean workspace. You can:

- Create new folders for different departments or projects.

- Move Zaps between folders.

- Filter Zaps by folder in the sidebar.

5.2 Pinning Frequently Used Apps

In the "My Apps" section, you can **pin frequently used apps** for quick access. This is useful if you rely heavily on certain tools like Google Sheets, Slack, or Trello.

5.3 Adjusting Notifications

Zapier can send notifications for:

- **Failed Zaps** (useful for troubleshooting).

- **Billing reminders** (to avoid service interruptions).

- **New feature updates**.

You can enable or disable notifications in the **Settings** menu.

Conclusion

Navigating the Zapier Dashboard effectively is crucial to maximizing your automation experience. By understanding each section—**Navigation Bar, Main Workspace, and Top Bar**—you'll be able to:

✓ Quickly access and manage your Zaps.

✓ Connect and monitor app integrations.

✓ Optimize your workflow for better productivity.

2.2.3 Connecting Your First App

Once you have created a Zapier account and familiarized yourself with the dashboard, the next crucial step is connecting your first app. Zapier allows you to integrate thousands of popular apps, enabling them to work together seamlessly without requiring any coding. This section will guide you through the process of linking an app to Zapier, setting up permissions, and ensuring a successful connection.

1. Understanding App Connections in Zapier

Zapier acts as a bridge between different applications, allowing them to communicate and share data automatically. When you connect an app to Zapier, you are essentially granting it permission to access data and perform actions on your behalf.

How Zapier Connects to Apps

Zapier connects to apps in three primary ways:

1. **API Integrations** – Most apps use APIs (Application Programming Interfaces) to communicate with Zapier. When you authorize Zapier to access your app, it securely connects to the app's API.

2. **OAuth Authentication** – Many modern apps, such as Google Drive, Slack, and Dropbox, use OAuth, a secure authorization method that allows you to log in without sharing passwords.

3. **API Keys or Webhooks** – Some apps may require you to manually enter an API key or configure a webhook to enable automation.

2. Finding and Selecting an App in Zapier

Step 1: Access the "Apps" Section

1. Log in to your **Zapier account** at Zapier.com.

2. On the **Zapier Dashboard**, locate the **"Apps"** tab in the left sidebar and click on it.

3. This will take you to the **App Directory**, where you can browse through thousands of available integrations.

Step 2: Search for Your Desired App

1. Use the **search bar** at the top to type in the name of the app you want to connect (e.g., Google Sheets, Slack, Trello).

2. Click on the app when it appears in the search results.

3. You will be taken to the **App Overview Page**, where you can see a brief description, available triggers and actions, and example workflows (Zaps).

Step 3: Check App Compatibility and Requirements

Before proceeding with the connection, it's important to check:

- Whether the app requires a **premium Zapier plan** (some apps have premium features).

- Whether you need administrator permissions to connect certain business apps.

- If there are any specific **limitations or restrictions** (e.g., some apps have rate limits on API calls).

3. Authorizing an App Connection

Step 1: Start the Connection Process

1. Once you've selected your app, click the **"Connect"** or **"Add Account"** button.

2. A **popup window** will appear, asking you to log in to the app's account.

Step 2: Grant Permissions

1. Enter your **username and password** (if using OAuth authentication).

2. If prompted, **approve the required permissions** so Zapier can access the app's data.

3. Click **Authorize** or **Allow** (depending on the app).

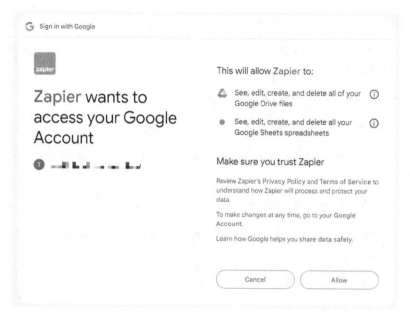

Step 3: Confirm the Connection

1. After authorization, Zapier will return to the dashboard and display a confirmation message.

2. You will now see your app listed under **"Connected Accounts"**.

3. Click **"Test Connection"** to ensure Zapier successfully links to your app.

4. Connecting Apps Requiring API Keys or Webhooks

Some apps do not support OAuth authentication and instead require API keys or webhooks. The setup process varies slightly.

Using API Keys

1. In the app's settings (outside of Zapier), navigate to the **API or Developer section**.

2. Copy the **API Key** provided by the app.

3. Return to Zapier, paste the API key into the connection field, and save.

Using Webhooks

1. Select **Webhooks by Zapier** as the app.

2. Choose whether you need a **Webhook Trigger** (Zapier listens for data) or **Webhook Action** (Zapier sends data).

3. Copy the provided **Webhook URL** and paste it into the third-party app's webhook settings.

4. Test the webhook by sending sample data and verifying the connection.

5. Managing and Organizing Your Connected Apps

Once you have connected an app, you may need to manage or update the connection over time.

Viewing Your Connected Apps

1. Select **"Apps"**

2. You will see a list of all your linked apps and services.

Reconnecting or Updating an App

If an app stops working due to a password change or security update, you may need to reconnect it.

1. Locate the app under **Connected Accounts**.

2. Click **"Reconnect"** and follow the authentication steps again.

Removing an App Connection

1. Find the app under **Connected Accounts**.

2. Click **"Disconnect"** or **"Remove"**.

3. Confirm your choice to remove the app from Zapier.

6. Testing Your Connected App

Before building your first Zap, it's important to test your connected app to ensure that it works correctly.

Step 1: Create a Test Zap

1. Click **"Create a Zap"** on the dashboard.

2. Choose the app you just connected as the **Trigger App**.

3. Select a **Trigger Event** (e.g., new email in Gmail).

4. Click **"Test Trigger"** to check if Zapier can pull sample data from the app.

Step 2: Verify Data Accuracy

- Ensure the sample data matches the expected format.

- If no data appears, check the app's settings or try reconnecting the app.

Step 3: Save and Continue

- Once you verify the connection, click **"Continue"** to proceed with creating your Zap.

7. Troubleshooting Common Connection Issues

Even with a straightforward process, you might encounter issues when connecting an app. Here are some common problems and solutions:

Issue	Possible Cause	Solution
App not connecting	Incorrect login credentials	Double-check username and password
Zapier can't access data	Insufficient permissions	Ensure your account has admin rights
Connection times out	Server issues or API limits	Wait a few minutes and retry
Missing expected data	API restrictions or filters	Verify settings and permissions in the app

If you continue facing issues, visit Zapier's **Help Center** or reach out to **Zapier Support**.

8. Next Steps: Building Your First Zap

Now that you have successfully connected your first app, you are ready to build an automation (Zap). In the next chapter, we will walk through the process of creating your first Zap, including selecting triggers and actions, configuring workflows, and testing your automation.

Coming up next: Chapter 2 - Creating Your First Zap!

Final Thoughts

By following these steps, you have taken the first major step in mastering Zapier. With your first app connected, you are now prepared to automate repetitive tasks and streamline workflows efficiently.

2.3 Zapier Plans and Pricing

Zapier offers various pricing plans designed to accommodate different user needs, from individuals automating small tasks to businesses managing complex workflows. Understanding the differences between the plans is essential to choosing the right one for your needs. In this section, we will explore the available plans, their features, and how to decide which one is best suited for your workflow automation requirements.

2.3.1 Free vs. Paid Plans

Admin controls		Free	Professional	Team	Enterprise
Two-factor authentication	ⓘ	✓	✓	✓	✓
Pay-per-task for overage tasks	ⓘ	–	✓	✓	✓
Static IP	ⓘ	–	✓	✓	✓
Audit log	ⓘ	–	✓	✓	✓
Owner access	ⓘ	–	–	✓	✓
SAML SSO	ⓘ	–	–	✓	✓
User provisioning (SCIM)	ⓘ	–	–	–	✓
Domain capture	ⓘ	–	–	–	✓
Super Admin	ⓘ	–	–	–	✓
Advanced admin permissions	ⓘ	–	–	–	✓
App restrictions New	ⓘ	–	–	–	✓
Action restrictions Beta	ⓘ	–	–	–	✓
Custom data retention	ⓘ	–	–	–	✓
Observability API New	ⓘ	–	–	–	✓
Analytics New	ⓘ	–	–	–	✓
Annual task limits New	ⓘ	–	–	–	✓

Collaboration tools		Free	Professional	Team	Enterprise
Seats	ⓘ	1	1	25	Unlimited
Shared app connections	ⓘ	–	–	✓	✓
Shared workspace	ⓘ	–	–	✓	✓
Folder permissions	ⓘ	–	–	✓	✓
Approval requests **Beta**	ⓘ	–	–	–	✓

Support		Free	Professional	Team	Enterprise
Email support	ⓘ	–	✓	✓	✓
Live chat*	ⓘ	–	✓	✓	✓
Premier support	ⓘ	–	–	✓	✓
Designated Technical Support	ⓘ	–	–	–	✓

Add-ons		Free	Professional	Team	Enterprise
Zapier Interfaces	ⓘ	✓	✓	✓	✓
Zapier Tables	ⓘ	✓	✓	✓	✓
Zapier Chatbots **Beta**	ⓘ	✓	✓	✓	✓

Add-ons		Free	Professional	Team	Enterprise
Zapier Interfaces	ⓘ	✓	✓	✓	✓
Zapier Tables	ⓘ	✓	✓	✓	✓
Zapier Chatbots **Beta**	ⓘ	✓	✓	✓	✓

Zaps		Free	Professional	Team	Enterprise
Unlimited Zaps	ⓘ	✓	✓	✓	✓
Steps	ⓘ	Two-step	Multi-step	Multi-step	Multi-step
Polling time	ⓘ	15 min	2 min	1 min	1 min
Visual editor	ⓘ	✓	✓	✓	✓
AI power-ups	ⓘ	✓	✓	✓	✓
Custom test records	ⓘ	✓	✓	✓	✓
Filters & Paths	ⓘ	–	✓	✓	✓
Formatter	ⓘ	–	✓	✓	✓

Zap Management		Free	Professional	Team	Enterprise
Drafts	ⓘ	✓	✓	✓	✓
Autoreplay	ⓘ	–	✓	✓	✓
Customized error settings	ⓘ	–	✓	✓	✓
Customized polling time	ⓘ	–	✓	✓	✓
Flood protection settings	ⓘ	–	✓	✓	✓
Versions	ⓘ	–	✓	✓	✓
Compare Versions New	ⓘ	–	–	–	✓
Alerts New	ⓘ	–	–	–	✓

Integrations		Free	Professional	Team	Enterprise
Custom actions (with AI) Beta	ⓘ	✓	✓	✓	✓
Unlimited premium apps	ⓘ	–	✓	✓	✓
Connections via webhooks	ⓘ	–	✓	✓	✓

Zapier provides both free and paid plans, each with distinct benefits and limitations. The Free Plan is a great starting point for beginners, but as your automation needs grow, upgrading to a paid plan may become necessary to unlock advanced features and higher usage limits. Below, we will examine each plan in detail, comparing their key features and helping you determine which plan best suits your needs.

1. The Free Plan: A Beginner's Starting Point

The Free Plan is ideal for individuals who are new to Zapier and want to experiment with automation without any financial commitment. Here's what you get with the Free Plan:

Key Features of the Free Plan:

- **5 Single-Step Zaps:** You can create up to five active Zaps at a time, but they must be single-step (meaning each Zap consists of only one trigger and one action).

- **100 Tasks per Month:** Each time Zapier performs an action as part of a Zap, it counts as one task. The Free Plan allows up to 100 tasks per month.

- **15-Minute Update Time:** Zaps on the Free Plan check for new trigger events every 15 minutes, meaning there may be a delay in automation execution.

- **Basic Apps Only:** While the Free Plan includes many commonly used apps, some premium integrations (like Salesforce, QuickBooks, and Shopify) are not available.

Limitations of the Free Plan:

- **No Multi-Step Zaps:** You cannot create complex workflows with multiple steps; each Zap can only have one trigger and one action.

- **Limited Task Allowance:** If you require more than 100 tasks per month, you will need to upgrade.

- **No Filters, Paths, or Advanced Features:** These advanced automation tools, which allow conditional logic and branching workflows, are not available on the Free Plan.

- **No Premium App Access:** Certain business-critical apps are only available on paid plans.

Who Should Use the Free Plan?

- Individuals who want to test Zapier before committing to a paid plan.

- Users with basic automation needs, such as simple notifications or data transfers between apps.

- Small personal projects where automation frequency is low.

2. Paid Plans: Unlocking More Automation Power

Zapier offers several paid plans with progressively more features and capacity. Below, we will examine the key benefits of each plan, helping you choose the one that best fits your needs.

Zapier Starter Plan

Price: Typically around $19.99/month (billed annually) or $29.99/month (billed monthly).

Key Features:

- **20 Zaps:** Allows up to 20 active Zaps at a time.

- **Multi-Step Zaps:** Unlocks the ability to create complex workflows with multiple actions per Zap.

- **750 Tasks per Month:** A substantial increase in task allowance compared to the Free Plan.

- **Premium App Integrations:** Access to business-critical apps like Salesforce, QuickBooks, Shopify, and more.

- **15-Minute Update Time:** The same as the Free Plan, meaning Zaps refresh every 15 minutes.

Who Should Choose This Plan?

- Individuals and small businesses that need slightly more automation capacity.

- Users who want to integrate premium apps into their workflows.

- Anyone who needs Multi-Step Zaps for more complex automation.

Zapier Professional Plan

Price: Typically around $49/month (billed annually) or $73/month (billed monthly).

Key Features:

- **Unlimited Zaps:** No restriction on the number of Zaps you can create.
- **2,000 Tasks per Month:** Increased task allowance for more automation activity.
- **2-Minute Update Time:** Faster trigger detection and Zap execution.
- **Filters & Formatters:** Enables advanced logic for refining automation.
- **Paths (Conditional Logic):** Allows you to create Zaps with multiple outcome branches.

Who Should Choose This Plan?

- Professionals and businesses needing frequent and complex automation.
- Users requiring faster task execution for time-sensitive workflows.
- Businesses handling data manipulation with filters and formatters.

Zapier Team Plan

Price: Typically around $69/month per user (billed annually).

Key Features:

- **Everything in Professional, Plus:** Higher task limits and better performance.
- **50,000+ Tasks per Month:** Designed for high-volume automation.
- **1-Minute Update Time:** Near real-time automation.
- **Shared Workspaces:** Enables team collaboration with shared automation setups.
- **Role-Based Access:** Assign permissions to team members.

Who Should Choose This Plan?

- Businesses requiring large-scale automation and workflow collaboration.
- Teams that need shared access to workflows with permission controls.

- Users dealing with frequent and high-volume data automation.

Zapier Company Plan

Price: Custom pricing, depending on business needs.

Key Features:

- **Enterprise-Grade Security:** Advanced security compliance, including SOC 2 and HIPAA.

- **Unlimited Task Allowance:** No restrictions on task usage.

- **Advanced Admin Controls:** Full control over workflows, permissions, and data security.

- **Dedicated Account Manager & Priority Support:** Personalized assistance for automation setup.

- **Custom Data Retention & Audit Logs:** Enhanced data tracking for compliance.

Who Should Choose This Plan?

- Large enterprises with mission-critical automation needs.

- Organizations requiring strict security and compliance measures.

- Businesses that need priority support and custom solutions.

How to Choose the Right Zapier Plan for You

When selecting a Zapier plan, consider the following factors:

1. Task Usage

- If you need only 100 tasks per month, the Free Plan may be enough.

- If you automate several processes daily, consider at least the Starter or Professional Plan.

2. Complexity of Automation

- If you only need basic automation (one trigger + one action), the Free Plan is fine.

- If you need workflows with multiple actions or conditional logic, upgrade to a paid plan.

3. Access to Premium Apps

- If your business relies on premium apps (Salesforce, QuickBooks, Shopify, etc.), a paid plan is necessary.

4. Update Speed Requirements

- If 15-minute delays are acceptable, Free or Starter is fine.

- If you need near real-time automation, Professional or higher is recommended.

5. Team Collaboration

- If you work alone, individual plans suffice.

- If you need shared workflows, opt for the Team or Company Plan.

Conclusion

Zapier offers flexible pricing plans to accommodate different automation needs. The Free Plan is a good entry point for beginners, but as you automate more tasks, upgrading to a paid plan becomes necessary to unlock advanced features. By understanding your automation goals, task volume, and app integration needs, you can select the best Zapier plan to maximize productivity and efficiency.

2.3.2 Choosing the Right Plan for Your Needs

Choosing the right Zapier plan is essential to ensuring that your workflow automation needs are met efficiently without unnecessary costs. Zapier offers different pricing tiers, each designed to cater to varying levels of automation, from individual users with simple needs to large businesses requiring advanced workflows. In this section, we will explore each plan in detail, compare their features, and provide guidance on selecting the best plan for your specific use case.

1. Overview of Zapier Pricing Plans

Zapier currently offers several pricing tiers, which can change over time. As of the latest update, the primary plans available are:

1. **Free Plan** – For beginners and light users.

2. **Starter Plan** – For individuals with moderate automation needs.

3. **Professional Plan** – For professionals and small businesses.

4. **Team Plan** – For teams that require collaboration and more automation power.

5. **Company Plan** – For enterprises needing advanced features and security.

Each plan has specific limitations and advantages, which we will examine in detail.

2. Free vs. Paid Plans: Understanding the Key Differences

Before diving into which plan suits you best, let's break down the key differences between the **Free** and **Paid** plans.

Feature	Free Plan	Paid Plans
Number of Zaps	Limited (e.g., 5 Zaps)	Unlimited (varies by tier)
Multi-Step Zaps	✗ Not available	✓ Available
Update Speed	15 minutes	As fast as 1 minute
Premium Apps	✗ Not available	✓ Available
Advanced Features (Paths, Filters, Formatter, Webhooks)	✗ Not available	✓ Available
Support	Standard support	Priority support (varies by tier)

From this comparison, it's clear that the **Free plan** is best for testing simple automations, while **Paid plans** unlock the true potential of Zapier.

3. Choosing the Best Plan for Your Needs

To determine the right Zapier plan, consider these key factors:

How Many Zaps Do You Need?

- If you only need a few simple automations, the Free Plan may suffice.

- If you require dozens or hundreds of automations, you should consider at least the Starter or Professional plan.

Do You Need Multi-Step Zaps?

- If your workflows only require a single trigger and action, the Free Plan works fine.

- If you want complex automation with multiple steps (e.g., trigger → email notification → add to Google Sheets → Slack alert), you need a Professional Plan or higher.

How Fast Do You Need Zaps to Run?

- **Free Plan**: Runs every **15 minutes**.

- **Starter Plan**: Runs every **15 minutes** (same as free).

- **Professional Plan**: Runs every **2 minutes**.

- **Team & Company Plans**: Runs every **1 minute**.

If timing is critical (e.g., instant notifications, live updates, or real-time processing), then a Professional Plan or higher is necessary.

Do You Need Access to Premium Apps?

Zapier allows connections to thousands of apps, but some advanced apps require a **paid plan**.
Examples of **Premium Apps**:

- Salesforce

- QuickBooks

- Shopify

- SQL Server

- Zendesk

- PayPal

If your automation depends on these apps, you must upgrade to at least the **Starter Plan**.

Are You a Team or an Individual User?

- If you're an individual, Starter or Professional Plan is sufficient.

- If you need collaboration features (e.g., multiple team members managing Zaps), you need at least the Team Plan.

Do You Need Advanced Features (Filters, Paths, Webhooks)?

Advanced features allow **more intelligent automation**, such as:

- **Filters**: Run a Zap **only under specific conditions**.

- **Paths**: Allow **conditional branching** (e.g., if a lead is from the US → add to CRM; if from Europe → send an email).

- **Webhooks**: Allow connections to **custom applications** or APIs.

If you need these, go for at least the **Professional Plan**.

---

4. Breakdown of Each Zapier Plan

Now, let's go through each plan in more detail.

Free Plan

Best for: Individuals testing Zapier, simple automations.
Limitations:

- Maximum **5 Zaps**.

- **Single-step Zaps only** (no multi-step workflows).

- Runs every **15 minutes**.

- No **Premium Apps**.

- Limited support.

✓ **Recommended for basic automation needs.**

Professional Plan

Best for: Power users, businesses needing advanced automation.
Upgrades from Starter Plan:

✓ Allows **100+ Zaps**.
✓ Runs every **2 minutes**.
✓ Adds **Filters, Paths, and Webhooks**.
✓ Offers **Priority Support**.

✓ **Recommended for businesses that need fast, advanced automation.**

Team Plan

Best for: Small-to-medium teams needing collaboration.
Upgrades from Professional Plan:
✓ **Unlimited Zaps**.
✓ **1-minute Zap execution speed**.
✓ **Multi-user access** (team collaboration).
✓ **Centralized Zap management**.

✓ **Best for teams managing automation across different departments.**

Company Plan

Best for: Large enterprises with high security and compliance needs.
Upgrades from Team Plan:
✓ **Advanced security features** (Single Sign-On, encryption).
✓ **Dedicated account manager**.
✓ **Custom integrations**.
✓ **Enterprise-grade support**.

✓ **Designed for businesses with strict security and compliance requirements.**

Summary: Which Plan Should You Choose?

User Type	Recommended Plan
Basic user, just testing Zapier	Free Plan

User Type	Recommended Plan
Business needing advanced automation	Professional Plan
Teams needing collaboration	Team Plan
Enterprise with security needs	Company Plan

6. Final Thoughts

Choosing the right Zapier plan depends on your workflow complexity, team size, app integrations, and automation speed requirements. If you're just starting, you can always begin with the Free Plan and upgrade as your automation needs grow.

For most individual professionals and small businesses, the Starter or Professional Plan is a great choice. If you're working in a team environment, the Team or Company Plan provides better collaboration and security options.

Whatever your choice, Zapier's flexibility ensures you can scale your automation as your needs evolve! 🚀

CHAPTER II
Creating Your First Zap

3.1 Step-by-Step Guide to Making a Zap

3.1.1 Choosing a Trigger App

Creating an automated workflow in Zapier starts with choosing a **Trigger App**. The **Trigger App** is the application that initiates the automation. In other words, when something happens in this app, Zapier detects the event and triggers the workflow to execute further actions.

For example:

- A new email arrives in **Gmail** → Trigger
- A new row is added in **Google Sheets** → Trigger
- A new customer is created in **Shopify** → Trigger

In this section, we will cover the following:

- Understanding trigger apps and events
- How to choose the right trigger app
- Configuring the trigger app in Zapier

1. Understanding Trigger Apps and Events

What is a Trigger App?

A **Trigger App** is an application that initiates an automation in Zapier. It serves as the starting point of your **Zap** (automation workflow). Each trigger app has specific **trigger events** that Zapier can monitor and respond to.

For example:

- **Gmail** can trigger a Zap when you receive a **new email**.

- **Google Drive** can trigger a Zap when a **new file is added to a folder**.

- **Trello** can trigger a Zap when a **new card is created**.

A **trigger event** is the specific action inside the app that causes the Zap to start. Different apps offer different trigger events.

Types of Trigger Events

There are two main types of trigger events in Zapier:

1. **Instant Triggers**

   o These triggers activate a Zap **immediately** when the event happens.

   o Example: A new lead is added in Facebook Lead Ads.

   o No waiting time is required.

2. **Polling Triggers**

   o These triggers check for new data **at intervals** (e.g., every 5 or 15 minutes).

   o Example: Zapier checks a Google Sheet for new rows every 15 minutes.

   o There may be a slight delay before the Zap runs.

Some advanced users may also use **Webhook Triggers**, which allow custom integrations, but for now, we will focus on standard app triggers.

---

2. How to Choose the Right Trigger App

Step 1: Identify Your Workflow Needs

Before selecting a trigger app, ask yourself:

✓ What action should start the automation?

✓ Which app contains the data that triggers the process?

✓ What specific event should act as the trigger?

For example, if you want to automate sending Slack messages when you receive an email, your trigger app should be **Gmail** and the trigger event should be **New Email Received**.

Step 2: Check Zapier's App Directory

Zapier supports thousands of apps. To check if your app is supported:

1. Go to **Zapier's App Directory** at zapier.com/apps.

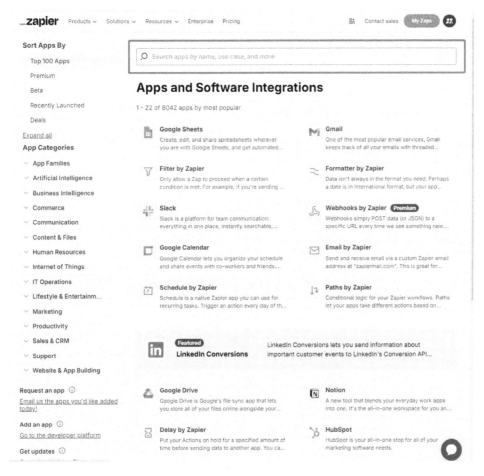

2. Search for the app you want to use.

3. Click on the app and check the available **trigger events**.

Some apps may offer only a few trigger events, while others provide multiple options.

Step 3: Choose a Reliable Trigger Event

Some apps offer multiple triggers, so select the one that best fits your needs. Here are some examples:

App	Trigger Event	Use Case
Gmail	New Email	Auto-save new emails to Google Drive
Google Sheets	New Row Added	Notify team via Slack when a new entry is added
Trello	New Card Created	Send an email notification when a new task is added
Shopify	New Order	Send a Slack message when a new order is received

3. Configuring the Trigger App in Zapier

Step 1: Start Creating a Zap

1. Log in to **Zapier** at zapier.com.

2. Click on **Create Zap** in the dashboard.

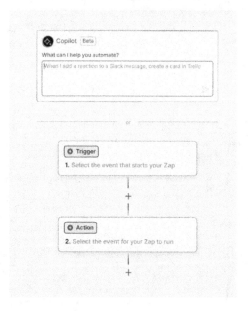

Step 2: Select a Trigger App

1. Click on the **Trigger** section.

2. Search for and select your trigger app (e.g., Gmail, Google Sheets, Trello).

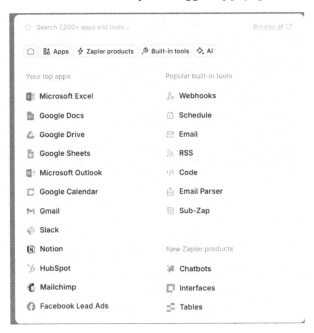

Step 3: Choose a Trigger Event

1. Select a **Trigger Event** from the dropdown menu.

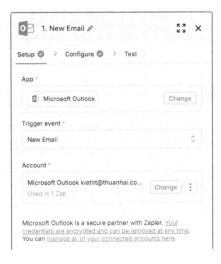

2. Click **Continue** to proceed.

Example: If you choose **Gmail**, the trigger event could be **New Email in Inbox**.

Step 4: Connect Your App Account

1. Click **Sign in to (App Name)** to connect your account.

2. Grant Zapier the necessary permissions.

3. Once connected, click **Continue**.

Example: If you choose **Google Sheets**, Zapier will ask for access to your Google Drive.

Step 5: Set Up Trigger Details

Some triggers require additional details, such as:

- **Folder Selection** (e.g., choose which Gmail inbox to monitor).

- **Filtering Options** (e.g., trigger only for emails with specific subject lines).

- **Spreadsheet Selection** (e.g., choose which Google Sheet to monitor).

Step 6: Test the Trigger

1. Click **Test Trigger** to check if Zapier can find recent data from the app.

2. If successful, Zapier will display the retrieved data.

3. Click **Continue** to move to the next step.

Example: Setting Up a Gmail Trigger in Zapier

Let's walk through an example where we set up **Gmail** as a trigger app:

1. Creating the Zap

- Log in to **Zapier**.

- Click **Create Zap**.

2. Selecting Gmail as the Trigger App

- In the **Trigger** section, search for **Gmail**.

- Click **Gmail** to select it.

3. Choosing a Trigger Event

- Select **New Email** as the trigger event.

- Click **Continue**.

4. Connecting Gmail to Zapier

- Click **Sign in to Gmail**.

- Grant Zapier access to your Gmail account.

5. Setting Up Trigger Options

- Choose the inbox or label you want Zapier to monitor.

- Optionally, add filters (e.g., trigger only for emails from a specific sender).

- Click **Continue**.

6. Testing the Trigger

- Click **Test Trigger**.

- Zapier will fetch recent emails matching your settings.

- If successful, you will see sample email data.

- Click **Continue** to proceed to the next step (adding an action).

Final Thoughts

Choosing the right **Trigger App** is the foundation of every Zapier automation. By following these steps, you can confidently select and configure a trigger that fits your workflow needs. In the next section, we will explore how to set up an **Action App** to complete the automation.

🚀 **Next Up: 3.1.2 Setting Up a Trigger Event** – Learn how to refine your trigger settings for more precise automation!

3.1.2 Setting Up a Trigger Event

Creating a Zap in Zapier is one of the easiest and most powerful ways to automate workflows. The process begins with the essential concept of **triggers**. A trigger is an event in one app that kicks off an action in another app. Without a trigger, there is no automation, making it the first step in setting up your Zap. This section will guide you through the process of setting up a trigger event in Zapier, making sure you understand everything from selecting the correct trigger app to configuring it correctly.

Understanding the Role of Triggers in Automation

Before diving into the technicalities of setting up a trigger, it's important to grasp the role triggers play in automation. Think of a trigger as the **"event"** that starts the entire process. For example:

- **When a new email arrives in your Gmail inbox,**

- **When a new lead is added to your CRM,**

- **When a task is completed in Asana,**

These are all examples of trigger events. The trigger monitors a specific app or service for an event, and once that event happens, it sends the data to Zapier to initiate an action in another app. Triggers allow you to automate tasks that would otherwise require manual work, saving time and reducing the chance of human error.

In Zapier, each integration comes with a set of predefined triggers. Some apps might offer a wide range of triggers, while others might offer only a few basic ones. However, regardless of the app you're working with, understanding how to set up the right trigger is critical to ensuring your workflow runs smoothly.

Step 1: Selecting the Trigger App

The first step in setting up a trigger is to choose the right **Trigger App**. This is the app where the event (trigger) happens. In Zapier, the process of selecting a trigger app is simple, thanks to Zapier's easy-to-use interface.

1. **Log into your Zapier account.**

o   After you've logged into Zapier, click on **"Make a Zap"** to start the process.

2. **Search for your Trigger App.**

o   In the "Trigger" section of the Zap setup page, you will be prompted to choose an app. This is the app that will send the event (trigger).

o   Start typing the name of the app in the search bar, such as "Gmail," "Google Sheets," "Slack," etc.

o   If the app you want isn't available, you can check Zapier's extensive library of supported apps or use a **Webhooks** trigger for more advanced use cases.

3. **Select the app you want to trigger from the list.**

o   Once you select the app, Zapier will show a list of available triggers that this app supports. For instance, in Gmail, the available triggers could include "New Email," "New Attachment," or "New Label."

4. **Click on the trigger you want to use.**

o   Once you select your app, you'll be asked to choose a specific **Trigger Event** from a list of options available for that app.

Step 2: Connecting Your Trigger App to Zapier

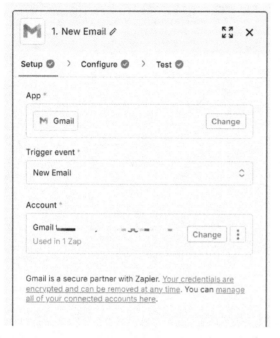

After selecting your app, the next step is to **connect it to your Zapier account**. This is an essential step, as it allows Zapier to communicate with your app and retrieve information.

1. **Click on "Connect" or "Sign In."**

    o   When you select your app, Zapier will often prompt you to log in or sign into your account for that app (for example, if you're using Gmail, you'll need to log into your Gmail account).

2. **Grant Permissions.**

    o   Zapier requires specific permissions to access your account in order to trigger workflows. For Gmail, for example, you may need to grant Zapier permission to access your emails, read messages, and send emails, depending on your chosen trigger.

3. **Confirm the Connection.**

    o   After you sign in and grant permissions, you'll see a confirmation message. In most cases, Zapier will test the connection to ensure everything is set up properly.

4. **Click "Continue" once the connection is confirmed.**

Step 3: Choosing the Trigger Event

Now that your app is connected, the next step is to **choose the specific trigger event**. This is where you select the event in your app that will start the automation process.

1. **Review Trigger Event Options.**

   o Each app offers a list of potential trigger events. Some apps have multiple triggers, while others only have one. For example, in Google Sheets, you could choose from triggers such as "New Spreadsheet Row," "Updated Spreadsheet Row," or "New or Updated Spreadsheet Row."

2. **Select the Correct Trigger.**

   o Think carefully about the event that will best trigger your workflow. Let's say you're using Gmail, and you want the Zap to trigger every time a new email comes in. The "New Email" trigger would be appropriate for this task.

   o In a CRM app, you might select "New Lead" if you want to automate actions every time a new lead enters your system.

3. **Understand Specific Trigger Event Details.**

o Some triggers require additional details to be configured. For instance, in Gmail, you might be asked to specify which label the trigger should apply to. In Google Sheets, you could set it to trigger only when new data is entered in a specific column.

Step 4: Configuring Trigger Filters and Options

Once you've chosen your trigger event, Zapier may give you the option to filter the data that flows into your Zap. This step is critical for customizing the automation to meet your needs.

1. **Apply Filters (Optional).**

   o Filters are incredibly useful for restricting when a trigger event should occur. For example, in Gmail, you can set filters based on specific criteria like subject lines or labels. This allows you to automate tasks only when certain conditions are met.

2. **Set up Trigger Options.**

   o Depending on the app, Zapier may provide additional options for your trigger. For instance, if you're using Google Sheets, you may be asked to choose which worksheet or range of cells should be monitored for new data.

   o These options help refine the trigger so that it is more specific to your use case, preventing unnecessary activations.

3. **Test the Trigger (Optional but Recommended).**

   o After setting up the trigger event, Zapier allows you to test it. By clicking the "Test Trigger" button, you'll see if the trigger is working properly.

   o For example, if your trigger is "New Email in Gmail," Zapier will check if it can find a recent email that matches your criteria.

Step 5: Troubleshooting the Trigger

If your trigger doesn't work as expected, you may need to troubleshoot:

1. **Check Permissions and Connectivity.**

   o Ensure that you've given Zapier the correct permissions to access your app's data.

   o Make sure that your app is properly connected to Zapier and that your account is active.

2. **Ensure the Correct Criteria Are Set.**

   o If your trigger isn't firing as expected, check that your criteria (such as labels, folders, or date ranges) are configured correctly.

3. **Consult Zapier's Support.**

   o If the trigger still isn't working after checking these factors, you can visit Zapier's help documentation or reach out to customer support for further assistance.

Conclusion: Mastering Triggers for Better Automation

Now that you understand how to set up a trigger, you've completed one of the most crucial steps in creating a Zap. Triggers serve as the backbone of your automation process, and setting them up correctly ensures that your workflows will run smoothly.

As you progress with Zapier, you'll encounter even more advanced options for triggers, such as multi-step workflows, filters, and custom webhooks. However, mastering the basics of trigger events is the foundation upon which all other automation will be built.

By carefully selecting the right trigger, configuring it correctly, and troubleshooting when necessary, you'll be on your way to automating repetitive tasks and boosting your productivity. So, let's move forward and explore the next steps in creating effective workflows with Zapier!

3.1.3 Selecting an Action App

Once you've selected your trigger app and configured the event that starts your workflow, the next crucial step in creating your first Zap is **Selecting an Action App**. This part of the process is essential because the action app is where the results of the trigger will be sent or executed.

In this section, we'll walk you through every detail of the **Action App selection**, explain the concept behind Action Apps, and guide you on how to choose and set up the app properly. By the end of this section, you'll have the knowledge to confidently select an Action App for any Zap and integrate it into your workflows.

What is an Action App?

An **Action App** is the second part of a Zap, which performs an action when the trigger event occurs. For instance, if your trigger app receives an email (let's say Gmail), the action could be to send that email to a specific Slack channel or create a new Trello card with details from that email.

Triggers initiate a workflow, and **actions** carry out the tasks that result from the trigger. The Action App essentially tells Zapier what to do with the data once it has been received from the trigger app.

There are two main components of an Action:

1. **Action App**: The application where the action takes place (e.g., Google Sheets, Slack, Gmail).

2. **Action Event**: The specific task the Action App will perform (e.g., creating a new row in Google Sheets, sending a message in Slack).

How to Select an Action App in Zapier

When it comes to selecting an Action App, you're provided with an extensive catalog of available apps within Zapier. Let's break down the process of choosing the right Action App step by step:

Step 1: Search for Your Desired Action App

Once you've configured your trigger, the next screen prompts you to **choose an Action App**. Zapier will show you an extensive list of apps that can be used in this stage. You can either browse through the entire list or use the **search bar** to find the app that matches the task you want to perform.

For example, if your trigger app is Gmail and your goal is to post an email to a Slack channel, you can search for "Slack" in the search bar. The available Slack actions will appear, and you can choose the one that suits your needs.

Step 2: Choose the Right Action Event

Once you've selected the Action App, you'll be asked to choose an **Action Event**. This is the specific task you want the Action App to perform. Different apps offer various action events, and it's important to select the right one for your workflow.

For example, in Slack, the action event could be:

- **Send Channel Message**: This sends a message to a specific channel in Slack.

- **Send Direct Message**: This sends a message to a specific user.

In Gmail, the action events could include:

- **Send Email**: This sends an email based on the information in your trigger.

- **Create Draft**: This creates a draft email in your Gmail account.

Step 3: Authenticate and Connect the Action App

Once you've chosen your desired Action App and the action event, the next step is to authenticate the app. If you've already connected the Action App in Zapier, you might skip this step. However, if it's your first time connecting it, Zapier will prompt you to sign in.

For instance, if you're setting up Slack as your Action App, Zapier will ask you to sign in to your Slack account. This is necessary because Zapier needs access to your Slack workspace to post messages or perform other actions.

Step 4: Customize the Action Event

After you've connected your Action App, Zapier will ask you to **map the data** from the trigger app to the action fields. This is where you tell Zapier how to use the data coming from the trigger to perform the action.

For example, if your trigger is receiving a new email in Gmail and your action is to send that email to Slack, Zapier will show you several fields that you can map:

- **Message Text**: In this field, you can pull in information from the Gmail trigger, such as the subject, body of the email, or the sender's name.

- **Channel**: You can specify which Slack channel you want the message to be posted in.

Mapping data is one of the most powerful aspects of Zapier, as it enables you to customize the way information flows between apps. It's important to understand how to pull the right data from your trigger app and send it to your Action App.

Step 5: Test Your Action

Before activating your Zap, Zapier will allow you to **test** your action. This test ensures that your Action App is properly receiving the data and executing the task as expected.

In the Slack example, the test might involve sending a message to the Slack channel you specified. If everything works fine, you'll see a confirmation that the message has been sent. If it fails, Zapier will show you an error and provide suggestions for troubleshooting.

Testing is a crucial step because it helps you spot any errors before your workflow is running live, which prevents disruptions in your automation.

Step 6: Activate Your Zap

After successfully testing your Zap and making sure the Action App is working as expected, the final step is to **activate your Zap**. Once activated, Zapier will automatically monitor the trigger event and perform the specified action whenever that trigger is activated.

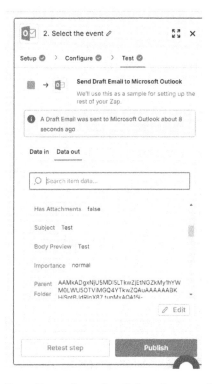

Best Practices for Selecting an Action App

- **Know Your Workflow**: Before selecting an Action App, make sure you understand the entire process of the workflow you're automating. This helps you determine which app and action will best suit your needs.

- **Start Simple**: If you're new to Zapier, it's best to start with simple workflows. For example, send an email from Gmail to a Google Sheet before trying more advanced integrations like multi-step zaps or custom APIs.

- **Use Built-In Zapier Apps**: Sometimes, Zapier offers its own internal tools like Formatter, Filter, or Delay, which can be very helpful for managing and transforming data before sending it to your Action App.

- **Test, Test, Test**: Always test your Zap before turning it on. This is essential to ensure that everything is working properly and that data is flowing between your trigger and action correctly.

Common Action Apps You Might Use

Here are a few examples of popular Action Apps and the action events they offer:

- **Gmail**: Send Email, Create Draft, Send Reply

- **Slack**: Send Channel Message, Send Direct Message, Create Reminder

- **Google Sheets**: Create Spreadsheet Row, Update Spreadsheet Row, Find Spreadsheet Row

- **Trello**: Create Card, Update Card, Add Comment to Card

- **Mailchimp**: Add Subscriber, Create Campaign, Send Campaign

- **Google Calendar**: Create Event, Update Event, Delete Event

Conclusion

Selecting an Action App is a key step in building your first Zap, and getting it right ensures your automation will work as expected. By following the steps outlined in this section— searching for the app, choosing the right action event, customizing your action, and testing it—you can confidently set up any Action App and create seamless workflows.

Remember, Zapier's power lies in its flexibility, allowing you to automate a wide variety of tasks and save significant time. With each new Action App you add, you increase the efficiency of your workflows, making your day-to-day tasks easier to manage.

By mastering the selection and configuration of Action Apps, you'll be able to fully harness the power of Zapier in your workflows.

3.1.4 Configuring Action Settings

Once you have chosen a trigger and an action for your Zap, the next crucial step is **configuring the action settings**. This step determines what happens when your Zap runs and ensures that the data is processed and transferred correctly between your apps.

In this section, we will break down the process of configuring action settings into clear, step-by-step instructions. By the end of this section, you will have a strong understanding of how to map fields, customize data, test outputs, and optimize your Zap for efficiency.

Understanding Action Settings in Zapier

When setting up an action in Zapier, you are essentially instructing Zapier on **what to do with the information** received from the trigger. This could be sending an email, updating a database, posting a message on Slack, or adding a new row to a spreadsheet.

Each action has its own settings, which typically include:

- **App selection** – The app where the action will take place.

- **Action event** – The specific event that will be executed (e.g., "Send Email" in Gmail, "Create Spreadsheet Row" in Google Sheets).

- **Data mapping** – Matching fields from the trigger event to corresponding fields in the action event.

- **Advanced customization** – Modifying text, dates, numbers, and other elements before sending them to the action app.

Example: Sending an Email via Gmail

Let's assume we are setting up an action where every time a new contact is added to a Google Sheet, Zapier will send an automated welcome email via Gmail.

1. **Choose Gmail as the action app**

   o In the **Action** step of the Zap editor, search for and select **Gmail**.

2. **Select an Action Event**

   o Choose **Send Email** as the action event, then click **Continue**.

3. **Connect Your Gmail Account**

   o If you haven't connected your Gmail account yet, you will be prompted to do so. Click **Sign in** and follow the authentication steps.

4. **Set Up Action Fields**

   o Here is where we configure the details of the email being sent.

Step-by-Step Guide to Configuring Action Settings

Step 1: Mapping Data Fields

Data mapping is the process of linking trigger data fields to action fields. Zapier automatically suggests mappings, but you should verify them carefully.

For example, when sending an email through Gmail, you must configure the following:

- **To:** (Recipient's email address)
- **Subject:** (Email subject line)
- **Body:** (Email content)
- **Attachments:** (Optional, if applicable)

Each of these fields can either be **manually entered** (static values) or **dynamically mapped** from the trigger event.

Example of Dynamic Data Mapping

If our trigger is a new contact in Google Sheets, we can map:

Action Field Data Source (from Google Sheets)

To: Email column in the sheet

Subject: "Welcome to Our Service"

Body: A personalized welcome message

To map a field:

1. Click inside the **To** field.
2. A dropdown will appear showing available trigger fields.
3. Select the field that contains the recipient's email.

Step 2: Customizing Text and Formatting

Many actions allow **custom text formatting** to make outputs more user-friendly. You can:

✓ **Use placeholders** for dynamic values
✓ **Apply basic text formatting** (e.g., bold, italic)
✓ **Use Zapier Formatter** for more advanced modifications

For example, in the email body:

Hello {{First Name}},

Thank you for signing up! We're excited to have you.

Best,

Your Company Team

Here, {{First Name}} dynamically pulls in the contact's first name from Google Sheets.

Step 3: Using Advanced Customization Features

A. Filters and Conditions

Sometimes, you may want to add conditions to an action.

For example:

- Only send an email **if the contact has opted in for email marketing**.

- Only create a Slack message **if a deal is worth more than $5000**.

To add a condition:

1. Click **+ Add a Condition** in the action setup.

2. Define the criteria (e.g., "Email Opt-in" = "Yes").

3. Save and test.

B. Delays and Scheduling

- You can delay an action (e.g., send a follow-up email **3 days later**).

- To add a delay, insert a **Delay by Zapier** step before the action.

C. Using Zapier Formatter

- Convert **dates** into different formats.

- Extract **specific words** from a text field.

- Format **phone numbers** into a consistent format.

Example: Converting "2025-02-18T14:30:00Z" into "Feb 18, 2025, 2:30 PM".

Step 4: Testing Your Action

Before activating your Zap, **always test the action**.

1.   Click **Test & Continue** to see if the email is correctly sent.

2.   If an error occurs, review the data mappings and fix any issues.

Common issues and fixes:

- **Incorrect email formatting** → Ensure a valid email address is provided.

- **Missing required fields** → Check if all mandatory fields are filled.

- **Authentication errors** → Reconnect the app and verify permissions.

Step 5: Saving and Activating Your Zap

Once your action settings are properly configured:

1.   Click **Turn on Zap** to activate it.

2.   Monitor Zap **task history** to check for errors.

3.   Optimize the Zap over time based on performance.

Summary

In this section, we covered:
✓ How to map trigger data to action fields
✓ Customizing outputs using placeholders and formatting
✓ Using filters, conditions, and delays
✓ Testing and troubleshooting common issues

By mastering action settings, you can build **powerful and efficient Zaps** that automate workflows seamlessly. Now, let's move on to managing and optimizing your Zaps in the next section!

3.1.5 Testing and Activating Your Zap

Now that you've set up your Zap by selecting a **trigger app**, configuring a **trigger event**, choosing an **action app**, and setting up the **action settings**, it's time to **test and activate your Zap**. This step is crucial because it ensures that your automation works correctly before it runs in the background.

This section will guide you through:
✓ How to test your Zap before activating it
✓ Understanding and troubleshooting test errors
✓ Activating and managing your Zap

1. Why Testing Your Zap is Important?

Before you activate your Zap, **testing is essential** for several reasons:

- **Ensures data is transferred correctly**: Testing confirms that your trigger app is sending the right data to the action app.

- **Identifies configuration errors**: If your trigger or action settings are incorrect, you can fix them before activating the Zap.

- **Prevents unnecessary task usage**: If your Zap runs incorrectly, it could consume unnecessary tasks, which may lead to exceeding your plan's limit.

- **Saves time troubleshooting later**: Identifying and fixing issues at the testing stage saves you from debugging issues after the Zap is active.

2. How to Test Your Zap in Zapier?

Zapier provides a built-in **testing tool** that lets you verify whether your Zap is set up correctly. Let's go step by step through the process of testing and activating your Zap.

Step 1: Test the Trigger

Once you've set up your trigger app and configured the trigger event, Zapier will prompt you to **test the trigger**.

How to Run a Trigger Test

1. **Click the "Test Trigger" button**: After setting up your trigger, Zapier will display a button labeled **"Test Trigger"**. Click it to proceed.

2. **Zapier fetches sample data**: Zapier will attempt to retrieve recent data from the trigger app.

3. **Review the sample data**: If successful, Zapier will show the data it retrieved. This is important because it ensures that Zapier is pulling the right kind of information.

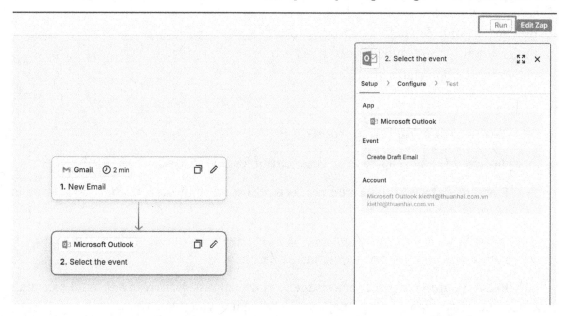

What If Zapier Can't Find Data?

If Zapier cannot fetch sample data from your trigger app, try these troubleshooting steps:

✅ **Ensure there is recent activity in the trigger app**: For example, if your trigger is "New Email in Gmail," ensure that a recent email is available in your inbox.

✅ **Manually create a test entry**: If your app doesn't have recent activity, create a new entry (e.g., send a test email, add a new spreadsheet row) and retry the test.

✅ **Check app permissions**: Make sure Zapier has the correct permissions to access your app. Sometimes, reconnecting the app can help.

✅ **Review trigger settings**: Double-check the trigger conditions. For example, if your trigger is "New Email with Label," make sure an email actually matches the label criteria.

If Zapier successfully retrieves sample data, move on to testing the **action step**.

Step 2: Test the Action

After setting up the action app and configuring the action, Zapier allows you to test the action step. This ensures that the data from the trigger is correctly processed and sent to the action app.

How to Run an Action Test

1. **Click the "Test & Review" or "Test & Continue" button**: Once the action step is configured, Zapier provides options to test it.

2. **Zapier sends the sample data**: Zapier will use the test data retrieved from the trigger app and send it to the action app.

3. **Check the test results**: If successful, Zapier will display confirmation that the data was sent to the action app.

How to Verify That the Action Worked?

✅ **Check the action app**: Open the action app and confirm that the automation ran as expected. For example:

- If the Zap is supposed to send an email, check your inbox.

- If the Zap adds a new Trello card, look for it in your Trello board.

- If the Zap updates a spreadsheet, verify that the new row appears.

✅ **Compare expected vs. actual results**: If the data doesn't appear as expected, review your Zap settings to ensure that all required fields are correctly mapped.

✅ **Review task history**: Zapier provides a **task history log** where you can see details about each step of the Zap.

---

3. Troubleshooting Common Test Errors

Sometimes, the test may fail due to misconfigurations or connectivity issues. Here's how to handle common issues:

Trigger Test Fails

◆ **Problem**: "Zapier could not find sample data."

✓ **Solution**: Manually create a test entry in the trigger app and retest.

♦ **Problem**: "App authentication failed."
✓ **Solution**: Reconnect your app in Zapier and ensure proper permissions.

♦ **Problem**: "Zapier can't access certain fields."
✓ **Solution**: Check that the trigger settings include the right data scope.

Action Test Fails

♦ **Problem**: "Zapier could not send data to the action app."
✓ **Solution**: Verify that the action app is connected correctly.

♦ **Problem**: "Required fields are missing."
✓ **Solution**: Ensure that all necessary fields in the action setup are properly mapped.

♦ **Problem**: "Action app is rejecting the data format."
✓ **Solution**: Use **Zapier Formatter** to format the data correctly before sending it.

---

4. Activating Your Zap

Once your Zap has been successfully tested, the final step is to **activate it** so that it runs automatically in the background.

How to Activate Your Zap

1. **Click the "Publish Zap" button**: This turns the Zap on, allowing it to run whenever the trigger conditions are met.

2. **Check the Zap status**: In your Zapier dashboard, ensure that the Zap status shows as **"On"**.

3. **Monitor the first few runs**: Check the task history to verify that your Zap is running smoothly.

Best Practices for Managing Active Zaps

✓ **Monitor task usage**: If you are on a free plan, ensure that your Zap isn't using up too many tasks quickly.

✓ **Set up notifications**: Zapier allows you to receive notifications if a Zap fails. This helps you quickly identify and fix issues.

✓ **Regularly review your Zaps**: As your workflow evolves, periodically review your Zaps to optimize and update them as needed.

Conclusion

Congratulations! You've successfully tested and activated your first Zap. 🎊 By following these steps, you ensure that your automation runs smoothly and efficiently.

◆ In the next section, we'll explore how to **edit and manage your Zaps**, including modifying existing Zaps, duplicating workflows, and organizing your automations.

🚀 **Ready to automate more tasks? Let's continue!** 🚀

3.2 Editing and Managing Your Zaps

3.2.1 Modifying an Existing Zap

Once you've created a Zap, you may find that you need to modify it to better fit your workflow. This could include changing a trigger, adjusting an action, adding new steps, or refining filters to improve automation efficiency. In this section, we'll go through the complete process of editing an existing Zap, from accessing the editor to implementing changes and troubleshooting potential issues.

Why Modify an Existing Zap?

There are several reasons why you might need to modify a Zap:

- **Business or workflow changes** – Your workflow may evolve, requiring adjustments to the Zap.

- **App updates** – The third-party apps you integrated may have new features or API changes.

- **Fixing issues** – If your Zap is not working correctly, you may need to debug and make corrections.

- **Optimization** – You may want to enhance the Zap's efficiency by refining triggers, actions, or adding new steps.

Accessing the Zap Editor

To modify an existing Zap, follow these steps:

1. **Log in to Zapier**

   o Go to Zapier's website and log in to your account.

   o Navigate to the **Dashboard** by clicking on "Zaps" from the left-hand menu.

2. **Find the Zap You Want to Modify**

o   Use the search bar or scroll through your list of Zaps to find the one you want to edit.

o   Click on the Zap's name to open the editor.

3. **Enter the Zap Editor**

o   The Zap Editor interface will appear, showing all steps in your automation.

o   Here, you can modify the trigger, actions, paths, and filters.

Editing the Trigger in a Zap

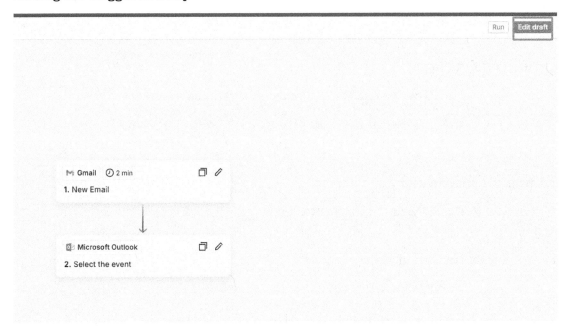

The trigger is the event that starts your Zap. If you need to change the trigger, follow these steps:

1. **Click on the Trigger Section**

   o The first step in the Zap Editor is your trigger. Click on it to open the settings.

2. **Modify the Trigger App**

   o If you need to change the app that triggers the Zap, click **Change App & Event** and select a new one.

3. **Adjust the Trigger Event**

   o Depending on the selected app, choose a new trigger event (e.g., "New Email" for Gmail or "New Row Added" for Google Sheets).

4. **Reconnect or Change the Account**

   o If necessary, update the connected account by clicking **Change Account** and re-authorizing a new integration.

5. **Update the Trigger Conditions**

   o Modify specific conditions, such as filtering emails by subject or selecting a particular folder in Google Drive.

6. **Test the Trigger**

   o Click **Test Trigger** to ensure the new settings work correctly.

   o If Zapier detects data successfully, click **Continue** to save the changes.

Editing an Action in a Zap

If you need to change what happens after the trigger fires, follow these steps to edit an action:

1. **Locate the Action Step**

   o Scroll down in the Zap Editor to find the action step you want to modify.

   o Click on the action block to expand its settings.

2. **Change the Action App (Optional)**

   o If you want to use a different app for the action, click **Change App & Event** and select a new app.

3. **Modify the Action Event**

   o Choose a different action event based on the selected app.

   o For example, if using Slack, you could change from "Send a Message" to "Create a Channel."

4. **Update the Connected Account**

   o If necessary, switch to a different account by selecting **Change Account** and reconnecting.

5. **Modify Action Fields**

   o Update data mapping between the trigger and action.

   o Ensure fields like message content, recipient email, or file destination are correct.

6. **Test the Action**

   o Click **Test & Review** to confirm the action is executed correctly.

   o If the test is successful, click **Continue** to save changes.

Adding a New Step to a Zap

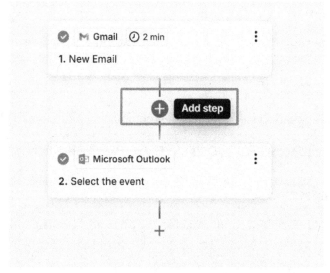

If you need to extend a Zap's functionality, you can add more steps:

1. **Click on the "+" Button**

   o   Find the section where you want to insert a new step.

   o   Click on the "**+**" icon to add an action.

2. **Choose an App for the New Step**

   o   Select an app for the new step (e.g., Google Drive, Trello, Salesforce).

3. **Set Up the Action or Filter**

   o   Choose the appropriate action (e.g., "Create File," "Add Card," "Send Email").

   o   Configure necessary settings and map data fields from previous steps.

4. **Test the New Step**

   o   Run a test to ensure the new step is working properly.

Using Filters and Paths to Refine Zaps

Filters and paths allow you to create advanced workflows by setting conditions.

1. **Adding a Filter**

    o Click **Add a Filter** and define rules to determine when the Zap should proceed.

    o Example: Only continue if an email subject contains "Urgent."

2. **Setting Up a Path**

    o Click **Add a Path** to create different branches in your Zap.

    o Example: If a customer type is "VIP," send an email; otherwise, log it in a spreadsheet.

3. **Testing the Conditions**

    o Run tests to confirm the filters and paths are working correctly.

Deleting or Disabling a Zap

If you no longer need a Zap, you can either disable or delete it.

1. **Disabling a Zap**

    o Go to the Zap Editor.

    o Toggle the **ON/OFF** switch to **OFF** to disable the Zap without deleting it.

2. **Deleting a Zap**

    o In the **Dashboard**, find the Zap.

    o Click the three-dot menu and select **Delete**.

    o Confirm the deletion (this action is permanent).

Testing and Troubleshooting After Modifications

After making changes, always test the Zap to ensure it works correctly.

1. **Run a Manual Test**

    o   Click **Test & Review** for each step in the Zap.

2. **Check the Zap History**

    o   Navigate to **Zap History** to review past runs.

    o   Look for errors or failed tasks and adjust settings accordingly.

3. **Use Zapier's Debugging Tools**

    o   Read error messages and troubleshoot based on Zapier's recommendations.

Best Practices for Editing Zaps

- **Always test changes before activating** to prevent automation failures.

- **Keep Zaps organized** by using folders and descriptive names.

- **Monitor Zap history** regularly to catch errors early.

- **Document changes** so team members understand updates.

Conclusion

Modifying an existing Zap is a crucial skill that allows you to optimize workflows, fix issues, and expand automation capabilities. By following these step-by-step instructions, you can confidently edit Zaps to improve efficiency and productivity.

Would you like to explore more advanced editing techniques, such as using Code by Zapier or integrating with APIs? Let's continue in the next section! 🚀

3.2.2 Duplicating and Deleting Zaps

Once you have created and refined your Zaps, you may find the need to duplicate or delete them. Duplicating a Zap can save time when you want to create similar workflows without starting from scratch. Deleting a Zap is useful when a workflow is no longer needed or is being replaced. This section will guide you through the process of duplicating and deleting Zaps effectively.

1. Why Duplicate a Zap?

Duplicating a Zap is a powerful feature that allows you to:

- **Save time** – Instead of recreating a workflow from scratch, you can duplicate an existing Zap and make necessary modifications.

- **Maintain consistency** – If you use similar workflows across different teams or projects, duplication ensures consistency in automation.

- **Test variations** – You can duplicate a Zap to experiment with different triggers, actions, or configurations without affecting the original workflow.

- **Scale automation** – When expanding your automation efforts, duplicating a Zap allows you to quickly replicate proven workflows.

Common Use Cases for Duplicating Zaps

1. **Similar Workflows for Different Teams**

   o Example: You have a Zap that sends Slack notifications when a new form submission is received. If multiple departments use different Slack channels, you can duplicate the Zap and adjust the destination channel.

2. **Different Trigger Conditions**

   o Example: You automate email notifications for new orders in Shopify. You duplicate the Zap to create another version that triggers only for high-value orders.

3. **Testing and Debugging**

   o Example: You want to modify an existing Zap but don't want to disrupt its functionality. Duplicating it allows you to test changes safely.

2. How to Duplicate a Zap

Duplicating a Zap in Zapier is a straightforward process. Follow these steps:

Step 1: Access Your Zaps

1. Log in to your Zapier account.

2. Navigate to the **Dashboard** by clicking on "Zaps" in the left-hand menu.

3. Locate the Zap you want to duplicate.

Step 2: Open the Zap Options

1. Find the Zap you wish to duplicate.

2. Click on the **three-dot menu (:)** located on the right side of the Zap.

3. Select **"Duplicate"** from the dropdown menu.

Step 3: Rename and Modify the Zap

1. After duplication, the copied Zap will appear in your Zaps list with "(Copy)" appended to its name.

2. Click on the duplicated Zap to open it.

3. Rename the Zap to reflect its new purpose by clicking the name at the top.

4. Modify the **Trigger App, Trigger Event, Action App, or Action Steps** as needed.

Step 4: Test and Activate the Duplicated Zap

1. Click **"Test"** to ensure the new Zap functions correctly.

2. Once verified, toggle the **"ON/OFF"** switch to activate the Zap.

◆ **Pro Tip:** If you are making minor changes to an existing Zap but want to preserve the original, duplicate the Zap first before making edits.

3. Why Delete a Zap?

Deleting Zaps helps you:

- **Declutter your workspace** – Over time, unused or obsolete Zaps can accumulate.

- **Avoid confusion** – Removing outdated workflows prevents mistakes and duplicate automation.

- **Optimize task usage** – Zapier plans limit the number of tasks per month. Deleting unnecessary Zaps prevents wasted tasks.

When Should You Delete a Zap?

✓ The Zap is outdated and no longer relevant.
✓ You created a new, improved version of the workflow.
✓ The connected app is no longer in use.
✓ The Zap is causing unintended automation issues.

4. How to Delete a Zap

Step 1: Locate the Zap to Be Deleted

1. Go to your **Zapier Dashboard**.

2. Click on **"Zaps"** in the left-hand menu.

3. Find the Zap you want to delete.

Step 2: Open the Zap Options

1. Click the **three-dot menu (⋮)** on the right side of the Zap.

2. Select **"Delete"** from the dropdown menu.

Step 3: Confirm Deletion

1. A pop-up window will appear asking you to confirm.

2. Click **"Yes, delete"** to permanently remove the Zap.

🏛 **Warning:** Deleted Zaps cannot be recovered. If you might need the workflow later, consider **turning it off** instead of deleting it.

◆ **Pro Tip:** Before deleting, **export the Zap's structure** by taking screenshots or noting key configurations if you plan to recreate it later.

5. Alternative: Turning Off a Zap Instead of Deleting It

If you are unsure whether to delete a Zap, you can **disable it temporarily** instead.

How to Turn Off a Zap

1. Locate the Zap in the **Dashboard**.

2. Toggle the **ON/OFF switch** next to the Zap's name.

3. The Zap is now disabled but still saved for future use.

✓ Use this option if:

- You might need the Zap later.

- You are troubleshooting and need to pause automation.

- You are switching to a different workflow but want to keep the old one as a backup.

---

6. Managing Multiple Zaps Efficiently

If you have numerous Zaps, managing them properly ensures a streamlined workflow. Here are some tips:

1. Organize Zaps into Folders

- Use folders to categorize Zaps by function (e.g., "Marketing," "HR Automation," "Finance").

- To create a folder, click **"+ New Folder"** in the Zapier Dashboard and drag relevant Zaps into it.

2. Use Naming Conventions

- Name your Zaps clearly, e.g., **"Slack Notification for New Trello Cards"** instead of **"Zap #3"**.

3. Regularly Review and Clean Up Zaps

- Set a schedule (e.g., monthly) to review active and inactive Zaps.

- Delete obsolete Zaps to keep your workspace efficient.

4. Document Key Zaps

- Keep a simple document (Google Docs, Notion) listing your active Zaps and their purposes.

7. Summary & Key Takeaways

- **Duplicating Zaps** saves time and ensures consistency across workflows.

- **To duplicate a Zap:** Go to the Dashboard → Click the three-dot menu → Select "Duplicate" → Rename and modify the Zap.

- **Deleting Zaps** helps declutter and optimize task usage.

- **To delete a Zap:** Go to the Dashboard → Click the three-dot menu → Select "Delete" → Confirm.

- **Instead of deleting, you can turn off a Zap** if you might need it later.

- **Organizing Zaps using folders and naming conventions** improves workflow management.

By following these steps, you can efficiently manage your Zaps, ensuring your automation remains organized and effective. 🚀

3.2.3 Organizing Zaps with Folders

As you create more Zaps to automate different tasks, managing them efficiently becomes crucial. Zapier provides a **Folders** feature that helps users categorize, sort, and locate Zaps more easily. By properly organizing your Zaps, you can enhance productivity, improve team collaboration, and avoid clutter in your Zapier dashboard.

This section will cover:

- Why organizing Zaps with folders is important

- How to create and manage folders

- Best practices for folder organization

- How to share and collaborate using folders

Why Organizing Zaps with Folders Is Important

When you start using Zapier, you might only have a few Zaps running. At this stage, managing them manually is easy. However, as your automation needs grow, you may end up with **dozens or even hundreds of Zaps**. Without a structured approach, you might face:

- **Difficulty finding specific Zaps** – Searching through an unorganized list can be frustrating.

- **Accidental duplication** – You might create similar Zaps because you can't easily find an existing one.

- **Collaboration challenges** – Team members may struggle to locate relevant Zaps.

- **Risk of disabling important Zaps** – If your Zaps are not categorized, you may accidentally turn off an essential one.

By using folders, you can **streamline your workflow, reduce errors, and save time** when managing your automation processes.

How to Create and Manage Folders in Zapier

Step 1: Accessing the Folders Feature

1. **Log in to your Zapier account.**

2. On the **Zapier dashboard**, navigate to the **Zaps** section.

3. Look at the left-hand panel where your Zaps are listed—this is where you'll find the **Folders** section.

Step 2: Creating a New Folder

1. Click on the **"+ Create Folder"** button.

2. A dialog box will appear prompting you to enter a **folder name**.

3. Choose a name that clearly describes the category or purpose of the Zaps you will store inside.

   o Example: **"Marketing Automations"** for all marketing-related Zaps.

4. Click **"Create"** to save the folder.

5. Your new folder will now appear in the **left-hand panel** under the **Folders** section.

Step 3: Moving Zaps into a Folder

1. Locate the Zap you want to move in your dashboard.

2. Click the **three-dot menu (⋮)** next to the Zap.

3. Select **"Move to Folder"** from the dropdown menu.

4. Choose the folder where you want to store the Zap.

5. Your Zap will now be organized under that folder.

◆ **Tip:** You can also drag and drop Zaps into folders for a quicker experience.

Step 4: Renaming or Deleting Folders

- To rename a folder: Click the **three-dot menu (⋮)** next to a folder and select **"Rename"**. Enter the new name and save.

- To delete a folder: Click the **three-dot menu (⋮)** and select **"Delete"**.

  o   ⚠ **Warning:** Deleting a folder **does not delete the Zaps inside it**—they will move back to the main **All Zaps** section.

Best Practices for Folder Organization

Proper organization of your folders helps you **stay efficient and avoid chaos**. Here are some best practices to follow:

1. Use Clear and Consistent Naming Conventions

When naming your folders, make them **descriptive and standardized** so you and your team can quickly understand their purpose.

✅ **Good Examples:**

- ♦ **Sales CRM Automations** (for all CRM-related Zaps)

- ♦ **Customer Support Workflows** (for Zaps that handle tickets and inquiries)

- ♦ **Social Media Posting** (for Zaps automating social media content)

✗ **Bad Examples:**

- ⚠ **Folder 1** (not descriptive)

- ⚠ **Zaps for Work** (too generic)

2. Categorize Folders by Function or Department

Organize your folders **based on your use case**. Some common structures include:

- **By Department:** Sales, Marketing, HR, Customer Support
- **By Function:** Lead Generation, Task Automation, Report Generation
- **By Frequency of Use:** Daily Zaps, Weekly Reports, Monthly Summaries

For example, if you run a business, you might have:

💼 **Sales CRM** – For Zaps related to HubSpot, Salesforce, or Pipedrive
💼 **Marketing Automation** – For Zaps handling email marketing and social media
💼 **Finance & Invoicing** – For Zaps connecting QuickBooks or Stripe

3. Create Subfolders for Further Organization

If you have many Zaps within a folder, consider breaking them down into **subcategories**:

📁 **Marketing Automations**

- 📄 **Email Marketing** (For Mailchimp, ActiveCampaign Zaps)

- 📄 **Social Media Posts** (For Facebook, Instagram Zaps)

📁 **HR & Recruitment**

- 📄 **New Hire Onboarding** (For new employee workflows)

- 📄 **Candidate Screening** (For Zapier integrations with job portals)

◆ **Note:** Zapier currently does not support subfolders **within the interface**, but you can simulate them by using **consistent folder names**.

Sharing and Collaborating Using Folders

1. Using Folders in Zapier Teams & Zapier for Companies

If you are using **Zapier for Teams** or **Zapier for Companies**, you can share and manage Zaps within folders more efficiently.

1. Click on a folder's **three-dot menu (⋮)**.

2. Select **"Share Folder"** and add team members.

3. Assign **view or edit permissions** depending on the level of access they need.

◆ **Tip:** For large teams, create a shared **"Master Folder"** with essential Zaps so all members have access.

2. Preventing Unauthorized Changes

- Set up **restricted access** to prevent accidental edits.

- Use **naming conventions** like **"[Do Not Edit]"** on folders containing critical automations.

- Regularly **audit** shared folders to ensure they are up to date.

Troubleshooting Folder Issues

Problem: I Can't Move a Zap into a Folder

✅ **Solution:** Ensure that the Zap is **active** and not in an error state. Try refreshing the page.

Problem: My Folder Disappeared

✅ **Solution:** Check if you **accidentally renamed** it. If you are on a team account, ensure another team member **did not delete** it.

Problem: My Zaps Are Not Well Organized

✅ **Solution:** Use a **consistent naming system** and review folder contents every **3-6 months** to remove outdated Zaps.

Final Thoughts

Organizing Zaps with folders is a simple yet powerful way to maintain a clean and efficient Zapier workspace. By following best practices such as using clear folder names, categorizing by function, and setting up proper access permissions, you can save time, avoid confusion, and optimize your automation workflow.

Now that you have mastered folder organization, let's move on to the next chapter, where we'll explore popular Zapier integrations and how they can enhance your productivity!

CHAPTER III
Exploring Popular Zapier Integrations

4.1 Automating Email and Communication

4.1.1 Gmail and Outlook Automations

Email is an essential tool for both personal and professional communication. However, managing emails manually can be time-consuming and inefficient, especially when handling repetitive tasks such as sending confirmations, sorting emails, or archiving important messages. Fortunately, Zapier enables you to automate Gmail and Outlook workflows, saving time and ensuring consistency in communication.

In this section, we will explore how to set up automations using Zapier for Gmail and Outlook, including:

- Setting up basic email automations

- Automating email organization and labeling

- Sending automated responses and follow-ups

- Integrating email with other tools

1. Understanding Zapier's Email Integrations

Zapier provides powerful integrations for both **Gmail** and **Outlook**, allowing users to create automated workflows that interact with emails. These integrations work by setting up a **Zap**, which consists of a **Trigger** (an event that starts the automation) and an **Action** (the task that Zapier performs in response).

Supported Triggers and Actions for Gmail

Zapier supports multiple triggers and actions for Gmail automation, including:

Triggers (What Starts an Automation in Gmail)

- **New Email** – Triggers when a new email is received.

- **New Email Matching Search** – Triggers when an email matching specific search criteria (e.g., subject line or sender) is received.

- **New Starred Email** – Triggers when an email is marked as starred.

- **New Labeled Email** – Triggers when an email is assigned a specific label.

Actions (What Zapier Does in Gmail)

- **Send Email** – Automatically sends an email from your Gmail account.

- **Create Draft Email** – Creates a draft email that you can review and send manually.

- **Add Label to Email** – Adds a label to a specific email for organization.

- **Reply to Email** – Automatically replies to an email with a pre-set response.

Supported Triggers and Actions for Outlook

Microsoft Outlook also has a wide range of automation options in Zapier.

Triggers (What Starts an Automation in Outlook)

- **New Email** – Triggers when a new email arrives in the inbox.

- **New Email Matching Search** – Triggers when an email that meets specific criteria is received.

- **New Event in Calendar** – Triggers when a new event is added to the Outlook calendar (useful for scheduling-related automations).

Actions (What Zapier Does in Outlook)

- **Send Email** – Sends an automated email from your Outlook account.

- **Create Draft Email** – Creates a draft email for manual review before sending.

- **Add Email to Folder** – Moves an email to a specific folder.

- **Reply to Email** – Sends an automated reply to an incoming email.

2. Setting Up Your First Email Automation

Now that we understand the available triggers and actions, let's walk through creating a **simple email automation** with Zapier.

Example 1: Sending an Automated Response for New Emails

Imagine you receive many inquiries via email and want to send an automatic acknowledgment message. Here's how you can do it:

Step 1: Create a New Zap

1. Log in to your **Zapier account**.

2. Click on **"Create a Zap"**.

Step 2: Set the Trigger (New Email in Gmail or Outlook)

1. Search for **Gmail** (or Outlook) and select it as the trigger app.

2. Choose **"New Email"** as the trigger event.

3. Click **"Continue"** and sign in to your Gmail or Outlook account.

4. Customize the trigger by selecting the inbox or folder where the email should be received.

Step 3: Set the Action (Send an Automated Response)

1. Search for **Gmail** (or Outlook) and select it as the action app.

2. Choose **"Send Email"** as the action event.

3. Click **"Continue"** and sign in to your email account.

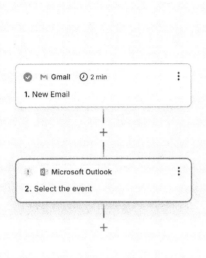
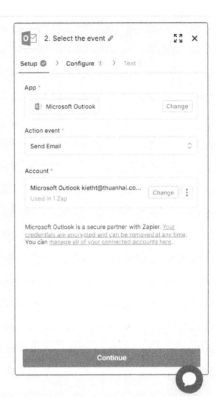

4. Set up the email content:

    o   **To:** Select the **"From"** field from the trigger step (this ensures the reply goes to the sender).

    o   **Subject:** Set it as **"Thank you for your email!"**

    o   **Body:** Write a response, such as:

"Hello,
Thank you for reaching out. We have received your message and will get back to you within 24 hours.
Best regards,
[Your Name]"

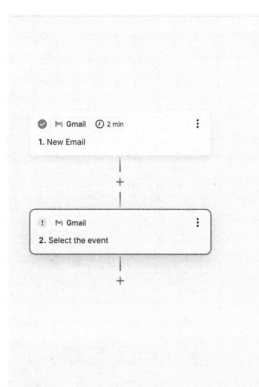

5.   Click **"Continue"**, test the Zap, and turn it on.

◈ **Outcome:** Whenever you receive a new email, an automatic reply will be sent, saving you time and ensuring prompt communication.

3. Automating Email Organization

If your inbox is cluttered with emails, you can use Zapier to **automatically categorize and organize incoming messages**.

Example 2: Auto-Labeling Emails from Important Clients

Step 1: Create a New Zap

- Go to Zapier and **create a new Zap**.

Step 2: Set the Trigger (New Email in Gmail with Specific Conditions)

- Select **Gmail** as the trigger app.

- Choose **"New Email Matching Search"** as the trigger event.

- Set search criteria, such as emails from a specific client (from:client@example.com).

Step 3: Set the Action (Add a Label to the Email)

- Select **Gmail** as the action app.

- Choose **"Add Label to Email"** as the action event.

- Select the label (e.g., "Important Clients").

- Test the Zap and turn it on.

◆ **Outcome:** Every time a client emails you, Zapier will **automatically label their emails**, keeping your inbox organized.

---

4. Advanced Email Automations

For more complex workflows, consider multi-step Zaps:

◈ **Send email attachments to Google Drive:** Automatically save attachments from Gmail or Outlook to Google Drive for easy access.
◈ **Add email senders to a Google Sheets contact list:** Store new email contacts in a Google Sheet for tracking purposes.
◈ **Forward important emails to Slack:** Get Slack notifications for critical emails.

---

5. Best Practices for Email Automation

- **Use filters carefully:** Avoid setting broad triggers that might cause unnecessary automations.

- **Personalize automated responses:** Make sure automated emails feel human and relevant.

- **Test before activating:** Run test emails to ensure accuracy.

- **Monitor automation logs:** Use Zapier's **Zap History** to track automation success and fix errors.

Conclusion

By leveraging **Zapier's Gmail and Outlook integrations**, you can **automate repetitive tasks**, improve efficiency, and streamline email management. Whether you're sending automatic replies, organizing your inbox, or integrating emails with other tools, Zapier makes email workflows smarter and faster.

💡 **Next Steps:** Try creating your own Zaps for different email scenarios and explore advanced automation features in the next section! 🚀

4.1.2 Slack and Microsoft Teams Workflows

In today's workplace, communication platforms like Slack and Microsoft Teams play a crucial role in collaboration, team discussions, and project management. By integrating these platforms with Zapier, you can automate various tasks, reduce manual effort, and ensure seamless communication across teams.

This section will cover:

- The benefits of automating Slack and Microsoft Teams workflows

- How to set up Slack and Microsoft Teams integrations with Zapier

- Common automation use cases and step-by-step guides

- Advanced automations with conditional logic and multi-step Zaps

1. Why Automate Slack and Microsoft Teams Workflows?

Slack and Microsoft Teams are powerful tools for team communication, but managing messages, notifications, and tasks manually can be time-consuming. Here's how automation with Zapier can help:

Increased Productivity

Instead of manually sending updates or reminders, Zapier can automate repetitive messaging tasks. For example:

- Automatically notify a Slack or Teams channel when a new task is created in Trello or Asana

- Send daily summary messages of new emails, form responses, or calendar events

Improved Collaboration

By integrating Slack and Teams with other productivity tools, you can ensure that everyone stays informed without switching between multiple apps.

Reduced Human Error

Automation helps eliminate the risk of missing important messages, forgetting to update team members, or sending duplicate notifications.

2. Setting Up Slack and Microsoft Teams in Zapier

Before creating automated workflows, you need to connect Slack and Microsoft Teams to Zapier.

Connecting Slack to Zapier

1. **Log in to Zapier** and navigate to the **Apps** section.

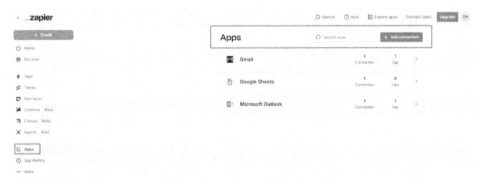

2. Search for **Slack** and click **Connect**.

3. Authorize Zapier to access your Slack workspace.

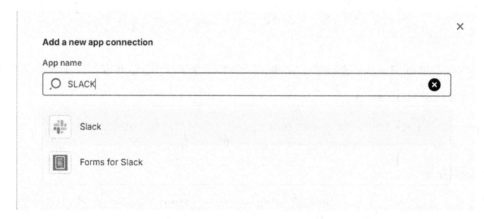

4. Select the channels or permissions Zapier will use.

Connecting Microsoft Teams to Zapier

1. In Zapier, search for **Microsoft Teams** and click **Connect**.

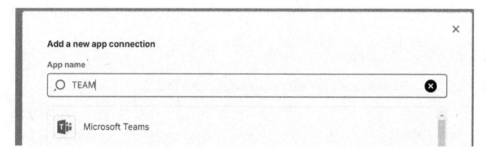

2. Sign in with your Microsoft 365 account.

3. Allow Zapier to access your Microsoft Teams environment.

4. Choose the Teams workspace and channels you want Zapier to interact with.

Once the connections are set up, you can start building Zaps to automate your workflows.

---

3. Common Slack and Microsoft Teams Automations

Here are some of the most useful automations that can enhance your team's efficiency:

Automatic Notifications for New Tasks

If your team uses project management tools like Trello, Asana, or Monday.com, you can automate task notifications in Slack or Teams.

Example: Send a Slack Message When a New Trello Card is Created

1. **Trigger**: Choose **Trello** → Select "New Card" in a specific board.

2. **Action**: Choose **Slack** → "Send Channel Message."

3. **Customize Message**: Use Trello data to include the task name, due date, and a link.

4. **Test and Activate**: Run a test, then enable your Zap.

◆ *Now, whenever a new Trello card is created, your Slack channel receives an update.*

Alert Teams When a New Lead Comes In

If your business collects leads through Google Forms, Typeform, or HubSpot, you can notify sales teams instantly via Slack or Teams.

Example: Notify a Microsoft Teams Channel When a Lead Fills Out a Form

1. **Trigger**: Choose **Google Forms** → "New Response in Spreadsheet."

2. **Action**: Choose **Microsoft Teams** → "Send Channel Message."

3. **Customize Message**: Include lead details such as name, email, and company.

4. **Test and Activate**: Run a test, then turn on your Zap.

◆ *Your sales team will receive an instant notification when a new lead submits a form.*

Automating Meeting Reminders

If you use Google Calendar or Outlook to schedule meetings, you can send automated reminders in Slack or Teams before the meeting starts.

Example: Send a Slack Reminder for Upcoming Meetings

1. **Trigger**: Choose **Google Calendar** → "Event Start."

2. **Action**: Choose **Slack** → "Send Direct Message."

3. **Customize Message**: Include meeting details and a Google Meet or Zoom link.

4. **Test and Activate**: Ensure messages are sent correctly, then enable your Zap.

◆ *Now, Slack will remind attendees 10 minutes before each meeting.*

---

4. Advanced Slack and Microsoft Teams Automations

For more complex workflows, you can use multi-step Zaps, conditional logic, and data formatting.

Multi-Step Zap: Assign Tasks Automatically

Instead of just notifying a channel, you can also assign a task based on predefined rules.

Example: When a High-Priority Support Ticket is Created, Notify a Slack Channel and Assign a Task in Asana

1. **Trigger**: Choose **Zendesk** → "New High-Priority Ticket."

2. **Action 1**: Choose **Slack** → "Send Channel Message."

3. **Action 2**: Choose **Asana** → "Create Task."

4. **Customize and Activate**: Ensure relevant details are passed between actions.

◆ *Your support team will be notified instantly, and a task will be assigned to the right person.*

Conditional Logic: Only Notify Certain Teams Based on Keywords

Using Zapier's **Filters**, you can send messages only when specific conditions are met.

Example: If a Message Contains "Urgent," Notify a Special Microsoft Teams Channel

1. **Trigger**: Choose **Slack** → "New Message Posted in Channel."

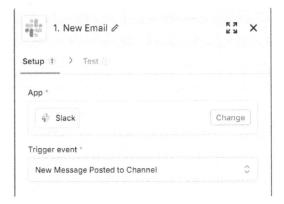

2. **Filter**: Use **Zapier Filter** → "Only continue if message contains 'Urgent'."

3. **Action**: Choose **Microsoft Teams** → "Send Message."

4. **Customize and Activate**: Ensure only urgent messages are forwarded.

◆ *Now, urgent messages will automatically be escalated to the right team.*

Using Webhooks for Custom Integrations

If an app isn't natively supported by Zapier, you can use **Webhooks** to connect it to Slack or Microsoft Teams.

Example: Receive a Slack Notification When a Custom API Sends Data

1. **Trigger**: Choose **Webhooks by Zapier** → "Catch Hook."

2. **Action**: Choose **Slack** → "Send Channel Message."

3. **Customize and Activate**: Format the incoming data and send it to Slack.

◆ *Now, Slack will receive data updates from any custom system.*

---

5. Best Practices for Slack and Teams Automations

Avoid Notification Overload

- Use **Filters** to limit unnecessary messages.

- Combine multiple updates into summary messages instead of sending each event separately.

Maintain Security and Compliance

- Be mindful of sensitive data shared in Slack or Teams.
- Use **Zapier's user permissions** to restrict access.

Monitor and Optimize Automations

- Regularly check your **Zap history** for errors.
- Use **Zapier's built-in logs** to troubleshoot issues.

6. Conclusion

Automating Slack and Microsoft Teams workflows with Zapier can transform how teams communicate and collaborate. Whether it's sending notifications, assigning tasks, or integrating with external tools, these automations can save time and boost efficiency.

4.1.3 Automating Notifications and Alerts

Effective communication is key to productivity, whether in a personal or business setting. However, manually checking emails, tracking updates, or staying informed of important events can be time-consuming. With **Zapier**, you can automate notifications and alerts across multiple platforms, ensuring you never miss a critical update.

This section will guide you through setting up automated notifications and alerts using **Zapier**, including:

- Understanding different types of notifications
- Setting up email and messaging alerts
- Automating notifications for project management updates
- Using Zapier to monitor and trigger important alerts

Understanding Different Types of Notifications

Before setting up automations, it's essential to understand the different types of notifications and their use cases. These include:

1. Email Notifications

- **Use case:** Receive an email when a specific event occurs, such as a form submission, payment received, or new lead.

- **Example:** Get an email alert when someone fills out a Google Form or signs up for a newsletter.

2. Slack or Microsoft Teams Alerts

- **Use case:** Get instant notifications in team collaboration tools for real-time communication.

- **Example:** Receive a Slack message when a new task is assigned to you in Trello.

3. SMS or Push Notifications

- **Use case:** Get an urgent alert on your phone for time-sensitive information.

- **Example:** Receive an SMS when a high-priority support ticket is created.

4. In-App or System Alerts

- **Use case:** Get notifications directly within business applications.

- **Example:** Receive a HubSpot CRM notification when a deal is closed.

Setting Up Email and Messaging Alerts with Zapier

One of the most common ways to automate notifications is through email and messaging platforms. Let's go step by step to create an automation that sends an email alert when a new row is added to a Google Sheet.

Example 1: Send an Email Notification for a New Google Sheet Entry

📌 **Scenario:** You maintain a Google Sheet where team members log new customer support requests. You want to receive an email notification whenever a new row is added.

Step 1: Create a New Zap

1. Log in to **Zapier**.

2. Click **Create Zap**.

Step 2: Set Up the Trigger (Google Sheets)

1. Select **Google Sheets** as the trigger app.

2. Choose **New Spreadsheet Row** as the trigger event.

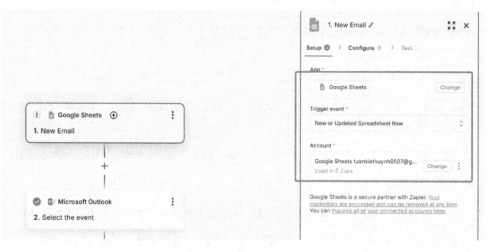

3. Connect your Google Sheets account.

4. Select the specific spreadsheet and worksheet to monitor.

Step 3: Set Up the Action (Send an Email Notification)

1. Select **Gmail** as the action app.

2. Choose **Send Email** as the action event.

3. Connect your Gmail account.

4. Configure the email details:

   o **To:** Your email address (or team members)

   o **Subject:** "New Support Request Logged"

   o **Body:** Include dynamic data such as the customer's name and issue description.

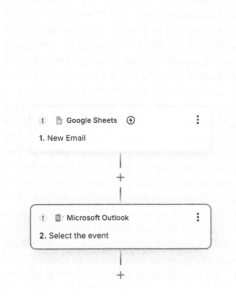

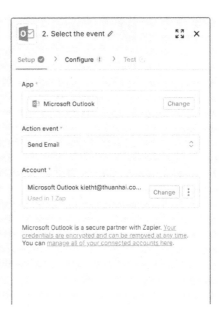

Step 4: Test and Activate the Zap

1. Click **Test & Continue** to ensure the Zap works correctly.

2. Click **Turn on Zap** to start automating notifications.

✅ *Now, every time a new row is added to the spreadsheet, an email notification will be sent automatically.*

Automating Slack or Microsoft Teams Alerts

For real-time collaboration, setting up alerts in **Slack** or **Microsoft Teams** can keep your team informed without flooding inboxes.

Example 2: Send a Slack Alert When a New Lead is Captured in HubSpot

📌 **Scenario:** Your sales team wants to receive a **Slack notification** whenever a new lead is added to **HubSpot CRM**.

Step 1: Set Up the Trigger (HubSpot CRM - New Contact Added)

1. Choose **HubSpot** as the trigger app.

2. Select **New Contact** as the trigger event.

3. Connect your HubSpot account.

4. Select the contact list you want to monitor.

Step 2: Set Up the Action (Slack Notification)

1. Select **Slack** as the action app.

2. Choose **Send Channel Message** as the action event.

3. Connect your Slack account.

4. Configure the Slack message details:

   o **Channel:** #sales-team

   o **Message:** " New lead captured: [Lead Name] from [Company]. Contact at: [Email]"

5. Click **Test & Continue** to verify.

Step 3: Activate the Zap

1. Click **Turn on Zap** to enable automatic Slack notifications.

✅ *Now, every time a new lead is added to HubSpot, the sales team will get an instant Slack message!*

Automating Project Management Alerts

Keeping track of project updates manually can be overwhelming. **Zapier** allows you to automate alerts for changes in Trello, Asana, ClickUp, and Monday.com.

Example 3: Get a Microsoft Teams Notification When a Trello Card is Updated

📌 **Scenario:** You want to get a **Microsoft Teams alert** whenever a Trello card is moved to "Completed."

Step 1: Set Up the Trigger (Trello - Card Moved to a Specific List)

1. Choose **Trello** as the trigger app.

2. Select **Card Moved to List** as the trigger event.

3. Connect your Trello account.

4. Select the **Board** and **Completed List** to monitor.

Step 2: Set Up the Action (Microsoft Teams Notification)

1. Choose **Microsoft Teams** as the action app.

2. Select **Send Message** as the action event.

3. Connect your Microsoft Teams account.

4. Configure the message:

   o **To:** Project Management Channel

   o **Message:** "🎉 A Trello task has been completed: [Card Name]"

Step 3: Activate the Zap

1. Click **Turn on Zap** to start receiving automated alerts in Teams.

✅ **Now, whenever a task is marked as completed in Trello, your team will get a Microsoft Teams notification!**

Using Zapier to Monitor and Trigger Important Alerts

Beyond standard notifications, **Zapier** can be used for monitoring important metrics and sending alerts when thresholds are met.

Example 4: Get an SMS Alert for Low Inventory in Shopify

📌 **Scenario:** You want to receive a **text message** when a product's stock falls below 10 units in **Shopify**.

Step 1: Set Up the Trigger (Shopify - Low Stock Alert)

1. Choose **Shopify** as the trigger app.

2. Select **Updated Product Inventory** as the trigger event.

3. Connect your Shopify account.

4. Set a filter to trigger when stock is **less than 10**.

Step 2: Set Up the Action (Send SMS via Twilio)

1. Choose **Twilio** as the action app.

2. Select **Send SMS** as the action event.

3. Connect your Twilio account.

4. Configure the SMS message:

   o **To:** Your phone number

   o **Message:** "⚠ Low Stock Alert: [Product Name] has only [Stock Count] left!"

Step 3: Activate the Zap

1. Click **Turn on Zap** to start receiving automated SMS alerts.

✅*Now, you'll receive an instant SMS whenever stock runs low in Shopify!*

Conclusion

Automating notifications with **Zapier** can significantly enhance productivity and efficiency. Whether you need email updates, Slack messages, SMS alerts, or project management notifications, Zapier allows you to set up seamless workflows.

🚀 **Next Steps:**

- Try out different integrations based on your needs.

- Experiment with multi-step Zaps for advanced automation.

- Explore Zapier's built-in tools like **Filters and Paths** to refine notifications.

By implementing these automations, you'll never miss an important update again! ✅

4.2 Streamlining Project Management

4.2.1 Trello and Asana Integrations

Effective project management is essential for productivity, collaboration, and ensuring that tasks are completed efficiently. Trello and Asana are two of the most widely used project management tools, helping individuals and teams organize tasks, track progress, and manage workflows. However, manually updating tasks across multiple platforms, ensuring that team members are notified, and integrating these tools with other applications can be time-consuming.

Zapier offers a powerful way to automate these processes, allowing users to connect Trello and Asana with hundreds of other apps. By integrating these tools with Zapier, you can reduce manual work, eliminate redundant data entry, and create seamless workflows that keep your projects moving forward.

1. Introduction to Trello and Asana

Before diving into automation, let's briefly introduce both platforms:

- **Trello** is a visual project management tool that organizes tasks using boards, lists, and cards. It is highly flexible and works well for teams that need an intuitive, drag-and-drop task management system.

- **Asana** is a more structured project management tool that helps teams plan, track, and manage work. It offers features like task dependencies, project timelines, and advanced reporting tools.

Both tools serve similar functions, but their interfaces and features cater to different project management styles. Regardless of which one you use, integrating them with Zapier can enhance their capabilities and streamline your workflow.

2. Benefits of Automating Trello and Asana with Zapier

By using Zapier, you can automate a variety of tasks in Trello and Asana, such as:

✅ **Automatically creating tasks and cards** – Generate Trello cards or Asana tasks from emails, form submissions, or other applications.

✅ **Syncing Trello and Asana** – Ensure that updates in one tool reflect in the other, so you never miss important task changes.

✅ **Automating notifications** – Send Slack messages, emails, or push notifications when tasks are updated or completed.

✅ **Tracking deadlines effortlessly** – Create calendar events when tasks reach their due dates.

✅ **Reducing manual data entry** – Automatically log project updates in spreadsheets or databases.

With these automations in place, you can save time, reduce errors, and keep your projects on track without constantly switching between apps.

---

3. Setting Up Zapier Integrations for Trello

3.1 Connecting Trello to Zapier

Before setting up automations, follow these steps to connect Trello to Zapier:

1. **Log in to Zapier** – If you don't have an account yet, sign up at Zapier.com.

2. **Click on "Create a Zap"** – This will start a new automation workflow.

3. **Choose Trello as a Trigger App** – Search for Trello in Zapier's app directory and select it.

4. **Select a Trigger Event** – Choose an event that will start your automation, such as:

   o **New Card Created** – Triggers when a new card is added.

   o **Card Moved to a List** – Triggers when a card moves to a specific list.

   o **New Activity** – Triggers when there's an update to a board or card.

5. **Connect Your Trello Account** – Log in to Trello and authorize Zapier to access your account.

6. **Test the Connection** – Zapier will pull in sample data to ensure it can access your Trello board.

3.2 Popular Trello Zaps

Here are some useful Zapier automations for Trello:

⬥ Create a Trello Card from an Email

- Trigger: New email in Gmail
- Action: Create a Trello card
- Use case: Automatically turn important emails into actionable Trello tasks.

⬥ Send a Slack Notification for a New Trello Card

- Trigger: New card added to a Trello list
- Action: Send a Slack message
- Use case: Notify your team instantly when a new task is assigned.

⬥ Sync Trello with Google Sheets

- Trigger: Card moved to a specific list
- Action: Add row to Google Sheets
- Use case: Maintain an automated log of completed tasks.

4. Setting Up Zapier Integrations for Asana

4.1 Connecting Asana to Zapier

To integrate Asana with Zapier, follow these steps:

1. **Log in to Zapier** – Go to Zapier.com and sign in.
2. **Click on "Create a Zap"** – This starts a new automation.
3. **Choose Asana as a Trigger App** – Search for Asana and select it.
4. **Select a Trigger Event** – Examples include:
   - **New Task Added** – Triggers when a task is created in a project.
   - **Task Completed** – Triggers when a task is marked as complete.
   - **Task Updated** – Triggers when task details change.

5. **Connect Your Asana Account** – Log in to Asana and grant access to Zapier.

6. **Test the Connection** – Zapier will pull in sample data from your Asana workspace.

4.2 Popular Asana Zaps

Here are some powerful Asana automations you can set up:

◆ Turn New Form Responses into Asana Tasks

- Trigger: New response in Google Forms

- Action: Create an Asana task

- Use case: Automatically create project tasks when a new form submission is received.

◆ Send an Email When an Asana Task is Assigned

- Trigger: New task assigned to a user

- Action: Send an email via Gmail

- Use case: Notify team members instantly when they receive a new task.

◆ Sync Asana with Google Calendar

- Trigger: Task due date approaching

- Action: Create an event in Google Calendar

- Use case: Automatically schedule reminders for important deadlines.

5. Syncing Trello and Asana with Zapier

If your team uses both Trello and Asana, keeping them in sync can prevent confusion and ensure seamless collaboration. Here's how you can connect them using Zapier:

5.1 Setting Up a Trello-Asana Sync

1. **Create a Zap** – Start a new automation in Zapier.

2. **Set Trello as the Trigger App** – Choose an event such as "New Card Added" or "Card Moved."

3. **Select Asana as the Action App** – Choose an event like "Create Task" to add a new task in Asana.

4. **Map the Data** – Ensure task details from Trello are correctly transferred to Asana (e.g., card name → task title).

5. **Test and Activate** – Run a test and turn on the Zap to keep your tools in sync.

5.2 Popular Trello-Asana Syncs

◆ Create an Asana Task from a New Trello Card

- Trigger: New Trello card created

- Action: Create Asana task

- Use case: Keep project updates consistent across both platforms.

◆ Mark a Trello Card as Done When an Asana Task is Completed

- Trigger: Task marked as complete in Asana

- Action: Move Trello card to "Done" list

- Use case: Ensure finished tasks are reflected in both tools.

Conclusion

By integrating Trello and Asana with Zapier, you can eliminate repetitive tasks, streamline project management, and enhance team collaboration. Whether you need to automate task creation, sync multiple tools, or send automatic notifications, Zapier provides the flexibility to customize your workflows.

Now that you have a solid understanding of how to automate Trello and Asana, the next chapter will explore **calendar and scheduling integrations** to further optimize your productivity.

4.2.2 Monday.com and ClickUp Automation

Project management is a crucial aspect of business operations, whether you're managing small tasks, large-scale projects, or cross-functional teams. Monday.com and ClickUp are two of the most popular project management tools that help teams collaborate, assign tasks, and track project progress. However, manually updating tasks, moving data between tools, and keeping everything in sync can be time-consuming. This is where **Zapier automation** becomes a game-changer.

By integrating Monday.com and ClickUp with Zapier, you can:

- Automate task creation and updates

- Sync project information across platforms

- Send automatic notifications and alerts

- Enhance team collaboration without manual data entry

In this section, we'll walk you through how to automate workflows between Monday.com, ClickUp, and other apps using Zapier.

1. Understanding Monday.com and ClickUp Integrations in Zapier

Both Monday.com and ClickUp support Zapier integrations, allowing users to connect them with thousands of apps. Here's a quick overview of how each tool works with Zapier:

- **Monday.com Zapier Integration**:

    o   Triggers: When an item is created, when a status changes, when a new update is posted, etc.

    o   Actions: Create an item, update a column value, add a comment, move an item to a different group, etc.

- **ClickUp Zapier Integration**:

    o   Triggers: When a new task is created, when a task is updated, when a status changes, etc.

    o   Actions: Create a task, update a task, change task status, post a comment, etc.

With these integrations, you can **automate cross-platform task management**, ensuring that updates in one tool reflect in another automatically.

2. Setting Up Zapier Automation Between Monday.com and ClickUp

Now, let's go through a step-by-step guide on setting up Zapier automations between Monday.com and ClickUp.

Use Case 1: Automatically Creating a ClickUp Task from a New Monday.com Item

If you use Monday.com to manage projects but also have ClickUp as your task management tool, you might want to **automatically create a ClickUp task whenever a new Monday.com item is added**. Here's how:

Step 1: Create a New Zap

1. Log into your **Zapier** account.
2. Click on **Create a Zap**.

Step 2: Set Monday.com as the Trigger App

1. In the **Trigger** section, search for **Monday.com**.
2. Choose the trigger event: **"New Item in Board"**.
3. Connect your **Monday.com** account to Zapier.
4. Select the board where new items will trigger the automation.

Step 3: Set ClickUp as the Action App

1. In the **Action** section, search for **ClickUp**.
2. Choose the action event: **"Create Task"**.
3. Connect your **ClickUp** account to Zapier.
4. Select the **ClickUp Space and List** where the new task should be created.
5. Map the fields:
   - **Task Name** → Monday.com Item Name
   - **Task Description** → Monday.com Item Description
   - **Due Date** → Monday.com Date Column

     ○   **Priority** → Set a default priority if necessary

Step 4: Test and Activate the Zap

1. Click **Test & Review** to ensure everything works properly.

2. If the test is successful, click **Turn On Zap** to activate the automation.

📌 *Now, whenever a new item is added to Monday.com, a corresponding task will be created in ClickUp automatically!*

Use Case 2: Syncing Status Updates Between Monday.com and ClickUp

Many teams use **Monday.com for strategic planning** and **ClickUp for execution**. If you want to **synchronize task status changes between the two tools,** follow these steps:

Step 1: Create a New Zap

1. Click **Create a Zap** in Zapier.

Step 2: Set Monday.com as the Trigger App

1. Search for **Monday.com** and choose the trigger event: **"Item Updated"**.

2. Select the board where updates should trigger the Zap.

3. Choose the specific **column** (e.g., Status, Progress, Priority) that will trigger the automation.

Step 3: Set ClickUp as the Action App

1. Search for **ClickUp** and select the action event **"Update Task"**.

2. Choose the correct **ClickUp Space and List**.

3. In the **Task ID** field, use the Monday.com item's unique identifier to match it to the correct ClickUp task.

4. Map the **Monday.com status column** to ClickUp's **status field**.

Step 4: Test and Activate the Zap

1. Run a test to check if updates in Monday.com reflect in ClickUp.

2. If everything works fine, activate the Zap.

📌 *With this automation, when you update the status of a task in Monday.com, the corresponding ClickUp task will be updated automatically!*

3. Other Useful Monday.com and ClickUp Automations

Here are more powerful workflows you can create with Zapier:

Sending Notifications for New Monday.com Items

- **Trigger**: A new Monday.com item is added.
- **Action**: Send a Slack/Email notification to the assigned team members.

Creating a Monday.com Item from a New ClickUp Task

- **Trigger**: A new task is added in ClickUp.
- **Action**: Create a corresponding item in Monday.com.

Archiving Completed Tasks in ClickUp

- **Trigger**: A task in Monday.com is marked as "Done."
- **Action**: Move the corresponding ClickUp task to an archive list.

4. Best Practices for Automating Monday.com and ClickUp with Zapier

✅ **Use Naming Conventions** – Clearly label your Zaps to avoid confusion.

✅ **Test Before Deploying** – Run test Zaps to ensure data is mapped correctly.

✅ **Optimize Task Usage** – Be mindful of how many Zapier tasks you use to avoid exceeding plan limits.

✅ **Monitor and Maintain** – Regularly check your Zap history for errors and make adjustments as needed.

Conclusion

Monday.com and ClickUp are powerful project management tools, and when combined with Zapier, they eliminate repetitive tasks, ensure data consistency, and enhance collaboration. Whether you're automating task creation, syncing status updates, or sending notifications, these integrations help your team stay focused on what matters most.

Now, try setting up these automations in your own workspace and experience the power of smart project management with Zapier!

4.2.3 Syncing Tasks Between Apps

Effective project management relies on seamless task synchronization across multiple tools. Many teams use different platforms to manage their workflows—Trello for brainstorming, Asana for execution, ClickUp for tracking, or Microsoft To Do for personal productivity. Manually updating tasks across these tools is time-consuming and error-prone.

With Zapier, you can automate task synchronization, ensuring that updates in one app reflect across all necessary platforms. This chapter will walk you through setting up automated workflows for syncing tasks between project management tools.

---

1. Why Sync Tasks Across Apps?

Before diving into the technical setup, let's explore the benefits of automating task synchronization:

Improved Efficiency

Manually updating tasks in different platforms wastes time. Automating the process eliminates redundant work, so your team can focus on execution rather than administration.

Reduced Errors and Overlooked Tasks

When tasks aren't updated consistently, team members might work with outdated information. Syncing tasks ensures real-time updates across platforms, reducing communication gaps.

Enhanced Team Collaboration

Different departments may prefer different project management tools. For example, a marketing team might use Trello, while a product development team relies on Asana. Syncing tasks between these platforms ensures all teams stay aligned.

2. How Zapier Helps Sync Tasks

Zapier enables integration between various project management tools without requiring any coding. By creating **Zaps**, you can:

✅ Automatically create new tasks in one app when they are added to another.

✅ Update existing tasks across multiple platforms.

✅ Synchronize task status, deadlines, and assignees.

Here's how you can use Zapier to connect Trello, Asana, ClickUp, and Microsoft To Do.

3. Setting Up Task Syncing with Zapier

This section will walk you through setting up Zapier workflows to sync tasks between popular project management tools.

Example: Syncing Trello and Asana

Step 1: Create a New Zap

1. Log into your Zapier account.
2. Click **Create a Zap**.
3. Choose **Trello** as the Trigger App.

Step 2: Configure the Trigger

1. Select **New Card** as the trigger event (this means the Zap will activate when a new Trello card is created).
2. Connect your Trello account and choose the board and list to monitor.
3. Click **Test Trigger** to verify the connection.

Step 3: Set Up the Action in Asana

1. Select **Asana** as the Action App.

2. Choose **Create Task** as the action event.

3. Connect your Asana account and select the correct project.

4. Map Trello card details (e.g., title, description, due date) to Asana task fields.

Step 4: Test and Activate the Zap

1. Click **Test Action** to ensure tasks are created in Asana when a new Trello card is added.

2. If the test is successful, click **Publish Zap**.

Now, every time a new card is added to Trello, an identical task is automatically created in Asana.

Example: Syncing ClickUp and Microsoft To Do

Step 1: Create a Zap with ClickUp as the Trigger

1. In Zapier, click **Create a Zap**.

2. Choose **ClickUp** as the Trigger App.

3. Select **New Task** as the trigger event.

Step 2: Configure ClickUp Trigger

1. Connect your ClickUp account and select the workspace, folder, and list to monitor.

2. Click **Test Trigger** to confirm it works.

Step 3: Set Up the Action in Microsoft To Do

1. Select **Microsoft To Do** as the Action App.

2. Choose **Create Task** as the action event.

3. Connect your Microsoft account.

4. Map task details from ClickUp to Microsoft To Do (e.g., title, due date).

Step 4: Test and Activate

1. Click **Test Action** to verify that a new task is created in Microsoft To Do.

2. If successful, click **Publish Zap**.

Now, any new task created in ClickUp will automatically appear in Microsoft To Do.

4. Advanced Task Synchronization Techniques

Beyond basic task syncing, you can enhance your workflow with additional Zapier features.

Two-Way Task Syncing with Zapier

By default, Zapier creates **one-way** automations (e.g., from Trello to Asana). However, you can create another Zap to sync in the opposite direction:

1. Set Asana as the **Trigger App** with the event **New Task**.

2. Select Trello as the **Action App** and create a **New Card** event.

3. Map details from Asana to Trello.

This ensures changes in either tool reflect in the other.

Updating Task Status Across Platforms

You can create Zaps to update task status when completed:

1. Use **Task Completed** in Trello as a trigger.

2. Set Asana's **Update Task** as the action.

3. Map task IDs to ensure correct updates.

Using Filters to Sync Specific Tasks

Zapier allows you to filter tasks before syncing.

- Use **Filters** to sync only tasks assigned to a specific team member.

- Exclude tasks marked with certain labels.

5. Best Practices for Task Synchronization

Choose the Right Syncing Approach

- **One-way sync** is simple and avoids conflicts.

- **Two-way sync** ensures full alignment but requires careful setup to prevent duplicates.

Prevent Duplicate Tasks

- Enable Zapier's **deduplication feature** to avoid creating duplicate entries.

- Use task IDs to match existing tasks instead of creating new ones.

Maintain Data Accuracy

- Regularly review your Zaps to ensure they are functioning correctly.

- Use **Zapier's Task History** to troubleshoot failed syncs.

6. Summary

In this chapter, we explored how to sync tasks between project management tools using Zapier. You learned:

✔ The benefits of syncing tasks across apps.

✔ How to set up Zaps to integrate Trello, Asana, ClickUp, and Microsoft To Do.

✔ Advanced techniques like two-way sync, status updates, and filtering tasks.

By automating task synchronization, you can reduce manual work, enhance collaboration, and ensure your entire team stays updated in real time.

4.3 Boosting Productivity with Calendar and Scheduling Tools

4.3.1 Google Calendar and Outlook Sync

Introduction to Calendar Automation

Calendars are essential for managing schedules, appointments, and deadlines. Many professionals rely on Google Calendar or Microsoft Outlook to keep their work and personal lives organized. However, manually updating calendars, adding events, and syncing information across platforms can be time-consuming and prone to errors.

With **Zapier**, you can automate many calendar-related tasks, such as:

- Syncing events between **Google Calendar** and **Outlook Calendar**

- Automatically adding events from emails, form submissions, or other sources

- Sending event reminders or notifications via Slack, email, or SMS

- Creating calendar entries from tasks in **Trello**, **Asana**, or other project management tools

By using Zapier, you can eliminate manual effort, reduce missed appointments, and ensure that all events are accurately recorded in your preferred calendar application.

Understanding Google Calendar and Outlook Integration

Google Calendar and **Outlook Calendar** are two of the most widely used scheduling tools. Many businesses and professionals use both platforms, especially when working with different teams or clients. However, they do not natively sync with each other, which can cause scheduling conflicts.

Zapier allows you to **automatically sync events between Google Calendar and Outlook**, ensuring that your schedules stay up to date across platforms. Here's how the integration works:

1. **One-Way Sync** – New events from Google Calendar are added to Outlook (or vice versa), but changes made in one calendar do not reflect in the other.

2. **Two-Way Sync** – Events are updated in both calendars whenever a change is made in either platform.

In this guide, we will set up a **one-way sync from Google Calendar to Outlook** using Zapier.

Step-by-Step Guide: Syncing Google Calendar with Outlook

Step 1: Connect Google Calendar and Outlook to Zapier

1. **Log in to Zapier** – Go to Zapier.com and sign in to your account.

2. **Create a New Zap** – Click on **"Create Zap"** to start building your automation.

3. **Choose Google Calendar as the Trigger App** – In the search bar, type **"Google Calendar"** and select it.

4. **Select a Trigger Event** – Choose **"New Event"** as the trigger. This means Zapier will trigger an action every time a new event is created in Google Calendar.

5. **Connect Your Google Account** – Click **"Sign in to Google"** and authorize Zapier to access your calendar.

Step 2: Configure the Google Calendar Trigger

1. **Select the Calendar** – If you have multiple Google Calendars, choose the one you want to sync.

2. **Set Up Event Filters** – You can apply filters to sync only specific events (e.g., only events with a certain keyword in the title).

3. **Test the Trigger** – Click **"Test Trigger"** to check if Zapier can retrieve your latest event. If successful, move to the next step.

Step 3: Set Up Outlook as the Action App

1. **Choose Outlook as the Action App** – In the search bar, type **"Microsoft Outlook"** and select it.

2. **Select an Action Event** – Choose **"Create Event"** as the action. This will create a new event in Outlook every time a new event is added to Google Calendar.

3. **Connect Your Outlook Account** – Click **"Sign in to Microsoft"** and authorize Zapier to access your Outlook Calendar.

Step 4: Customize the Event Details

1. **Match Google Calendar Fields to Outlook Fields:**

   ○ **Event Title:** Select **"Summary"** from Google Calendar

   ○ **Event Description:** Select **"Description"**

   ○ **Start Time:** Select **"Start Date & Time"**

   ○ **End Time:** Select **"End Date & Time"**

   ○ **Location:** Select **"Location"**

2. **Set Up Additional Options (Optional):**

   ○ Choose event reminders (e.g., email notifications)

   ○ Set default event duration

   ○ Add attendees automatically

3. **Test the Action** – Click **"Test & Review"** to ensure the event is successfully created in Outlook.

Step 5: Activate and Monitor the Zap

1. **Turn on the Zap** – Click **"Publish Zap"** to activate it.

2. **Monitor the Zap** – Check the **Zap History** to ensure events are syncing properly.

3. **Make Adjustments if Needed** – If you encounter any issues, tweak the filters or settings to match your workflow.

Advanced Zap Customization

1. Two-Way Sync Between Google Calendar and Outlook

To enable **bi-directional syncing**, create another Zap with:

- **Trigger:** Outlook Calendar → New Event
- **Action:** Google Calendar → Create Event

This ensures that changes in Outlook Calendar are also reflected in Google Calendar.

2. Adding Event Reminders via Slack or Email

You can enhance your workflow by sending reminders to yourself or your team:

- **Trigger:** New Google Calendar Event
- **Action:** Send a notification via Slack or Gmail

Example use cases:
✅ Receive a Slack message 15 minutes before a meeting.
✅ Get a summary email of the next day's events.

3. Syncing Calendar Events with a Task Management Tool

If you use tools like **Trello, Asana, or ClickUp**, you can automate task creation:

- **Trigger:** New Google Calendar Event
- **Action:** Create a task in Trello/Asana

This ensures that meetings and deadlines are reflected in your project management tool.

Troubleshooting Common Issues

Issue	Solution
Events are not syncing	Check if the Zap is turned on and running properly
Duplicate events appearing	Add filters to prevent unnecessary event duplication
Events missing details	Ensure all fields (title, time, description) are correctly mapped
Delays in syncing	Upgrade to a **Zapier Premium Plan** for faster sync times

Conclusion

Automating **Google Calendar and Outlook** integration with Zapier saves time and ensures that all appointments, meetings, and reminders stay updated across platforms. Whether you need a simple one-way sync or a more advanced multi-step automation, Zapier provides the flexibility to optimize your workflow.

✅ **Next Steps:**

- Try additional integrations, such as Slack reminders and CRM automation.

- Explore Zapier's premium features for faster syncing and advanced filtering.

- Customize Zaps based on your team's specific scheduling needs.

By implementing these automations, you can **boost productivity, eliminate manual work, and ensure you never miss an important event again.** 🚀

4.3.2 Automating Meeting Scheduling with Calendly

Introduction

Scheduling meetings can be a time-consuming process, involving multiple back-and-forth emails to find a mutually convenient time. Calendly, a popular scheduling tool, simplifies this by allowing users to set their availability and letting invitees book meetings without conflicts. By integrating Calendly with Zapier, you can automate even more aspects of the scheduling process, such as sending follow-up emails, updating CRM records, and notifying team members automatically.

In this section, we'll walk through how to integrate Calendly with Zapier, explore common automation use cases, and provide a step-by-step guide to setting up effective Zaps to streamline your scheduling process.

1. Understanding Calendly and Its Integration with Zapier

Calendly is a scheduling platform that enables users to set their availability, create meeting types, and share scheduling links with others. It integrates with popular calendar apps like Google Calendar, Outlook, and iCloud to prevent double bookings.

With Zapier, you can extend Calendly's capabilities by triggering automated workflows based on scheduling events, such as:

- Sending confirmation or reminder emails when someone books a meeting.

- Adding new events to task management tools like Trello, Asana, or ClickUp.

- Updating CRM records in HubSpot or Salesforce when a new lead schedules a call.

- Notifying team members in Slack or Microsoft Teams when a meeting is booked.

To use Calendly with Zapier, you'll need:

- A **Calendly** account (Free, Essentials, Professional, or Teams plan).

- A **Zapier** account (Free or Paid, depending on the complexity of your Zaps).

- An active integration with your preferred calendar service (Google Calendar, Outlook, etc.).

2. Connecting Calendly to Zapier

Before creating automation, you need to connect your Calendly account to Zapier.

Step 1: Log in to Zapier and Create a New Zap

1. Go to Zapier and log in to your account.

2. Click the **"Create a Zap"** button.

Step 2: Set Up Calendly as a Trigger

1. Search for **Calendly** in the trigger app search bar.

2. Select **Calendly** and choose a trigger event:

   o **"Invitee Created"** – triggers when someone books a meeting.

   o **"Invitee Canceled"** – triggers when a meeting is canceled.

3. Click **Continue**, then sign in to your Calendly account.

4. Allow Zapier to access your Calendly data.

5. Choose your Calendly event type (e.g., 30-minute meeting, 60-minute consultation).

6. Click **Test Trigger** to fetch recent bookings.

3. Popular Calendly Automations with Zapier

Now that you've connected Calendly, let's explore some powerful automations.

Send a Confirmation Email via Gmail or Outlook

You can automatically send a personalized confirmation email when a meeting is scheduled.

Steps:

1. Add **Gmail** or **Outlook** as the action app.

2. Choose the **"Send Email"** action.

3. Map the invitee's email from Calendly to the recipient field.

4. Personalize the email body using details from the booking (date, time, meeting link).

5. Test and activate the Zap.

📌 **Example Use Case:** A consultant wants to send automatic confirmations and preparation materials to clients after they book a session.

Add Scheduled Meetings to a Task Management App

If you use **Trello**, **Asana**, or **ClickUp**, you can automatically create a task for every scheduled meeting.

Steps:

1. Select your task management tool as the action app.

2. Choose **"Create Task"** as the action event.

3. Map the invitee name, meeting time, and link from Calendly to the task fields.

4. Set due dates, assign tasks to a specific team member, and add meeting notes.

5. Test and activate the Zap.

📌 **Example Use Case:** A sales team can automatically log client meetings in Trello to ensure follow-ups are scheduled.

Notify Your Team via Slack or Microsoft Teams

You can send instant notifications to your team's communication platform when a new meeting is scheduled.

Steps:

1. Select **Slack** or **Microsoft Teams** as the action app.

2. Choose **"Send Message"** as the action event.

3. Select the channel or team member to notify.

4. Personalize the message with meeting details.

5. Test and activate the Zap.

📌 **Example Use Case:** A customer support team gets real-time Slack notifications when a customer schedules a support call.

Update Your CRM (HubSpot, Salesforce, Pipedrive, etc.)

Automatically create or update a contact in your CRM when a meeting is booked.

Steps:

1. Choose your CRM (HubSpot, Salesforce, etc.) as the action app.

2. Select **"Create or Update Contact"** as the action event.

3. Map the invitee's name, email, and other relevant details.

4. Test and activate the Zap.

★ **Example Use Case:** A sales team keeps track of new leads in HubSpot when potential customers book a demo.

Send Automated Reminders Before the Meeting

Reduce no-shows by sending automated reminders before the scheduled time.

Steps:

1. Select **Zapier Delay** as an action and set it for 24 hours before the meeting.

2. Add **Gmail**, **Outlook**, or **SMS provider (Twilio, ClickSend, etc.)** as the next action app.

3. Choose **"Send Email"** or **"Send SMS"** as the action event.

4. Personalize the reminder message and include meeting details.

5. Test and activate the Zap.

★ **Example Use Case:** A coaching business sends SMS reminders to clients a day before their session.

4. Troubleshooting Common Issues

While Zapier makes automation easy, you might encounter issues. Here's how to troubleshoot:

Meeting Details Not Populating Correctly

✅ Double-check that the correct Calendly event type is selected in the trigger.
✅ Ensure the invitee fields are mapped correctly in Zapier.

Emails Not Sending Automatically

✅ Verify that Gmail/Outlook has the correct permissions in Zapier.

✅ Check your Zap history to see if errors are occurring.

Duplicate Entries in CRM or Task Apps

✅ Enable "Find or Create" options in Zapier to avoid duplicate contacts.

✅ Use filters to process only relevant meeting types.

5. Best Practices for Calendly and Zapier Automation

◆ **Use descriptive Zap names** – Helps in organizing and managing multiple workflows.

◆ **Test your Zaps thoroughly** – Before activating, run multiple test cases.

◆ **Regularly review and update Zaps** – Business needs change, so ensure automations remain relevant.

◆ **Utilize Paths and Filters** – Add logic to handle different scenarios efficiently.

Conclusion

By integrating Calendly with Zapier, you can streamline scheduling, reduce administrative work, and ensure a seamless experience for both you and your invitees. Whether you're automating email confirmations, updating your CRM, or notifying your team, Zapier's no-code automation makes scheduling effortless.

Next Steps:

✅ Experiment with different Zap combinations.

✅ Explore advanced Zapier features like Multi-Step Zaps and Webhooks.

✅ Continuously optimize workflows to improve efficiency.

4.3.3 Creating Task Reminders Automatically

Staying organized and ensuring that important tasks are completed on time can be challenging, especially when managing multiple responsibilities. Fortunately, **Zapier** allows you to automate task reminders by integrating various apps like **Google Calendar, Outlook, Trello, Asana, Slack, and email services**. This automation helps you avoid missing deadlines and keeps you on top of your schedule without manual effort.

In this section, we'll explore **how to create automatic task reminders** using Zapier. We'll cover:

- Setting up a simple task reminder in **Google Calendar**

- Sending reminders via **Slack or Email**

- Automating reminders for project management tools like **Trello and Asana**

- Advanced workflows for **custom reminder notifications**

1. Why Automate Task Reminders?

Manually setting up reminders can be **time-consuming** and **prone to human error**. With automation, you can:

✓ Ensure you never miss important deadlines

✓ Reduce repetitive work of setting manual reminders

✓ Keep team members informed of upcoming tasks

✓ Improve productivity by staying focused on what matters

Common Use Cases for Automated Task Reminders

- **Daily Work Reminders**: Get a Slack or email notification about key tasks at a specific time.

- **Meeting Preparation**: Receive a reminder before a scheduled meeting with relevant documents attached.

- **Deadline Alerts**: Notify yourself or your team when a project milestone is approaching.

- **Follow-Up Tasks**: Set up automatic follow-ups after client meetings or support tickets.

2. Setting Up a Task Reminder with Google Calendar

One of the simplest ways to create automated reminders is by using **Google Calendar** with Zapier. You can set up a workflow that sends you notifications before an event starts.

Step-by-Step Guide: Creating a Google Calendar Reminder Zap

Step 1: Choose a Trigger App (Google Calendar)

1. Log in to **Zapier** and click **Create a Zap**.

2. In the **Trigger** step, search for **Google Calendar** and select it.

3. Choose the trigger event: **"Event Start"**.

4. Connect your **Google Calendar account** and grant Zapier the necessary permissions.

5. Select the **specific calendar** where you want to track events.

6. Set up the trigger conditions, such as the reminder time (e.g., **15 minutes before** the event starts).

7. Click **Test Trigger** to ensure Zapier can detect upcoming events.

Step 2: Choose an Action App (Email, Slack, or Notifications)

Now, decide how you want to receive the reminder:

Option 1: Send an Email Reminder

1. Choose **Gmail** or **Outlook** as the action app.

2. Select the action event **"Send Email"**.

3. Connect your email account.

4. Set up the email details:

   o **To:** Your email address (or a team member's).

   o **Subject:** "Reminder: [Event Title] Starts Soon!"

   o **Body:** Include event details like time, location, and attendees.

5. Click **Test & Continue** to check if the email is sent correctly.

Option 2: Send a Slack Notification

1. Choose **Slack** as the action app.

2. Select **"Send Channel Message"** or **"Send Direct Message"**.

3. Connect your Slack account and select the appropriate **channel** or **user**.

4. Customize the message:

      o Example: "🗓 Reminder: Your meeting with [Client Name] starts in 15 minutes!"

5. Click **Test & Continue** to ensure the notification is working.

Option 3: Use Zapier's Built-In Notifications

Zapier offers a **built-in notification tool** to send push alerts to your phone.

1. Choose **Pushbullet** or **SMS by Zapier** as the action app.

2. Enter your **phone number** or **notification settings**.

3. Customize the message and test the Zap.

Once everything is set up, **turn on the Zap**, and your reminders will now be sent **automatically** before each event!

---

3. Automating Task Reminders in Trello and Asana

If you use **Trello** or **Asana** for task management, you can **automatically receive reminders** when a task is due soon.

Example 1: Sending a Reminder for a Trello Task

Step 1: Set Up the Trigger

1. Create a new Zap and select **Trello** as the trigger app.

2. Choose the trigger event **"Card Due Soon"**.

3. Connect your **Trello account** and select the relevant board.

4. Choose when the reminder should trigger (e.g., **1 hour before the due date**).

5. Test the trigger to make sure Zapier detects an upcoming task.

Step 2: Choose the Action

Now, select how you want to be reminded:

- **Slack Message** → "Reminder: Task '[Card Name]' is due soon!"

- **Email Reminder** → Subject: "Trello Task Alert", Body: "Complete '[Card Name]' before [Due Date]!"

Step 3: Activate the Zap

Once tested, **turn on the Zap**, and you'll receive automatic reminders whenever a task is about to be due!

---

4. Advanced Reminder Workflows with Zapier

For more complex workflows, you can:

Use Multi-Step Zaps for Advanced Reminders

Example: **Send a Slack reminder, then log the task in Google Sheets.**

1. **Trigger:** Task due in Trello

2. **Action 1:** Send Slack notification

3. **Action 2:** Add a row to a Google Sheet for tracking

Use Paths to Send Different Reminders

Example: **Different reminders for different people.**

- If the task is marked **High Priority**, send a reminder to the **Manager**.

- If the task is marked **Normal**, send a reminder to the **Team Member**.

Use Webhooks for Custom Notifications

If you work with a **custom CRM or project tool**, use **Webhooks** to send reminders directly into your system.

---

5. Best Practices for Automated Task Reminders

To ensure reminders are effective, follow these tips:

✅ **Avoid Notification Overload** – Too many reminders can be counterproductive.

✅ **Use Clear and Concise Messages** – Make sure the reminder provides all necessary details.

✅ **Test Your Zaps Regularly** – Ensure automations are working as expected.

✅ **Integrate with the Right Tools** – Choose the notification method that best fits your workflow.

Conclusion

With Zapier, automating task reminders helps you stay organized, meet deadlines, and reduce manual work. Whether you need simple event reminders or advanced task alerts, Zapier offers flexible solutions.

Next Step: Try building your own task reminder automation and experiment with different integrations!

4.4 E-Commerce and Marketing Automation

4.4.1 Connecting Shopify and WooCommerce

In the world of e-commerce, efficiency and automation are crucial for success. Whether you are managing an online store on Shopify or WooCommerce, Zapier can help automate essential tasks like order processing, customer notifications, inventory updates, and marketing campaigns. By integrating Shopify and WooCommerce with other business tools, you can save time, reduce manual effort, and enhance customer experience.

This section provides a step-by-step guide to connecting Shopify and WooCommerce with Zapier, along with practical automation ideas that can improve your e-commerce workflow.

1. Why Automate Shopify and WooCommerce with Zapier?

Both **Shopify** and **WooCommerce** are powerful e-commerce platforms, but they do not always integrate seamlessly with other business tools. Managing multiple apps manually can lead to errors, wasted time, and inefficiencies. Zapier helps bridge this gap by connecting Shopify and WooCommerce to thousands of other applications.

Key Benefits of Automation:

- **Save Time:** Reduce repetitive tasks like manually entering customer details or sending order confirmations.

- **Improve Customer Experience:** Automate notifications, shipping updates, and abandoned cart recovery.

- **Enhance Marketing Efforts:** Sync sales data with email marketing tools, CRM systems, and social media platforms.

- **Optimize Inventory Management:** Automatically update stock levels across multiple sales channels.

- **Streamline Order Processing:** Connect with payment gateways, accounting software, and shipping providers.

2. Setting Up Shopify and WooCommerce in Zapier

Before creating automations (Zaps), you need to connect your Shopify or WooCommerce account to Zapier.

Step 1: Connecting Shopify to Zapier

1. **Log in to Zapier:** Go to Zapier's website and sign in to your account.

2. **Add a New Zap:** Click the **"Create Zap"** button.

3. **Select Shopify as the Trigger App:**

   o   In the **Trigger** section, search for **Shopify**.

   o   Choose a trigger event (e.g., "New Order", "New Customer", "Product Updated").

4. **Connect Your Shopify Account:**

   o   Click **"Sign in to Shopify"** and enter your store URL.

   o   Grant Zapier the necessary permissions.

5. **Test the Connection:** Zapier will fetch sample data to ensure the connection works properly.

Step 2: Connecting WooCommerce to Zapier

1. **Install the Zapier Plugin:**

   o   Log in to your WooCommerce WordPress dashboard.

   o   Navigate to **Plugins > Add New** and search for **Zapier for WooCommerce**.

   o   Install and activate the plugin.

2. **Get API Credentials:**

   o   Go to **WooCommerce > Settings > Advanced > REST API**.

   o   Click **Add Key**, set permissions to **Read/Write**, and generate the API keys.

3. **Connect WooCommerce to Zapier:**

   o   In Zapier, select WooCommerce as the Trigger app.

o Enter your API credentials when prompted.

4. **Test the Connection:** Fetch sample data to confirm integration success.

---

3. Automating Shopify and WooCommerce Workflows with Zapier

Once Shopify or WooCommerce is connected, you can create powerful automations to improve efficiency. Here are some practical Zap ideas:

Order Processing Automation

Automate Order Notifications

☞ **Trigger:** New order in Shopify/WooCommerce
☞ **Action:** Send a Slack message, email, or SMS notification

★ *Example:* When a customer places an order, Zapier automatically sends a notification to the fulfillment team via Slack.

Sync Orders with Google Sheets

☞ **Trigger:** New order in Shopify/WooCommerce
☞ **Action:** Create a new row in Google Sheets

★ *Example:* Keep track of all Shopify or WooCommerce orders in a Google Sheets spreadsheet for easy reporting and analysis.

Send New Orders to an Accounting System

☞ **Trigger:** New paid order in Shopify/WooCommerce
☞ **Action:** Create an invoice in QuickBooks/Xero

★ *Example:* Automatically generate an invoice in QuickBooks when a new order is received in Shopify.

Inventory and Product Management Automation

Sync Inventory Across Platforms

☞ **Trigger:** Product updated in Shopify/WooCommerce

☞ **Action:** Update stock levels in another system

📌 *Example:* When inventory changes in Shopify, it automatically updates stock levels in a WooCommerce store or an ERP system.

Send Low-Stock Alerts

☞ **Trigger:** Low-stock warning in Shopify/WooCommerce

☞ **Action:** Send an email or Slack message

📌 *Example:* When a product reaches low stock in WooCommerce, an automatic Slack alert is sent to the inventory manager.

Customer Communication and Engagement Automation

Send Order Confirmation Emails via Gmail or Outlook

☞ **Trigger:** New order in Shopify/WooCommerce

☞ **Action:** Send an email confirmation via Gmail

📌 *Example:* Instead of relying on Shopify's default email, customize and send order confirmations through Gmail with a personalized touch.

Follow Up with Customers Using CRM

☞ **Trigger:** New customer in Shopify/WooCommerce

☞ **Action:** Create a contact in HubSpot or Salesforce

📌 *Example:* When a new customer places an order, Zapier automatically adds them to HubSpot for future marketing campaigns.

Send Post-Purchase Surveys

☞ **Trigger:** Order completed in Shopify/WooCommerce

☞ **Action:** Send a Typeform or Google Forms survey

📌 *Example:* After a customer receives their order, an automated survey is sent to gather feedback.

Marketing and Promotions Automation

Abandoned Cart Recovery Emails

☞ **Trigger:** Cart abandoned in Shopify/WooCommerce
☞ **Action:** Send an email reminder via Mailchimp

★ *Example:* If a customer leaves items in their cart without checking out, Zapier triggers an automated email with a discount offer.

Sync Shopify and WooCommerce Sales with Facebook Ads

☞ **Trigger:** New purchase in Shopify/WooCommerce
☞ **Action:** Add customer to a Facebook Ads custom audience

★ *Example:* Retarget customers who made a purchase by automatically adding them to a Facebook Ads audience.

Automate Social Media Posts for New Products

☞ **Trigger:** New product added in Shopify/WooCommerce
☞ **Action:** Post on Twitter, Facebook, or Instagram

★ *Example:* When a new product is added to the store, Zapier posts an announcement on social media.

---

4. Troubleshooting Shopify and WooCommerce Zaps

Even with proper setup, issues may arise in automation workflows. Here are some common problems and solutions:

Problem: Orders Are Not Syncing Properly

✓ Check API permissions and reconnect the app in Zapier.
✓ Ensure the Zap trigger is correctly set (e.g., "New Paid Order" instead of "New Order").

Problem: Delayed or Failed Notifications

✓ Check Zap history in Zapier to find errors.
✓ Ensure notification apps (Slack, email) have proper permissions.

Problem: Inventory Levels Not Updating

✅ Ensure the correct fields are mapped between Shopify/WooCommerce and the inventory tool.

✅ Test the Zap manually to verify the update process.

5. Conclusion

Integrating Shopify and WooCommerce with Zapier enables powerful automation that saves time and improves efficiency. By automating order processing, inventory management, customer communication, and marketing efforts, businesses can focus more on growth and customer satisfaction.

Next Steps:

✅ Experiment with different Zapier templates for e-commerce.

✅ Explore advanced workflows using multi-step Zaps.

✅ Monitor and optimize your automations for better efficiency.

By leveraging Zapier's automation capabilities, you can create a seamless, optimized e-commerce experience. Happy automating!

4.4.2 Automating Social Media Posts

Social media is a crucial part of modern marketing, allowing businesses and individuals to engage with audiences, promote products, and share valuable content. However, managing multiple social media accounts and posting consistently can be time-consuming. This is where **Zapier** comes in, enabling you to automate social media posting by connecting different apps and scheduling posts automatically.

In this section, we will cover:

✅ Why automate social media posts with Zapier

✅ Setting up Zapier for different social media platforms

✅ Creating Zaps for automatic posting

✅ Managing and optimizing automated workflows

Why Automate Social Media Posting?

Manual social media posting requires logging into different platforms, copying and pasting content, and keeping track of schedules. This process is inefficient and prone to errors, such as missing posts or inconsistent posting times. Automating social media with Zapier offers several key benefits:

- **Saves Time** – Reduce repetitive tasks and free up time for strategic marketing.

- **Ensures Consistency** – Maintain a regular posting schedule without manual effort.

- **Reduces Errors** – Prevent mistakes like missing posts or posting at the wrong time.

- **Increases Engagement** – Post at optimal times to reach a wider audience.

- **Integrates with Other Marketing Tools** – Connect your CRM, email marketing, or content management system (CMS) to streamline your workflow.

With these advantages in mind, let's explore how you can set up Zapier to automate social media posts.

Setting Up Zapier for Social Media Platforms

Zapier supports integrations with all major social media platforms, including:

- **Facebook** (Facebook Pages and Facebook Groups)

- **Twitter (X)**

- **Instagram** (Business accounts only)

- **LinkedIn** (Profiles and Pages)

- **Pinterest**

- **YouTube**

Before creating your first Zap, ensure you have:
- A Zapier account (Free or Paid)
- Social media accounts connected to Zapier
- A source for your social media content (Google Sheets, RSS Feeds, WordPress, etc.)

Now, let's go step by step to create an automated posting workflow.

Creating an Automated Social Media Posting Zap

Step 1: Choose a Trigger

The first step in setting up a social media automation is defining what will trigger the post. Common triggers include:

- **New Row in Google Sheets** – Each new row represents a new post.

- **New Blog Post in WordPress** – Automatically share your latest blog article.

- **RSS Feed Update** – Share news updates from an RSS feed.

- **New Entry in Airtable** – Schedule posts from a content database.

☞ **Example: Automating Social Media Posts from Google Sheets**
We will create a Zap that posts to Twitter every time a new row is added to a Google Sheet.

1. **Go to Zapier Dashboard** and click **Create Zap**.

2. **Choose Google Sheets as the Trigger App**.

3. **Select "New Spreadsheet Row" as the Trigger Event**.

4. **Connect your Google Account and select the correct spreadsheet**.

5. **Test the trigger** to ensure Zapier detects new rows.

Step 2: Set Up the Action (Post to Social Media)

Once the trigger is set, you need to define the action, which is the social media post itself.

Posting to Twitter (X)

1. **Choose Twitter as the Action App**.

2. **Select "Create Tweet" as the Action Event**.

3. **Connect your Twitter account** to Zapier.

4. **Customize the Tweet** by mapping fields from Google Sheets:

    o Tweet Content = Column A (Text from Google Sheet)

- Image URL (optional) = Column B (Link to an image)

5. **Test the Zap** to ensure it successfully posts to Twitter.

6. **Turn on the Zap** to automate future tweets.

Posting to Facebook Pages

1. **Choose Facebook Pages as the Action App.**

2. **Select "Create Page Post" as the Action Event.**

3. **Connect your Facebook account.**

4. **Customize the post** by adding:

   - Message = Column A (Post Content)

   - Link (optional) = Column B (URL to be shared)

   - Image URL = Column C (Image for the post)

5. **Test and activate the Zap.**

Advanced Social Media Automation Techniques

1. Scheduling Posts with Zapier and Buffer

Instead of posting immediately, you can integrate **Buffer** to schedule posts at optimal times.

1. **Trigger: New row in Google Sheets.**

2. **Action 1: Add post to Buffer queue.**

3. **Buffer schedules the post** based on your posting times.

This method ensures your social media is active without overwhelming followers with too many posts at once.

2. Cross-Posting Across Multiple Platforms

Want to post on **Twitter, Facebook, and LinkedIn simultaneously**? You can create a **Multi-Step Zap:**

1. **Trigger: New post in WordPress.**

2. **Action 1: Create Tweet on Twitter.**

3. **Action 2: Create Facebook Post.**

4. **Action 3: Create LinkedIn Post.**

This setup ensures content is distributed across all major platforms without extra effort.

3. Automating Hashtags and Mentions

- Use Zapier Formatter to **automatically add hashtags** based on keywords in your post.

- Mention users by setting dynamic username fields in the Google Sheets database.

Managing and Optimizing Automated Posts

After setting up automation, it's crucial to track its effectiveness and make improvements.

1. Monitor Performance Metrics

- Use Google Analytics and UTM parameters to track traffic from social media posts.

- Check **Facebook Insights, Twitter Analytics, and LinkedIn Analytics** for engagement trends.

2. Avoid Spammy or Over-Posting Behavior

- Use **delays** in Zapier to space out posts.

- Rotate hashtags and post formats to avoid looking automated.

3. Handling Errors and Troubleshooting

- If a post fails, check **Zap History** in Zapier to find the issue.

- Use **Zapier Filters** to ensure posts meet quality standards before being published.

Conclusion

Automating social media posting with Zapier can **save time, ensure consistency, and boost engagement** without manual effort. By leveraging tools like **Google Sheets, WordPress, Buffer, and social media APIs**, you can create a seamless workflow that keeps your content strategy on track.

Key Takeaways:

✔ Use Google Sheets, RSS feeds, or WordPress as triggers for posts.
✔ Connect Zapier with Facebook, Twitter, LinkedIn, and Instagram for automation.
✔ Utilize Buffer for scheduling and avoid over-posting.
✔ Monitor performance metrics and tweak automation for better results.

Now that you've mastered **social media automation with Zapier**, you're ready to streamline your marketing workflow and focus on **engagement and strategy** instead of repetitive posting tasks! 🚀

4.4.3 CRM and Lead Management with Zapier

Introduction to CRM and Lead Management Automation

Customer Relationship Management (CRM) and lead management are essential for businesses looking to grow and maintain strong customer relationships. With the increasing number of digital tools used in sales and marketing, managing leads effectively can be time-consuming and complex.

Zapier simplifies CRM and lead management by connecting various apps and automating workflows, ensuring that no lead slips through the cracks. Whether you are capturing leads from web forms, nurturing them through automated emails, or syncing them across different platforms, Zapier can help streamline the process and boost efficiency.

This section will cover:

- The importance of automating CRM and lead management

- Common CRM-related Zapier workflows

- Step-by-step instructions for setting up key automations

- Best practices for using Zapier with CRM systems

Why Automate CRM and Lead Management?

Manually handling leads and customer data can be inefficient and error-prone. Here's why automation is crucial:

1. Faster Response Times

Studies show that responding to leads within five minutes increases conversion rates significantly. Automating lead capture and follow-ups ensures prospects receive timely responses.

2. Improved Data Accuracy

Manually entering lead information into a CRM can lead to errors and inconsistencies. Automating this process ensures accurate and up-to-date records.

3. Seamless Integration Across Tools

Sales and marketing teams use multiple tools—email platforms, web forms, social media, and CRMs. Zapier bridges the gap between these tools, ensuring data flows smoothly.

4. Time and Resource Savings

Automation reduces repetitive tasks, freeing up sales and marketing teams to focus on high-value activities like engaging with prospects and closing deals.

Common CRM and Lead Management Workflows in Zapier

Below are some of the most popular Zapier workflows for CRM and lead management:

1. Capturing Leads Automatically

- **Google Forms to CRM**: Automatically send lead details from Google Forms to HubSpot, Salesforce, or Zoho CRM.

- **Facebook Lead Ads to CRM**: Capture leads from Facebook ads and push them directly into your CRM.

- **Website Form to CRM**: Sync leads from Typeform, JotForm, or Gravity Forms to CRM platforms.

2. Automating Lead Nurturing

- **CRM to Email Marketing**: When a new lead is added to the CRM, add them to an email sequence in Mailchimp, ActiveCampaign, or ConvertKit.

- **Lead Score Alerts**: Notify sales reps via Slack or email when a lead reaches a certain score.

3. Syncing CRM Data Across Apps

- **CRM to Google Sheets**: Automatically update a Google Sheet when new leads are added to the CRM.

- **Multi-CRM Sync**: Sync leads and contacts between HubSpot, Salesforce, and Pipedrive.

4. Scheduling Follow-Ups and Tasks

- **New Lead to Calendar**: Automatically create follow-up tasks in Google Calendar or Outlook when a new lead enters the CRM.

- **CRM to Task Manager**: Assign tasks in Asana, Trello, or ClickUp based on new leads.

Step-by-Step Guide: Setting Up a CRM Automation with Zapier

Let's go through a step-by-step example of automating lead capture from Facebook Lead Ads to HubSpot CRM.

Step 1: Connect Your Facebook Lead Ads Account

1. Log into Zapier and click **Create a Zap**.
2. Choose **Facebook Lead Ads** as the trigger app.
3. Select the **New Lead** trigger event.
4. Connect your Facebook account and choose the lead form you want to use.

Step 2: Configure the Action in HubSpot

1. Select **HubSpot CRM** as the action app.
2. Choose **Create Contact** as the action event.
3. Connect your HubSpot account.

4. Map the Facebook lead fields (name, email, phone number, etc.) to the corresponding HubSpot fields.

Step 3: Test and Activate Your Zap

1. Click **Test & Review** to ensure the lead data transfers correctly.

2. If the test is successful, turn on the Zap.

3. Monitor Zap history to confirm leads are being captured properly.

Advanced CRM Automations with Zapier

Once you master basic automations, you can build more advanced workflows to improve CRM efficiency.

1. Multi-Step Lead Qualification

- Step 1: Capture leads from a web form.
- Step 2: Use Zapier's **Formatter** to clean and standardize lead data.
- Step 3: Use a **Filter** to send high-quality leads to a sales rep while lower-priority leads enter an automated nurturing sequence.

2. Automated Lead Assignment

- Step 1: New leads enter the CRM.
- Step 2: Use **Zapier Paths** to assign leads to different sales reps based on criteria (e.g., location, industry, or company size).
- Step 3: Notify the assigned rep via Slack or email.

3. Lead Scoring Automation

- Step 1: New leads enter the CRM.
- Step 2: Use **Zapier Webhooks** to pull additional data (e.g., LinkedIn profile, company size).
- Step 3: Use **Zapier Formatter** to calculate a lead score.
- Step 4: If the lead score is above a threshold, trigger an alert in Slack.

Best Practices for CRM Automation with Zapier

To maximize the benefits of CRM automation, follow these best practices:

1. Keep Data Clean and Organized

- Use Zapier Formatter to standardize data.
- Regularly review and clean up your CRM.

2. Use Filters to Reduce Noise

- Avoid unnecessary Zaps by filtering out incomplete or duplicate leads.
- Ensure only high-quality leads enter sales workflows.

3. Monitor and Optimize Zaps Regularly

- Check Zap History to identify any failures.
- Optimize Zaps to reduce unnecessary tasks and stay within Zapier's task limits.

4. Ensure Data Security and Compliance

- Use Zapier's built-in security features to protect sensitive lead data.
- Follow GDPR and other data protection regulations when handling customer data.

Conclusion

Zapier provides powerful tools for automating CRM and lead management, allowing businesses to capture, nurture, and track leads more efficiently. By integrating your CRM with other tools, you can ensure a smooth, automated workflow that enhances productivity and improves customer relationships.

Whether you're a solo entrepreneur or part of a large sales team, Zapier's automation capabilities can save time, reduce errors, and help convert more leads into loyal customers.

CHAPTER IV
Advanced Zapier Features

5.1 Multi-Step Zaps and Conditional Logic

5.1.1 Creating a Multi-Step Zap

Zapier is not just about creating simple one-step automations; its true power lies in **Multi-Step Zaps**, which allow you to connect multiple apps and automate complex workflows. In this section, we will explore how to create a Multi-Step Zap, understand its benefits, and go through a step-by-step guide to building one.

What is a Multi-Step Zap?

A **Multi-Step Zap** is an automation in Zapier that consists of more than one action after the trigger. Unlike **Single-Step Zaps**, which only allow for one action per trigger, Multi-Step Zaps enable a sequence of multiple actions, transforming a simple automation into a more advanced workflow.

For example, instead of just **saving an email attachment to Google Drive**, a Multi-Step Zap could:

1. **Trigger** when an email with an attachment arrives in Gmail.

2. **Upload the attachment** to a designated folder in Google Drive.

3. **Send a Slack notification** to your team about the new file.

4. **Log the email details** in a Google Sheet for record-keeping.

This makes it possible to **automate entire workflows**, reducing manual work and improving efficiency.

Benefits of Using Multi-Step Zaps

1. Increased Efficiency

Multi-Step Zaps eliminate the need for repetitive manual tasks by automating multiple actions at once. Instead of handling tasks separately, they happen seamlessly in the background.

2. Greater Flexibility

You can customize Multi-Step Zaps to fit different needs by adding actions like **data filtering**, **formatting text**, or even **applying conditional logic** (which we will explore in the next section).

3. Improved Accuracy

Manual data entry can lead to mistakes. Automating workflows with Multi-Step Zaps ensures consistent data transfer and reduces errors.

4. Saves Time and Resources

By automating time-consuming workflows, Multi-Step Zaps allow you to focus on higher-priority tasks, helping businesses scale more efficiently.

Step-by-Step Guide to Creating a Multi-Step Zap

Let's go through the process of creating a **Multi-Step Zap** in Zapier using a real-world example:

Scenario: You want to automate the process of collecting new leads from a Google Form, adding them to your CRM (HubSpot), sending a follow-up email, and notifying your sales team on Slack.

Step 1: Choose a Trigger App

1. Log in to **Zapier** and click on **"Create a Zap."**

2. Under **"Choose App & Event,"** search for **Google Forms** (or any form tool you use).

3. Select **"New Form Response"** as the trigger event.

4. Click **"Continue."**

5. Connect your **Google Forms account** and select the form you want to use.

6. Click **"Test Trigger"** to ensure Zapier detects recent form responses.

Step 2: Add the First Action – Create a New Contact in HubSpot

1. Click on **"+"** to add an action step.

2. Search for **HubSpot** and select **"Create Contact"** as the action event.

3. Click **"Continue."**

4. Connect your **HubSpot account** and configure the fields:

   o **First Name:** Map it to the name field from the form response.

   o **Email:** Select the email from the form response.

   o **Phone Number:** If applicable, map the phone number field.

5. Click **"Test & Continue"** to confirm the data is being sent correctly.

Step 3: Add the Second Action – Send a Follow-Up Email

1. Click on **"+"** to add another action step.

2. Search for **Gmail** (or another email provider like Outlook).

3. Select **"Send Email"** as the action event.

4. Click **"Continue."**

5. Connect your **Gmail account** and configure the email:

   o **To:** Map the email field from the form response.

   o **Subject:** "Thank You for Signing Up!"

   o **Body:** "Hi {{First Name}}, thank you for reaching out. Our team will contact you soon."

   o **From Name:** Your company name.

6. Click **"Test & Continue"** to check if the email is sent correctly.

Step 4: Add the Third Action – Notify the Sales Team on Slack

1. Click on **"+"** to add another action.

2. Search for **Slack** and select **"Send Channel Message"** as the action event.

3. Click **"Continue."**

4. Connect your **Slack account** and select a channel (e.g., #sales-leads).

5. Customize the message:

   o **Message Text:** "New lead received! Name: {{First Name}}, Email: {{Email}}"

   o **Bot Name:** Zapier

   o **Icon Emoji:** ✉

6. Click **"Test & Continue."**

Step 5: Activate Your Multi-Step Zap

1. Review all steps to ensure the correct data mapping.

2. Click **"Turn On Zap."**

🎊 **Your automation is now live!** Every time a new lead fills out the form, Zapier will automatically add them to HubSpot, send a follow-up email, and notify your sales team on Slack!

Best Practices for Multi-Step Zaps

✅ **Use Filters to Process Only Relevant Data**

- If you only want to process leads from specific countries, add a **Filter Step** that only allows the Zap to continue if the "Country" field matches a certain value.

✅ **Use Formatter to Clean and Standardize Data**

- If form submissions have inconsistent capitalization (e.g., "john DOE"), use **Zapier Formatter** to apply proper case formatting.

✅ **Add a Delay if Needed**

- If you want to send a follow-up email **after 24 hours**, use the **Delay by Zapier** feature.

✅ **Test Your Zap Regularly**

- Ensure your Zap is running smoothly by checking **Zap History** for errors or failed executions.

Conclusion

In this section, we explored how to create a **Multi-Step Zap**, from setting up a trigger to executing multiple actions across different apps. By leveraging **Multi-Step Zaps**, you can automate complex workflows, improve efficiency, and enhance productivity.

Next, we will dive into **Conditional Logic in Zapier**, where we explore how to **use Paths and Filters** to create dynamic workflows that can handle different scenarios. 🚀

5.1.2 Using Paths for Conditional Workflows

One of the most powerful features in Zapier is the ability to create **conditional workflows** using **Paths**. Paths allow you to introduce **if-then logic** into your automations, meaning that a Zap can take different actions based on the data it processes. This is particularly useful for automating **complex workflows** that require different responses depending on specific conditions.

In this section, we will explore:

- What Paths are and how they work

- When to use Paths in your workflows

- Step-by-step instructions to create a Path

- Advanced use cases for Paths

- Best practices for using Paths effectively

What Are Paths in Zapier?

Paths in Zapier allow you to create **conditional branching** in your workflows. Instead of every Zap following a single linear process, Paths enable different **outcomes based on**

conditions. You can think of them as decision trees where your Zap follows different branches depending on the data it receives.

For example, suppose you run an online store and receive **customer inquiries**. Using Paths, you could set up the following logic:

- If the customer asks about **order status**, send an email with tracking information.

- If the customer has a **billing issue**, notify the finance team.

- If the customer is inquiring about **new products**, add them to a marketing campaign.

This **intelligent automation** ensures that each type of inquiry is handled correctly without human intervention.

When to Use Paths in Zapier

Paths are useful in many real-world scenarios, especially when your workflows involve **multiple possible actions** based on incoming data. Common use cases include:

1. Customer Support Automation

- Direct **support tickets** to the right department based on keywords in the request.

- Assign **urgent** tickets to a high-priority queue while routing general inquiries to the FAQ section.

2. Lead Management and Sales Automation

- Categorize leads into **hot, warm, and cold** based on engagement levels.

- Send high-value leads directly to a **sales rep**, while lower-priority leads receive an automated follow-up email.

3. HR and Employee Onboarding

- Route **new hire forms** to the HR department.

- If the employee is full-time, assign them company benefits.

- If the employee is a freelancer, send them a different onboarding package.

4. Marketing and E-commerce

- If a customer purchases a **high-value item**, trigger a VIP discount for their next order.

- If a customer abandons their shopping cart, send a **reminder email**.

Paths allow your workflows to become **dynamic**, responding intelligently to different inputs rather than executing a one-size-fits-all process.

How to Create a Path in Zapier: Step-by-Step Guide

Now, let's go through the process of setting up **Paths in Zapier**. We'll create a workflow that categorizes new support tickets and routes them accordingly.

Step 1: Create a New Zap

1. Log into your **Zapier account**.

2. Click **"Create Zap"**.

3. Choose a **Trigger App** (e.g., Gmail for new customer emails).

4. Set the **Trigger Event** (e.g., "New Email Received").

5. Connect your Gmail account and test the trigger to make sure it's working.

Step 2: Add the Paths Step

1. Click on the **"+"** button to add a new action.

2. Select **"Paths"** from the list of actions.

3. Zapier will now create **Path A** and **Path B** by default (you can add more if needed).

Step 3: Define Conditions for Each Path

Each Path needs rules to determine when it should be triggered.

Path A: If the Email Contains "Billing" → Forward to Finance Team

1. Click on **Path A** and rename it **"Billing Inquiries"**.

2. Set the condition:

   o **Condition Type:** Text Contains

- o **Field:** Email Subject
- o **Value:** "Billing"

3. Add an **Action**:

- o Choose **Gmail** (or Slack, Teams, etc.).
- o Select **"Send Email"** to forward the inquiry to the finance team.

4. Test and save this path.

Path B: If the Email Contains "Order Status" → Send Tracking Info

1. Click on **Path B** and rename it **"Order Status Requests"**.

2. Set the condition:

- o **Condition Type:** Text Contains
- o **Field:** Email Subject
- o **Value:** "Order Status"

3. Add an **Action**:

- o Choose **Google Sheets** (or your CRM).
- o Select **"Find Tracking Info"** based on the customer's email.
- o Send an automated email with the tracking details.

4. Test and save this path.

Step 4: Add More Paths if Needed

- You can create additional Paths for **General Inquiries, Technical Support**, etc.
- Each Path can have multiple **conditions** (e.g., email contains multiple keywords).

Step 5: Test and Activate Your Zap

1. Run a test using sample emails.

2. Check if the Paths are executing correctly.

3. If everything looks good, **turn on** the Zap!

Your workflow is now live, and all new support emails will be categorized and processed automatically.

Advanced Use Cases for Paths

Paths can be combined with **other Zapier features** to build even more powerful automations:

1. Using Paths with Multi-Step Zaps

- You can add **multiple actions** within each Path (e.g., notify multiple teams at once).
- Example: If a lead is high-value, send an **email, Slack alert**, and **CRM update** in the same Path.

2. Combining Paths with Filters

- Filters can refine when a Zap **runs in the first place**, reducing unnecessary automation.
- Example: Only trigger the Path if the email **comes from a VIP client**.

3. Paths and Formatter for Data Processing

- Use **Formatter** to clean and format data before applying Paths.
- Example: Convert messy date formats before sending them to different departments.

Best Practices for Using Paths in Zapier

To maximize efficiency and avoid **Zap complexity**, follow these best practices:

✓ **Limit the Number of Paths:** Too many Paths can slow down execution and become hard to manage.

✓ **Use Clear Naming Conventions:** Name each Path based on its purpose (e.g., "High-Priority Leads").

✓ **Test Each Path Thoroughly:** Run test data through different scenarios to ensure expected outcomes.

✓ **Monitor and Optimize:** Regularly check Zap **task usage** to prevent unnecessary automation runs.

✓ **Use Nested Paths Only When Necessary:** Avoid deep nesting, as it makes troubleshooting harder.

Conclusion

Zapier's **Paths** feature unlocks powerful **conditional logic**, making workflows more **dynamic and intelligent**. Whether you're managing **customer inquiries, sales leads, HR processes, or marketing automation**, Paths can help **customize** the automation experience based on specific data inputs.

By mastering Paths, you'll take your **Zapier automation skills to the next level**, enabling **smarter, more efficient workflows** with minimal manual effort.

Next Step: In the next section, we'll dive into **Webhooks and Custom Integrations**, helping you extend Zapier's functionality beyond standard app connections.

5.1.3 Implementing Filters to Refine Automations

When building automated workflows in Zapier, not all data should trigger an action. Sometimes, you need to filter out certain information to ensure that only relevant tasks are executed. This is where **Zapier's Filter feature** comes into play. Filters allow you to **set conditions** so that a Zap continues only if specific criteria are met.

This section will walk you through the fundamentals of **Zapier Filters**, explain their importance, and provide a **step-by-step guide** on how to implement them effectively. We will also explore **real-world use cases** and **troubleshooting tips** to help you create refined and efficient automations.

---

1. Understanding Zapier Filters

What Are Filters in Zapier?

Filters are **conditional rules** that determine whether a Zap should proceed to the next step or stop. If the filter condition is met, the automation continues. If not, the Zap stops without performing the subsequent actions.

For example, let's say you receive email inquiries through Gmail and want to send automatic responses only if the subject contains the word **"urgent."** You can set up a Zapier filter to check the subject line and proceed only if it includes "urgent."

Why Are Filters Important?

Filters help refine workflows by:
✓ **Reducing unnecessary tasks** – Prevents your Zap from running when conditions aren't met, saving automation tasks.
✓ **Improving accuracy** – Ensures that only relevant data is processed.
✓ **Saving time and resources** – Prevents irrelevant actions from being triggered.

---

2. Step-by-Step Guide: How to Use Filters in Zapier

Let's go through a detailed process of setting up a **Zap with a Filter** step by step.

Example Scenario:

Imagine you have a form on **Google Forms** where users submit support requests. You want to send an email notification **only if the request is marked as "High Priority."**

Step 1: Create a New Zap

1. Log in to **Zapier** and click **"Create a Zap."**
2. Select **Google Forms** as the trigger app.
3. Choose **"New Response in Spreadsheet"** as the trigger event.
4. Connect your Google account and select the form you want to use.
5. Test the trigger to make sure Zapier pulls in a sample response.

Step 2: Add a Filter Step

1. Click **"+"** to add a new action and select **"Filter by Zapier."**
2. Define the filter conditions:
   - **Field:** Select the form field where users indicate priority.
   - **Condition:** Choose **"Text Exactly Matches."**
   - **Value:** Enter **"High Priority."**

This setup ensures that only form submissions labeled as **High Priority** will proceed to the next step.

Step 3: Add an Action Step

1. Click **"+"** and select **Gmail** (or another email service).

2. Choose **"Send Email"** as the action event.

3. Connect your Gmail account.

4. Set up the email template:

   o **To:** Enter your support team's email.

   o **Subject:** "New High Priority Support Request!"

   o **Body:** Include details from the form submission.

5. Test the action to verify the email sends correctly.

Step 4: Activate Your Zap

1. Click **"Turn on Zap."**

2. Submit a test form with different priority levels to ensure the filter works as expected.

---

3. Advanced Filtering Techniques

Using Multiple Filter Conditions

Sometimes, a single filter isn't enough. Zapier allows you to set **multiple conditions** using **AND** or **OR** logic.

Example 1: Using AND Logic

You want to notify the sales team only if:

- The form submission contains the keyword "Enterprise."

- The customer is from the United States.

Setup:

✓ Condition 1: **Form Field "Plan Type"** – Text contains "Enterprise."

✓ Condition 2: **Form Field "Country"** – Text exactly matches "United States."

→ The Zap **runs only** if **both** conditions are met.

Example 2: Using OR Logic

You want to follow up with a lead if:

- The lead's budget is above $10,000, **OR**

- The lead requests a demo.

Setup:

✓ Condition 1: **Budget Field** – Number is greater than 10,000.

✓ **OR** Condition 2: **Request Type Field** – Text exactly matches "Demo Request."

→ The Zap **runs if either condition** is met.

Combining Filters with Paths for More Complexity

If you need **more complex decision-making**, consider using **Zapier Paths** instead of filters. Paths allow for **branching workflows** based on multiple conditions.

---

4. Real-World Use Cases of Zapier Filters

1. Automating Lead Qualification

Scenario: You receive leads via a **Typeform survey** but only want to follow up with leads who indicate a **strong interest** in your product.

✓ Filter Condition: **"Interest Level" is "Very Interested."**

✓ Action: Add the lead to your CRM and send a personalized email.

2. Managing Job Applications

Scenario: You use **Google Forms** to collect job applications but only want to notify the HR team if the applicant has more than **5 years of experience.**

✓ Filter Condition: **"Years of Experience" is greater than 5.**

✓ Action: Forward the application via Slack to HR.

3. Filtering Spam from Contact Forms

Scenario: You receive submissions from a website **contact form** but want to block messages containing **spam keywords** like "SEO services" or "guest post."

✓ Filter Condition: **Message contains "SEO" OR "guest post."**

✓ Action: Stop the Zap if the condition is met.

5. Troubleshooting Common Issues with Filters

1. The Zap Is Not Running as Expected

✓ Check if the sample data meets the filter condition.

✓ Ensure the field format (text, number, boolean) is correct.

2. The Filter Is Too Strict

✓ Use **"Contains"** instead of **"Exactly Matches"** to allow variations.

✓ Add multiple conditions using **OR** logic to be more flexible.

3. The Zap Runs Too Often

✓ Refine conditions to reduce unnecessary triggers.

✓ Use additional filters or **delays** to control automation timing.

Conclusion

Zapier Filters are a powerful way to **refine your automations**, ensuring that only relevant data triggers the next steps. By **using multiple conditions**, **combining filters with paths**, and **troubleshooting issues**, you can create **smarter** and **more efficient workflows**.

Now that you've mastered filtering, let's move on to **5.2 Using Webhooks and Custom Integrations** to explore even more advanced automation possibilities!

5.2 Using Webhooks and Custom Integrations

5.2.1 Introduction to Webhooks in Zapier

What Are Webhooks?

Webhooks are a method of communication between different applications, allowing one app to send real-time data to another when a specific event occurs. Unlike APIs, which require regular polling to fetch new data, webhooks work by automatically sending updates whenever an event is triggered. This makes them highly efficient for automation, as they enable instant data transfer without unnecessary API calls.

In the context of Zapier, webhooks allow you to **send and receive data** between applications that may not have built-in Zapier integrations. With webhooks, you can:

- Trigger workflows based on external events.

- Send custom data to other applications.

- Capture real-time updates from third-party services.

How Webhooks Work in Zapier

Zapier provides two main webhook functionalities:

1. **Catch Hook (Incoming Webhooks)** – Listens for data from external sources and triggers a Zap.

2. **POST Webhooks (Outgoing Webhooks)** – Sends data to external applications when a Zap is executed.

These webhook actions are available through **Zapier's Webhooks by Zapier** app, which allows users to integrate with almost any web service that supports webhooks.

Understanding Incoming Webhooks (Catch Hook)

How an Incoming Webhook Works

An incoming webhook listens for data from an external service and starts a Zap when new data is received. This is useful when you need Zapier to respond instantly to an event in another app.

Example Use Cases for Incoming Webhooks

- A form submission in **Google Forms** sends data to **Google Sheets**.

- A payment confirmation in **Stripe** triggers an email notification.

- A new customer signup on a **website** creates a contact in **HubSpot CRM**.

How to Set Up an Incoming Webhook in Zapier

Follow these steps to create an incoming webhook in Zapier:

Step 1: Create a New Zap

1. Go to your Zapier dashboard and click **"Create a Zap."**

2. In the **Trigger** step, search for **Webhooks by Zapier** and select it.

3. Choose **Catch Hook** as the trigger event.

4. Click **Continue.**

Step 2: Get Your Webhook URL

1. Zapier will generate a unique **Webhook URL**.

2. Copy this URL – you will need it to send data from an external app.

Step 3: Send a Test Request

To ensure the webhook works, send test data from an external application. You can do this by:

- Using **Postman** to send a manual request.

- Configuring an external service (e.g., Stripe, Google Forms, or Typeform) to send data to this URL.

Step 4: Verify the Data

1. Go back to Zapier and click **"Test Trigger."**

2. If the webhook is set up correctly, Zapier will display the received data.

3. Click **Continue** to proceed with setting up an action.

Step 5: Define the Zap's Action

Once the webhook captures data, you need to define what happens next. Some common actions include:

- Storing data in **Google Sheets**.

- Sending an email via **Gmail**.

- Creating a task in **Asana or Trello**.

Step 6: Activate Your Zap

After configuring the action, click **Publish Zap** to activate the webhook. Now, every time the external service sends data to the webhook URL, the Zap will execute automatically.

Understanding Outgoing Webhooks (POST, GET, PUT, DELETE Requests)

What Is an Outgoing Webhook?

An outgoing webhook sends data from Zapier to another application when a Zap is triggered. This is useful when you need to:

- Update records in an external database.

- Send data to a custom-built application.

- Automate interactions with APIs that don't have a Zapier integration.

Types of Outgoing Webhook Requests

- **POST** – Sends data to an external service (e.g., creating a new record).

- **GET** – Retrieves data from an external service.

- **PUT** – Updates existing data.

- **DELETE** – Removes data from an external service.

Example Use Cases for Outgoing Webhooks

- Automatically sending data to a **custom CRM system**.

- Creating a new **order** in an e-commerce platform.
- Notifying an external system when a **Zap completes**.

How to Set Up an Outgoing Webhook in Zapier

Step 1: Create a Zap and Set Up a Trigger

1. In Zapier, click **"Create a Zap."**
2. Choose a trigger app (e.g., **Google Forms** submission).
3. Configure the trigger event and click **Continue.**

Step 2: Add the Webhook Action

1. In the **Action** step, search for **Webhooks by Zapier** and select it.
2. Choose **POST**, **GET**, **PUT**, or **DELETE** as the request type, depending on your use case.

Step 3: Configure the Webhook Request

- Enter the URL of the external API or service.
- Define **headers** (e.g., authorization tokens).
- Set the **payload format** (e.g., JSON, form data).
- Include necessary **parameters** and data fields.

Step 4: Test and Activate the Zap

1. Click **Test & Review** to check if the webhook is working.
2. If the request is successful, click **Publish Zap** to activate it.

Best Practices for Using Webhooks in Zapier

1. Secure Your Webhooks

- Use authentication (e.g., API keys) to prevent unauthorized access.
- Only accept data from **trusted sources**.

2. Optimize Webhook Performance

- Minimize unnecessary data to reduce processing time.

- Use **filters** in Zapier to refine incoming data.

3. Handle Errors Gracefully

- Use **Zapier's built-in error handling**.

- Implement retries for failed requests.

Conclusion

Webhooks provide a **powerful way** to integrate Zapier with almost any app, even those without native Zapier integrations. By understanding how to use **incoming and outgoing webhooks**, you can create **custom automation workflows** tailored to your needs. Whether you're capturing real-time data or sending automated requests, webhooks can unlock **new automation possibilities** and enhance your workflow efficiency.

In the next section (**5.2.2 Setting Up a Webhook Trigger**), we'll dive deeper into how to configure different webhook triggers and troubleshoot common issues.

5.2.2 Setting Up a Webhook Trigger

Introduction to Webhook Triggers

Webhooks are one of the most powerful tools in Zapier, enabling real-time automation by allowing apps to communicate instantly. Unlike traditional API-based integrations, which often rely on scheduled checks for new data, webhooks push data automatically when a specific event occurs.

In Zapier, a **Webhook Trigger** listens for incoming data from an external service and starts a Zap when new information arrives. This allows you to create highly responsive automations, eliminating the need to wait for periodic updates.

Why Use Webhook Triggers in Zapier?

Webhook triggers provide several advantages, including:
✅ **Real-Time Data Transfer** – Information is sent instantly instead of waiting for Zapier's scheduled polling intervals.

✓ **Greater Flexibility** – Can be used with almost any app or service that supports webhooks, even those not natively supported by Zapier.

✓ **Efficiency** – Reduces API calls, making automation faster and more efficient.

✓ **Custom Integration Possibilities** – Allows you to integrate with custom-built applications or lesser-known services.

In this section, we'll go step by step through the process of setting up a **Webhook Trigger** in Zapier.

Step 1: Creating a Zap with a Webhook Trigger

To start, we'll create a new Zap that listens for data from an external service via a webhook.

1.1 Navigate to Zapier and Create a New Zap

1.   Log in to your Zapier account.

2.   Click **"Create Zap"** in the top-left corner of your dashboard.

3.   In the **"Trigger"** section, search for **"Webhooks by Zapier"** and select it.

1.2 Choose the Webhook Trigger Event

Zapier provides three different types of Webhook Triggers:

- **Catch Hook** – Receives data from an external source when an event occurs. This is the most commonly used trigger.

- **Catch Raw Hook** – Similar to Catch Hook but receives unprocessed data. Useful for advanced users working with raw JSON.

- **Retrieve Poll** – Periodically checks an endpoint for new data. This is less common and primarily used when an API does not support webhooks.

For this tutorial, select **"Catch Hook"** as it allows external applications to send data to Zapier automatically. Click **"Continue"** to proceed.

Step 2: Obtaining and Testing the Webhook URL

After selecting the **"Catch Hook"** trigger, Zapier will generate a **Webhook URL**. This is the endpoint that external applications will send data to.

2.1 Copy the Webhook URL

1. After selecting **"Catch Hook"**, Zapier will display a unique Webhook URL.

2. Click **"Copy"** to save it to your clipboard.

This URL acts as a unique address where data from external sources will be sent. Any service that supports webhooks can send data to this URL.

2.2 Configuring an External Application to Send Data

To test the Webhook Trigger, we need to send data from an external application. Here's how you can configure some popular tools:

Example 1: Sending Data from Slack

1. Open **Slack** and navigate to **Workflow Builder** (found under "Tools").

2. Click **"Create a Workflow"** and choose **"Webhook Trigger"**.

3. Paste the **Webhook URL** from Zapier.

4. Define the event that will send data (e.g., when a new message is posted in a specific channel).

5. Save the changes and activate the workflow.

Example 2: Sending Data from Google Forms

1. Open **Google Forms** and install the **"Webhook for Google Forms"** add-on.

2. Set up a new webhook and paste the **Zapier Webhook URL** as the endpoint.

3. Configure the form to send responses to this URL whenever a new submission is made.

4. Submit a test response to check if the webhook is working.

Example 3: Sending Data from a Custom API

If you're working with a custom API, you can send a POST request using tools like **Postman** or writing a simple script:

```
curl -X POST -H "Content-Type: application/json" -d '{"name": "John Doe", "email": "john@example.com"}' "https://hooks.zapier.com/hooks/catch/123456/"
```

2.3 Test the Webhook Trigger in Zapier

Once the external application sends data to the webhook, return to Zapier and click **"Test Trigger"**.

If everything is set up correctly, you should see the data that was sent. If no data appears, double-check the webhook setup in the external application.

Step 3: Processing the Webhook Data

After successfully capturing webhook data, you can now process it and pass it to other apps.

3.1 Parsing Webhook Data

Zapier will display the data structure received from the webhook. This may include multiple fields such as:

- **Name**
- **Email**
- **Phone Number**
- **Message**

You can select specific fields to use in the next steps of your Zap.

3.2 Adding an Action Step

Once the webhook trigger is working, you need to define what happens next. Click **"Add an Action"** and choose an app to process the data.

Example Use Cases

- **Send an Email** – Forward the captured data to Gmail to notify someone.
- **Create a Spreadsheet Entry** – Log the webhook data into Google Sheets for record-keeping.
- **Post a Message in Slack** – Automatically notify a team when new webhook data arrives.
- **Add to CRM** – Store leads in HubSpot, Salesforce, or another CRM.

3.3 Configuring the Action Step

1. Select an app (e.g., Gmail, Google Sheets, Slack).

2. Map the webhook fields to the corresponding fields in the selected app.

3. Test the action to ensure data is processed correctly.

Step 4: Activating and Monitoring the Zap

4.1 Turn on the Zap

After configuring and testing the action step, click **"Publish Zap"** to activate it.

4.2 Monitoring Zap Performance

To ensure the Zap is running smoothly:
✓ Check the **Zap History** to review execution logs.
✓ Look for any **errors** in the Zapier dashboard.
✓ Adjust settings if necessary (e.g., adding filters or formatters).

4.3 Debugging Common Webhook Issues

If the Zap isn't working as expected, consider the following:
- **No data received?** – Ensure the external app is correctly sending requests.
- **Unexpected data format?** – Use the Zapier **Formatter** tool to clean up data.
- **Webhook URL mismatch?** – Verify the correct URL is being used in the external service.

Conclusion

Setting up a Webhook Trigger in Zapier opens up endless automation possibilities, allowing seamless integration between applications. By following these steps, you can build powerful real-time workflows tailored to your needs.

Next Steps

⚡ Explore more **advanced webhook integrations** using authentication methods.
⚡ Experiment with **multi-step Zaps** to create complex workflows.
⚡ Learn how to **connect APIs** with Zapier for even more customization.

5.2.3 Connecting APIs with Zapier

Introduction to API Integrations in Zapier

Zapier is a powerful automation tool that allows users to connect different apps without writing code. While Zapier provides built-in integrations for thousands of apps, sometimes you need to connect to an application that isn't natively supported. This is where **APIs (Application Programming Interfaces)** come in.

By using APIs with Zapier, you can interact with external applications, retrieve data, send commands, and create powerful automations that go beyond the standard Zapier capabilities. This section will guide you through:

- Understanding how Zapier interacts with APIs

- Using Webhooks to send and receive data

- Setting up API requests with Zapier's **Webhooks by Zapier** feature

- Practical examples of API-based automations

Understanding How Zapier Interacts with APIs

An API is a set of rules that allows different applications to communicate. In the context of Zapier, APIs enable automation by allowing you to:

- **Send data to an external application** (e.g., create a new contact in a CRM).

- **Retrieve data from an external application** (e.g., fetch recent orders from an e-commerce store).

- **Update or delete data in an application** (e.g., modify a database record).

Zapier interacts with APIs primarily using **Webhooks**, which allow Zapier to send and receive data via HTTP requests. The most common API request methods are:

- **GET** – Retrieve data from an external system.

- **POST** – Send new data to an external system.

- **PUT** – Update existing data.

- **DELETE** – Remove data from an external system.

Understanding these request types is crucial for successfully integrating APIs with Zapier.

Using Webhooks in Zapier to Connect APIs

Zapier provides a built-in app called **Webhooks by Zapier**, which allows you to send and receive API requests. Let's break down the different ways you can use Webhooks to connect APIs in Zapier.

1. Sending Data to an API (POST Requests)

A **POST request** sends new data to an API. This is useful for:

- Creating a new customer in a CRM
- Submitting form responses to a database
- Sending messages to a chat application

Example: Creating a New Contact in a CRM

Let's say you want to automatically add new leads from a Google Form to a CRM that doesn't have a native Zapier integration. Here's how to set up a POST request:

1. **Create a new Zap** and choose **Google Forms** as the trigger.
2. Select **"New Form Response"** as the trigger event.
3. Add an **action step** and choose **Webhooks by Zapier**.
4. Select **POST** as the request type.
5. In the **URL** field, enter the API endpoint of your CRM (e.g., https://api.examplecrm.com/v1/contacts).
6. In the **Headers** section, add an API key for authentication (e.g., Authorization: Bearer YOUR_API_KEY).
7. In the **Data** section, map the form fields to the API parameters (e.g., "name": {{Name from Google Form}}").
8. Click **Test & Review** to verify the request.

Once the Zap is activated, new form submissions will automatically create contacts in your CRM.

2. Retrieving Data from an API (GET Requests)

A **GET request** is used to fetch data from an API. This can be useful for:

- Pulling recent orders from an e-commerce platform

- Retrieving the latest blog posts from a website

- Checking the status of a project

Example: Fetching New Orders from an E-Commerce API

Let's say you want to retrieve the latest orders from an online store. Here's how to set up a GET request:

1. **Create a new Zap** and choose **"Schedule by Zapier"** as the trigger.

2. Set it to run every hour.

3. Add an **action step** and select **Webhooks by Zapier**.

4. Choose **GET** as the request type.

5. Enter the API URL to retrieve orders (e.g., https://api.onlinestore.com/orders?status=new).

6. Add any necessary authentication headers.

7. Click **Test & Review** to ensure the API returns data correctly.

8. Use the retrieved data in subsequent steps, such as adding it to a Google Sheet.

This setup ensures that new orders are automatically recorded in your preferred system without manual checks.

3. Updating Data via API (PUT Requests)

A **PUT request** updates existing data in an application. Use this when:

- Updating lead statuses in a CRM

- Modifying project details in a management tool

- Changing a customer's subscription plan

Example: Updating a Lead's Status in a CRM

Imagine you want to update a lead's status in a CRM when they book a sales call. Here's the process:

1. **Trigger:** Use **Calendly** to detect a new booking.

2. **Action:** Add a **Webhooks by Zapier** step.

3. **Request Type:** Choose **PUT**.

4. **URL:** Enter the CRM's API endpoint for lead updates.

5. **Data:** Include the lead ID and the new status ("status": "Booked Call").

6. **Test & Activate** the Zap.

Now, every time a sales call is booked, the lead's status updates automatically.

---

4. Deleting Data via API (DELETE Requests)

A **DELETE request** removes data from an external system. This is useful when:

- Deleting outdated customer records

- Removing completed tasks from a project management tool

- Unsubscribing users from a mailing list

Example: Removing a User from a Mailing List

If you want to automatically remove unsubscribed users from a mailing list:

1. **Trigger:** Detect an **unsubscribe event** from Mailchimp.

2. **Action:** Add **Webhooks by Zapier** and select **DELETE**.

3. **URL:** Use the API endpoint for removing subscribers.

4. **Data:** Pass the user's email ID in the request.

5. **Test & Activate** the Zap.

This ensures that your mailing list stays up-to-date without manual intervention.

Best Practices for API Integrations in Zapier

When working with APIs in Zapier, keep these best practices in mind:

✓ **Check API Documentation** – Always read the API documentation to understand request methods, authentication, and response formats.
✓ **Use API Keys Securely** – Store API keys in a safe place and never expose them in shared workflows.
✓ **Test API Calls First** – Use tools like Postman to test API requests before setting them up in Zapier.
✓ **Monitor Zap History** – Regularly check your Zapier logs for failed API calls and troubleshoot errors.
✓ **Optimize API Requests** – Limit unnecessary API calls to avoid exceeding rate limits or incurring extra costs.

Conclusion

By leveraging **Webhooks by Zapier**, you can connect virtually any API and automate workflows beyond Zapier's built-in integrations. Whether you're sending, retrieving, updating, or deleting data, API integrations unlock powerful automation possibilities for businesses and individuals alike.

Ready to take your Zapier skills to the next level? In the next section, we'll explore how **Zapier Formatter** can further enhance your automated workflows by cleaning and structuring data before passing it between apps.

5.3 Working with Zapier Formatter

5.3.1 Formatting Text and Numbers

When working with automation in Zapier, one of the most common challenges is ensuring that the data passed between different apps is in the correct format. Raw data often needs adjustments—whether it's cleaning up text, standardizing number formats, or extracting specific information.

Zapier's **Formatter** tool provides a set of powerful options to manipulate text and numbers, making your workflows more efficient and reducing the need for manual intervention. This section will guide you through various ways to use Zapier Formatter to clean, modify, and enhance text and number fields in your Zaps.

---

1. Introduction to Zapier Formatter

Zapier Formatter is a built-in feature that allows users to transform data within a Zap before passing it to the next step. It acts as a middle layer that ensures data consistency, improving automation reliability.

The **Formatter** tool provides different types of formatting options:
✅ **Text Formatting** – Modifying capitalization, extracting words, removing whitespace, etc.
✅ **Number Formatting** – Adjusting decimal places, converting currencies, rounding numbers, etc.
✅ **Date/Time Formatting** – Converting date formats, calculating date differences, etc.
✅ **Utilities** – Performing advanced actions like splitting text, extracting numbers, and more.

In this section, we will focus on **Text Formatting** and **Number Formatting**, two of the most widely used features in Zapier automation.

---

2. Text Formatting in Zapier

Text formatting is useful when you need to:

- Convert all text to uppercase or lowercase.

- Remove extra spaces or unwanted characters.

- Extract a portion of text, such as a name or email domain.

- Replace specific words or characters in a string.

2.1 How to Use Text Formatting in Zapier

To apply text formatting, follow these steps:

1️ **Create a Zap** – Set up a trigger from an app that provides text data (e.g., Gmail, Google Sheets, Slack).
2️ **Add a Formatter Step** – Choose "Formatter by Zapier" as the action app.
3️ **Select "Text"** – In the event dropdown, choose "Text" to access formatting options.
4️ **Customize the Formatting** – Select the type of text modification you need.
5️ **Test and Save** – Run the test to see if the transformation works as expected.

2.2 Common Text Formatting Options

Below are some commonly used text formatting features in Zapier:

◆ Convert Text Case

You can automatically change the text to:

- **Uppercase** → Convert all letters to capital letters.

- **Lowercase** → Convert all letters to small letters.

- **Title Case** → Capitalize the first letter of each word.

Example:
📧 *Incoming data:* "hello world"
⬆ *Formatted result:* "Hello World" (Title Case)

◆ Remove Unnecessary Spaces

Zapier allows you to **trim spaces** from the beginning or end of a text string. This is useful when dealing with input fields that may contain accidental spaces.

Example:
📧 *Incoming data:* " Zapier Automation "
⬆ *Formatted result:* "Zapier Automation" (Trimmed)

◆ Extract Specific Text

You can extract parts of a string using predefined rules:

- **Extract Email Address** – Pulls the first email found in a text.

- **Extract Number** – Retrieves numbers from a string.

- **Extract URL** – Finds a URL in the text.

Example:
✉ *Incoming data:* "Contact us at support@example.com"
⬆ *Formatted result:* "support@example.com"

◆ Find and Replace Text

This feature helps replace specific words or characters within a text string.

Example:
✉ *Incoming data:* "Order Status: pending"
⬆ *Formatted result:* "Order Status: Processing" (after replacing "pending" with "Processing")

---

3. Number Formatting in Zapier

Number formatting is useful when dealing with numerical values, such as:

- Rounding numbers to a certain number of decimal places.

- Converting between different number formats.

- Formatting currency values.

3.1 How to Use Number Formatting in Zapier

To format numbers in a Zap, follow these steps:

1⬜. **Create a Zap** – Start with an app that provides numerical data (e.g., Google Sheets, QuickBooks, Stripe).
2⬜. **Add a Formatter Step** – Choose "Formatter by Zapier" as the action app.
3⬜. **Select "Numbers"** – In the event dropdown, choose "Numbers."

4️. **Customize the Formatting** – Select the number transformation you need.

5️. **Test and Save** – Ensure that the output matches your expected format.

3.2 Common Number Formatting Options

◆ **Rounding Numbers**

You can round numbers to the nearest whole number or to a fixed number of decimal places.

Example:

✉ *Incoming data:* 3.768

⬆ *Formatted result:* 3.77 (rounded to two decimal places)

◆ **Adding Thousand Separators**

This helps improve number readability by inserting commas.

Example:

✉ *Incoming data:* 1000000

⬆ *Formatted result:* 1,000,000

◆ **Converting Currency Formats**

Zapier can convert a plain number into a formatted currency string.

Example:

✉ *Incoming data:* 1500

⬆ *Formatted result:* $1,500.00 (if USD is selected)

◆ **Performing Basic Calculations**

Zapier can also do simple calculations, such as:

- Addition, subtraction, multiplication, and division.

- Percentage calculations.

Example:

✉ *Incoming data:* Price: 100 → Multiply by 1.15 (for a 15% tax)

⬆ *Formatted result:* 115

4. Practical Use Cases for Formatter in Zaps

Let's look at real-world examples where text and number formatting can improve your automation.

📌 Use Case 1: Standardizing Email Subjects

Scenario: A company receives emails from a form submission with inconsistent subject formats. Zapier can convert all email subjects to Title Case.

✉ *Incoming subject:* "urgent: customer support request"
⬆ *Formatted result:* "Urgent: Customer Support Request"

📌 Use Case 2: Formatting Invoice Amounts

Scenario: A business receives raw transaction amounts and needs to format them for accounting.

✉ *Incoming amount:* 1500
⬆ *Formatted result:* $1,500.00

📌 Use Case 3: Extracting Order Numbers

Scenario: A business receives order details via email, and Zapier extracts the order number for tracking.

✉ *Incoming text:* "Your order #345678 has been shipped."
⬆ *Formatted result:* 345678

5. Summary

In this section, we explored how to use Zapier Formatter to manipulate text and numbers efficiently. You have learned how to:
✓ Convert text case, trim spaces, extract data, and replace words.
✓ Round numbers, format currency, and perform calculations.
✓ Apply Formatter in real-world automation scenarios.

By mastering text and number formatting, you can make your Zaps smarter and eliminate the need for manual data cleanup. In the next section, we'll dive into **date and time formatting**, another essential skill for advanced automation.

5.3.2 Date and Time Conversions

Time is a crucial element in automation. Whether you are scheduling events, tracking deadlines, or managing customer interactions, handling date and time correctly ensures your workflows function as expected. In Zapier, working with date and time can become complex, especially when dealing with different time zones, formats, or required transformations. Fortunately, Zapier's **Formatter** tool provides a simple way to manipulate and convert date and time values within your Zaps.

In this section, we will cover:

- Understanding date and time formats

- Using Zapier Formatter to convert date and time

- Common use cases for date and time conversions

- Handling time zones effectively

- Formatting relative dates (e.g., "tomorrow," "next Monday")

- Troubleshooting date and time conversion issues

Understanding Date and Time Formats in Zapier

Zapier works with various date and time formats, but before using Formatter, it's essential to understand how dates are typically represented. Some common formats include:

Format	Example
MM/DD/YYYY	12/31/2025
DD/MM/YYYY	31/12/2025
YYYY-MM-DD	2025-12-31
Unix Timestamp	1704067200 (seconds since 1970-01-01 00:00:00 UTC)
RFC 2822	Wed, 31 Dec 2025 23:59:59 +0000
ISO 8601	2025-12-31T23:59:59Z

Different apps and services use different date formats. For example:

- Google Sheets might store dates as **MM/DD/YYYY** by default (depending on locale).

- Salesforce often uses **YYYY-MM-DDTHH:MM:SSZ** (ISO 8601 format).

- Many APIs return dates in **Unix Timestamp** format.

When moving data between different apps, you may need to **reformat** these dates for consistency.

Using Zapier Formatter for Date and Time Conversion

Step 1: Adding a Formatter Step in Zapier

1. In your Zap, click on **"+"** to add a new step.

2. Choose **"Formatter"** as the app.

3. Select **"Date/Time"** as the event.

4. Click **Continue** to configure the transformation.

Step 2: Configuring the Date/Time Transformation

1. **Select the Input Field**: Choose the date value from a previous step (e.g., from an email, form submission, or spreadsheet).

2. **Select the Transformation Type**: Choose from:

   o **Format**: Convert between date formats.

   o **Add/Subtract Time**: Adjust dates by adding or subtracting days, hours, minutes.

   o **Compare Dates**: Find differences between two dates.

3. **Specify the Input Format** (optional but recommended):

   o If Zapier cannot automatically detect the format, you can specify it.

   o Example: If your input date is **12/31/2025**, set the format as **MM/DD/YYYY**.

4. **Specify the Output Format**: Choose how you want the converted date to appear.

   o Example: Convert **12/31/2025** (MM/DD/YYYY) → **2025-12-31** (YYYY-MM-DD).

5. **Time Zone Selection**: Choose a time zone if applicable.

Step 3: Testing and Saving the Formatter Step

1. Click **Test & Review** to see the formatted output.

2. If the output looks correct, click **Continue** and proceed with the next Zap step.

3. If the output needs adjustment, edit the transformation settings.

Common Use Cases for Date and Time Conversions

1. Formatting Dates for Different Apps

- Problem: A CRM exports dates in **YYYY-MM-DD**, but you need **MM/DD/YYYY** for Google Sheets.

- Solution: Use Formatter to convert the format before sending data.

2. Adding or Subtracting Time

- Problem: You want to send reminders **3 days before** an event.

- Solution:

   o Use **"Add/Subtract Time"** in Formatter.

   o Input: **2025-12-31**

   o Add: **-3 days**

   o Output: **2025-12-28**

3. Handling Time Zones in Automations

- Problem: An event is in **UTC**, but you need local time for emails.

- Solution:

   o Input: **2025-12-31T15:00:00Z** (UTC)

- o Convert to: **America/New_York (EST)**

- o Output: **2025-12-31 10:00 AM EST**

4. Converting Relative Dates ("Tomorrow", "Next Monday")

- Problem: A user submits "next Monday" in a form, but your database needs an exact date.

- Solution:

  - o Input: **Next Monday**

  - o Formatter will convert it to the exact date (e.g., **2025-03-10**).

5. Calculating Time Differences

- Problem: You need to calculate the number of days between two dates.

- Solution:

  - o Use Formatter's **"Compare Dates"**

  - o Input: **Start Date: 2025-01-01**, **End Date: 2025-01-10**

  - o Output: **9 days**

Handling Time Zones Effectively

Understanding Zapier's Default Time Zone

Zapier uses **UTC (Coordinated Universal Time)** by default. If your apps are in different time zones, you may need to convert times.

Steps to Convert Time Zones in Formatter

1. In your Formatter step, select **"Date/Time"**.

2. Choose **"Format"** and set the desired output format.

3. Select the **original time zone** and the **new time zone** (e.g., UTC → PST).

4. Test and review the output.

Original Time (UTC) Converted to PST (-8h)

2025-12-31 15:00:00 2025-12-31 07:00:00

Troubleshooting Date and Time Issues

Issue	Cause	Solution
Date not converting	Wrong input format	Specify input format manually
Incorrect time zone	Defaulted to UTC	Set the correct time zone in Formatter
Output not changing	Cache issue	Refresh Zap, retest Formatter step
"Invalid date" error	Incorrect input format	Check and correct format

Conclusion

Date and time conversions in Zapier are essential for creating accurate and efficient workflows. Whether you need to adjust time zones, format dates for different applications, or calculate time differences, Zapier's Formatter provides a powerful, no-code solution. By mastering these functions, you can ensure that your automations run smoothly and deliver data in the exact format needed for your business processes.

Next Steps:
✓ Practice date formatting with sample Zaps.
✓ Experiment with adding/subtracting time.
✓ Explore complex use cases like scheduling reminders or syncing time zones.

By applying these skills, you can build **smarter, time-aware automations** that make your workflows more efficient!

5.3.3 Using Formatter for Data Cleaning

Data cleaning is an essential step in automation, ensuring that the information being transferred between apps is formatted correctly, consistent, and free of unnecessary clutter. Zapier's Formatter tool provides a variety of functions that help clean and refine data before it is passed to the next step in a Zap.

In this section, we will explore how to use Zapier Formatter for data cleaning, including text modifications, removing unwanted characters, restructuring data, and ensuring consistency across different systems.

1. Why is Data Cleaning Important in Automation?

When automating workflows, raw data often contains inconsistencies, errors, or unwanted elements. These issues can lead to problems such as:

- Mismatched formatting between different apps

- Redundant or incorrect information being stored

- Errors in numerical calculations or date/time conversions

- Unreadable or cluttered text fields

By cleaning data before passing it to another step in a Zap, users can improve the accuracy, efficiency, and reliability of their automated workflows.

2. Key Features of Zapier Formatter for Data Cleaning

Zapier Formatter offers various data transformation tools that help clean up and standardize information. Some of the most commonly used Formatter functions for data cleaning include:

2.1 Text Cleanup Functions

- **Trim Spaces**: Removes extra spaces from text fields.

- **Change Case**: Converts text to uppercase, lowercase, or title case.

- **Find and Replace**: Replaces specific words, characters, or patterns within a text field.

- **Extract Pattern**: Uses regular expressions (RegEx) to extract specific information from a text.

- **Remove HTML**: Strips out HTML tags from copied text.

2.2 Number and Date Formatting

- **Round Numbers**: Converts floating-point numbers into whole numbers or specific decimal places.

- **Convert Date Formats**: Changes date formats to match the requirements of the receiving app.

- **Extract Date Elements**: Pulls out specific parts of a date (e.g., year, month, day).

2.3 Data Parsing and Splitting

- **Split Text**: Breaks a string of text into multiple parts using a delimiter (e.g., commas, spaces).

- **Extract Email/Phone Number**: Identifies and extracts emails or phone numbers from a text.

- **Extract URL**: Finds and extracts URLs from a block of text.

---

3. Step-by-Step Guide: Cleaning Data with Zapier Formatter

Now, let's walk through how to use Zapier Formatter to clean up data within a Zap.

Step 1: Set Up a Zap with Raw Data Input

1. Go to Zapier and create a new Zap.

2. Select a trigger app that provides raw data input (e.g., Google Sheets, Typeform, Gmail).

3. Configure the trigger event (e.g., "New Response in Google Forms").

For example, let's say we receive names from a form where users enter their names inconsistently:

Name (Raw)

john doe

MARY SMITH

DaVid JoHnson

We need to standardize these names before storing them in a CRM system.

Step 2: Add the Zapier Formatter Step

1. Click the **"+"** button to add a new action step.

2. Search for **Formatter by Zapier** and select it.

3. Choose **"Text"** as the action event.

Step 3: Configure the Formatter to Clean Data

Example 1: Change Name Format to Title Case

1. In the **Transform** dropdown, select **"Change Case"**.

2. In the **Input** field, select the name field from the trigger app.

3. Choose **"Title Case"** to ensure names follow proper capitalization.

4. Click **"Test & Review"** to see the output.

Name (Formatted)

John Doe

Mary Smith

David Johnson

Example 2: Removing Extra Spaces from Input Data

If users accidentally enter extra spaces, we can trim them.

1. Choose **"Trim Whitespace"** in the Formatter tool.

2. Select the text input field.

3. Click **"Test & Review"** to see the cleaned data.

Before: " John Doe "
After: "John Doe"

Example 3: Replacing Incorrect Symbols

If a CSV file contains names separated by underscores instead of spaces:

- **Before:** "John_Doe"

- **After:** "John Doe"

1. Select **"Find and Replace"** as the transformation.

2. Input "_" in the **Find** field.

3. Input " " (a space) in the **Replace With** field.

4. Run the test to see the corrected output.

---

4. Cleaning Email, Phone Numbers, and URLs

Zapier Formatter can extract clean versions of emails, phone numbers, and URLs.

Extracting an Email from a Message

If an email contains unnecessary text:

Raw input:

"Hello, please contact us at support@example.com for help."

Formatter Configuration:

1. Select **"Extract Email Address"**.

2. Choose the text field containing the email.

3. Run the test.

Cleaned Output:

"support@example.com"

---

5. Automating Data Cleaning in Real Workflows

5.1 Cleaning Form Responses Before Saving to a Database

- A business receives customer feedback via Typeform.

- Names and emails need to be properly formatted before adding them to Google Sheets.

- A Zap runs Formatter functions (Change Case, Trim Spaces, Extract Email) before saving.

5.2 Standardizing Product Data for E-Commerce

- An online store receives product descriptions with extra spaces and inconsistent capitalization.

- A Zap cleans the descriptions before publishing them on Shopify.

5.3 Normalizing Contact Information for a CRM

- When users submit phone numbers in different formats:

    o   +1 (555) 123-4567

    o   555.123.4567

    o   555-123-4567

- A Zap standardizes all phone numbers into +15551234567 format.

6. Best Practices for Using Formatter in Data Cleaning

✓ **Use Multiple Formatter Steps** – Some transformations require chaining multiple actions (e.g., Trim → Change Case → Find & Replace).
✓ **Test with Sample Data** – Always test Formatter actions before activating a Zap.
✓ **Consider Webhooks for Complex Cleaning** – When Formatter's built-in tools are not enough, Webhooks can send data to external services for advanced processing.
✓ **Monitor Zap History** – Regularly check logs to ensure data is being cleaned correctly.

7. Conclusion

Cleaning data is a crucial part of any automated workflow. By leveraging Zapier's Formatter, users can ensure that their data is well-structured, accurate, and compatible with different apps. Whether it's formatting text, extracting useful information, or standardizing inputs, Zapier makes data cleaning easy and efficient.

With the skills learned in this section, users can build more reliable automations that prevent errors, improve consistency, and ultimately save time in their workflows.

CHAPTER V
Troubleshooting and Best Practices

6.1 Debugging Common Zapier Issues

6.1.1 Checking Zap History and Logs

When working with Zapier, issues can arise due to misconfigured triggers, incorrect action setups, app connection failures, or system errors. To effectively troubleshoot these issues, Zapier provides a **Zap History and Logs** feature, which records every execution attempt for each Zap. By understanding how to check these logs and interpret the data, you can quickly diagnose and resolve errors in your automated workflows.

Understanding Zap History in Zapier

Zap History is a powerful debugging tool that allows you to:

- See the status of your Zaps and determine if they ran successfully or failed.

- Review the data that was sent through each step of your Zap.

- Identify errors and the reasons why a Zap might not have executed properly.

- Manually replay failed Zaps after making corrections.

By analyzing your Zap History, you can pinpoint what went wrong and take corrective actions accordingly.

How to Access Zap History in Zapier

Follow these steps to access your Zap History:

Step 1: Navigate to Zap History

1. Log in to your Zapier account.

2. Click on **"Zap History"** from the left-hand menu.

3. You will see a list of all recent Zap executions, including their statuses.

The Zap History dashboard categorizes Zap runs into three statuses:

- **Success (Green Checkmark ✅)** – The Zap ran successfully without any issues.

- **Held (Yellow Pause Symbol ⏸)** – The Zap is paused due to conditions such as required manual review or approval.

- **Error (Red Exclamation Mark ✖)** – The Zap encountered an issue and failed to complete.

By filtering through these statuses, you can focus on troubleshooting only the problematic Zaps.

Interpreting Zap History Logs

Once inside the Zap History, click on any Zap run to see the detailed logs. Here's what you'll find:

1. Zap Run Summary

At the top, you will see a summary with key details, including:

- **Zap Name** – The specific workflow that was executed.

- **Run Time** – The exact timestamp of when the Zap ran.

- **Execution Duration** – How long it took for the Zap to complete.

- **Status** – Whether it was successful, held, or failed.

2. Trigger Data

- The first section shows the trigger event details, including:

    o The app that initiated the trigger.

- o The trigger event type (e.g., "New Email in Gmail," "New Row in Google Sheets").

  - o The data Zapier received from the trigger app.

- If your trigger is not working as expected:

  - o Click **"View Data In"** to see the raw input from the app.

  - o Ensure that the event correctly matches the expected format.

3. Action Steps and Data Flow

- Each action in your Zap is recorded separately.

- Clicking on any action step will reveal:

  - o The data received from the previous step.

  - o The data sent to the next step.

  - o Any error messages that may have occurred.

For example, if your Zap is supposed to send a Slack message but failed, you will see:

- The input data that was expected.

- The actual data received.

- Any error messages indicating why the action failed.

Common Issues Found in Zap History and How to Fix Them

Here are some frequent problems you may encounter and how to resolve them:

1. Zap Trigger Not Firing

If a Zap is not triggering:
✓ Check if the app's trigger event is correctly configured.
✓ Verify that the data in the source app meets the Zap's trigger criteria.
✓ Ensure the connected app has proper permissions to send data.

2. Zap Stuck in "Held" Status

A Zap may be held due to:

❧ Filters – The data doesn't meet the filter conditions. Adjust filter settings if needed.

❧ Approval Required – Some apps require manual review before executing an action.

3. Failed Actions Due to Invalid Data

If an action fails because of incorrect data:

☐☐ Check the input fields and compare them with the expected format.

☐☐ Use Zapier's Formatter tool to clean or reformat data before passing it to the action step.

4. Connection Issues with Third-Party Apps

If a Zap fails due to authentication issues:

☐ Reconnect the app under **My Apps** in Zapier.

☐ Verify API permissions and ensure the app allows third-party integrations.

Replaying Failed Zaps

Once you've identified and fixed an issue, you may want to **manually replay** failed Zaps instead of waiting for them to run again.

How to Replay a Failed Zap

1. Open **Zap History** and filter by **"Error"** status.

2. Click on the failed Zap entry.

3. Review the error details and correct the issue.

4. Click **"Replay Zap"** to rerun the failed instance.

Zapier will attempt to execute the workflow again using the original trigger data. If the issue has been resolved, the Zap should now complete successfully.

Best Practices for Managing Zap History

To keep your Zap History clean and organized, consider the following best practices:

1. Regularly Review Zap History

- Set a routine to check your Zap History for errors.

- Address failures as soon as possible to prevent disruptions.

2. Use Naming Conventions for Zaps

- Assign clear and descriptive names to your Zaps for easy identification.

- Example: **"New Lead from Google Forms → Add to HubSpot CRM"** instead of **"Zap #2345"**.

3. Enable Notifications for Zap Failures

- Set up email alerts for Zap failures under **Settings → Notifications**.

- This ensures that you are immediately informed when something goes wrong.

4. Archive Old Zap Runs

- Periodically archive or delete old Zap History logs to improve visibility and performance.

Conclusion

Zap History and Logs are essential tools for troubleshooting errors in Zapier. By regularly checking your Zap executions, understanding common issues, and following best practices, you can maintain a smooth and efficient automation system.

6.1.2 Resolving Connection Errors

Zapier is a powerful automation tool that connects various apps to streamline workflows. However, sometimes users encounter **connection errors**, preventing Zaps from running as expected. These errors typically occur when Zapier fails to authenticate an app, loses access due to permission changes, or faces API limitations.

This section will cover:

- **Common causes of connection errors**

- **How to diagnose and fix authentication issues**

- **Handling expired tokens and API rate limits**

- **Best practices to maintain stable connections**

---

1. Understanding Connection Errors in Zapier

Connection errors in Zapier usually fall into a few common categories:

Authentication Failures

These occur when Zapier cannot authenticate an app due to:

- Incorrect login credentials

- Expired or revoked access tokens

- Security settings that block third-party access

Example: If you connect Google Sheets to Zapier but change your Google password later, Zapier may lose access to your sheets.

API Restrictions and Rate Limits

Some services enforce rate limits, restricting how many requests Zapier can send in a specific timeframe. If you exceed this limit, the connection may temporarily fail.

Example: If you automate a high volume of emails with Gmail, Google may block further Zapier requests for a short period.

App Permission Issues

Some apps require specific user permissions for Zapier to function properly. If these permissions are missing, the Zap may fail.

Example: If you attempt to update a Trello board via Zapier but lack editing permissions, Zapier won't be able to make the changes.

Firewall or Security Restrictions

Some companies have security settings that prevent Zapier from accessing certain applications. Firewalls, VPNs, or enterprise security policies can block connections.

Example: If your company restricts API access to Salesforce, Zapier may be unable to sync your CRM data.

2. Diagnosing Connection Errors

To resolve connection issues, you first need to diagnose the problem. Here are key steps to identify what's wrong:

Check Zapier's Error Message

Zapier provides error messages that indicate the cause of the connection failure. Follow these steps:

1. Open **Zapier Dashboard** → Click on **Zaps**.

2. Find the Zap with issues (usually marked with an error icon ⚠☐).

3. Click on **Task History** to review error details.

4. Look for specific messages like:

    o *"Invalid credentials"*: Indicates incorrect login details.

    o *"Token expired"*: Requires re-authentication.

    o *"Permission denied"*: Suggests missing access rights.

    o *"Rate limit exceeded"*: The app has restricted requests.

Test the Connection Manually

If Zapier reports a connection error, try manually logging into the app:

- Visit the app's official website and log in with the same credentials used in Zapier.

- If you can't log in, reset your password and update it in Zapier.

- If login works but Zapier still fails, check API permissions (explained in the next section).

Check API Status and Service Outages

Sometimes, the issue is on the app's side, not Zapier's. To check if an app is experiencing downtime:

- Visit **Zapier's Status Page**. https://status.zapier.com/

- Check the app's official status page (e.g., *Google Workspace Status, Slack Status*).

- Look for recent reports of outages or degraded performance.

Reconnect the App in Zapier

A simple reconnection can often fix authentication-related errors. Follow these steps:

1. Go to **Zapier Dashboard** → Click on **My Apps**.

2. Find the problematic app and click **Reconnect**.

3. Enter your credentials again and authorize Zapier.

4. Run a test Zap to confirm the connection is restored.

3. Fixing Common Connection Issues

Resolving Authentication Failures

Solution: Update or Reset Login Credentials

- If you changed your password recently, update it in Zapier.

- Remove the old connection and add the app again.

Solution: Reauthorize the App in Zapier

- Some apps (e.g., Facebook, Google Drive) require periodic reauthorization.

- Go to **My Apps** → Click **Reconnect** → Follow the authentication steps.

Solution: Enable Two-Factor Authentication (2FA) If Required

- Some apps require 2FA for third-party access.

- If enabled, make sure you enter the correct verification code when reconnecting.

Fixing Expired Tokens and API Rate Limits

Solution: Refresh the Access Token

- If Zapier reports an expired token, disconnect and reconnect the app.

- Some platforms (e.g., Microsoft 365, Google) refresh tokens automatically, while others require manual reconnection.

Solution: Reduce API Requests

- If you hit an API rate limit, reduce the frequency of your Zaps.

- Instead of triggering a Zap every minute, try every 10 minutes.

- Use **Zapier Filters** to minimize unnecessary requests.

Solution: Use Webhooks for High-Frequency Tasks

- Webhooks allow direct app-to-app communication without excessive API calls.

- Many apps (e.g., Shopify, Stripe) support Webhooks via Zapier's **Webhook by Zapier** feature.

Addressing Permission and Security Issues

Solution: Check App-Specific Permissions

- Some apps require administrator-level permissions to allow Zapier integration.

- Go to the app's **Settings → Integrations** and ensure Zapier has the right access.

Solution: Whitelist Zapier in Firewalls

- If your company's firewall blocks Zapier, ask IT to whitelist **zapier.com** and related API domains.

- For Google Workspace or Microsoft 365, enable third-party app permissions in admin settings.

Solution: Use a Dedicated API Key

- Some apps allow users to generate API keys specifically for Zapier.

- Using a dedicated API key instead of a personal login can improve security and reliability.

4. Best Practices for Maintaining Stable Connections

Regularly Review Connected Apps

- Check **Zapier Dashboard → My Apps** every few months to ensure all connections are active.

Monitor Zap History for Errors

- Set up **Zapier Notifications** to get alerts when Zaps fail.

Use Backup Accounts for Critical Integrations

- If a key app (e.g., Gmail) is connected to a single account, consider using a second account as a backup in case of disruptions.

Conclusion

Connection errors in Zapier are common but can be easily resolved by:

✓ Diagnosing the issue using Zap History and error messages

✓ Reconnecting or reauthorizing apps when authentication fails

✓ Managing API rate limits by optimizing Zap frequency

✓ Checking permissions and security settings to prevent access issues

By following these steps, you can ensure that your Zapier automations run smoothly with minimal disruptions.

6.1.3 Fixing Failed Actions

Zapier is an incredibly powerful automation tool, but like any software, it's not immune to occasional errors and failed actions. A **failed action** in Zapier occurs when a step in your automation (Zap) encounters an issue that prevents it from executing properly. This can disrupt workflows, cause inefficiencies, and lead to missed opportunities.

In this section, we will explore the common reasons why Zapier actions fail, how to diagnose these failures, and the best methods to resolve them effectively.

1. Understanding Failed Actions in Zapier

What Is a Failed Action?

A failed action occurs when a step in your Zap does not complete successfully. Instead of executing as expected, it results in an error message, an incomplete process, or an incorrect output.

How Does Zapier Handle Failed Actions?

- **Zap History Logs:** Zapier provides detailed logs that show the status of each Zap execution, highlighting successful and failed steps.

- **Error Messages:** When a step fails, Zapier displays an error message explaining the issue.

- **Retry Options:** Depending on the failure type, you may have options to manually retry the action or make adjustments to prevent future failures.

2. Common Causes of Failed Actions and How to Fix Them

Incorrect or Expired App Connections

Problem:

- If a connected app (such as Gmail, Slack, or Google Sheets) requires authentication and the connection expires, Zapier may fail to execute the action.
- API tokens or credentials may have changed, leading to authentication failures.

Solution:

1. **Check Your App Connections:**
   - Go to **Zapier Dashboard > My Apps**
   - Look for any **disconnected** or **expired** apps.
   - Click **Reconnect** and enter updated credentials.

2. **Reauthorize the App:**
   - If reconnecting doesn't work, try removing the app connection and adding it again.
   - This forces Zapier to create a fresh connection with new authentication tokens.

3. **Enable API Access in the App Settings:**
   - Some apps require API access to be enabled before they can work with Zapier.
   - Check the settings of the connected app to ensure integration is allowed.

Incorrect Field Mapping

Problem:

- Data fields between apps don't match, causing Zapier to fail when sending or receiving data.

- Example: A Zap is set up to send data from Google Forms to Airtable, but the column names in Airtable don't match the form field names.

Solution:

1. **Verify Field Mapping in Your Zap:**

   o Open the **Zap Editor** and check each action step.

   o Ensure the correct fields are being pulled from the previous step.

2. **Check Data Sample Compatibility:**

   o Click **Test Action** to preview the data being sent.

   o If the test fails, adjust the field selections to match the receiving app's format.

3. **Use Zapier's Formatter to Adjust Data:**

   o If the format doesn't match, use **Zapier Formatter** to modify the output before sending it to the next step.

API Rate Limits and Usage Restrictions

Problem:

- Some apps impose limits on the number of API requests you can make within a given time frame.

- If Zapier exceeds this limit, actions may fail due to **"429 Too Many Requests"** errors.

Solution:

1. **Check API Limits of the Connected App:**

   o Refer to the app's API documentation to understand its rate limits.

2. **Use Zap Delays to Reduce API Calls:**

   o Add a **Delay by Zapier** step between actions to slow down requests.

- o Example: If sending data to a CRM, set a 5-second delay between submissions to avoid hitting the API limit.

3. **Batch Process Data Instead of Sending Individual Requests:**

   - o Instead of triggering a Zap for every single new entry, collect data and send it in bulk.

App-Specific Errors

Problem:

- Some apps may experience **downtime** or **service disruptions**, causing Zapier to fail when trying to send data.

- Example: If a Zap is supposed to create a Trello card, but Trello is down, the action will fail.

Solution:

1. **Check Zapier's Status Page:**

   - o Visit Zapier Status to see if the issue is on their end.

2. **Check the App's Status Page:**

   - o Many services (Google, Slack, Trello, etc.) have public **status pages** where you can check for outages.

3. **Enable Zapier's Auto-Retry Feature:**

   - o Zapier automatically retries failed actions **up to three times** before marking them as failed.

Missing Permissions in the Connected App

Problem:

- Zapier may fail to execute actions if the user account used for authentication **doesn't have the necessary permissions**.

- Example: A Zap is set up to create Google Calendar events, but the connected Google account doesn't have write access.

Solution:

1. **Verify App Permissions:**

   o   Check if the authenticated account has the required permissions.

2. **Use an Account with Proper Access:**

   o   If necessary, connect a different account with the right level of access.

3. **Grant Permissions Again:**

   o   Some apps require users to **reconfirm permissions** periodically.

---

3. Preventing Failed Actions in the Future

Enable Zapier's Error Notifications

- Go to **Zap Settings** and turn on **Email Notifications for Zap Errors**.
- This ensures you get alerts when a Zap fails.

Use Zapier's Built-In Error Handling Tools

- Use **Filters** to prevent actions from running when certain conditions aren't met.
- Use **Paths** for conditional workflows, ensuring actions only trigger when valid data is received.

Regularly Test and Monitor Your Zaps

- Check **Zap History** frequently to catch issues early.
- Periodically review and update Zaps to reflect any changes in the connected apps.

Conclusion

Fixing failed actions in Zapier requires a structured approach, from diagnosing the issue to implementing preventive measures. By understanding the common reasons for failures—

such as expired app connections, incorrect field mapping, and API rate limits—you can ensure your Zaps run smoothly.

Regular monitoring, using Zapier's built-in tools like **Error Notifications**, **Filters**, and **Paths**, and keeping up-to-date with app changes will help prevent disruptions and optimize your automation workflows.

With these troubleshooting strategies, you can maintain reliable and efficient Zaps, saving time and enhancing productivity.

6.2 Optimizing Zap Performance

6.2.1 Reducing Task Usage and Costs

Zapier operates on a task-based pricing model, where every successful action performed by a Zap counts as a task. If you're running multiple Zaps or automating complex workflows, your task count can quickly add up, leading to higher subscription costs. Optimizing task usage is crucial to ensuring efficiency and cost-effectiveness. In this section, we will explore various strategies to minimize task consumption without compromising automation effectiveness.

Understanding Task Consumption in Zapier

Before optimizing, it's important to understand how Zapier calculates tasks:

1. **Each action in a Zap counts as a task.**

    o Example: If a Zap triggers when a new email arrives and then sends a Slack message and updates a Google Sheet, it consumes **two** tasks—one for sending the message and one for updating the sheet.

2. **Multi-step Zaps consume more tasks.**

    o Each additional action adds to the task count.

3. **Filters, paths, and formatting actions also count as tasks.**

    o A filter that stops an unwanted Zap from running **still counts as a task** if the Zap triggers.

By being mindful of how tasks are counted, you can identify where optimizations are needed.

Strategies to Reduce Task Usage

1. Use Filters Effectively to Prevent Unnecessary Zaps

A Zap runs whenever its trigger conditions are met, even if the resulting action is not useful. One way to minimize unnecessary task consumption is to use **filters** wisely.

◆ Example: Filtering Emails for Important Notifications

- Suppose you have a Zap that sends a Slack notification whenever an email arrives in your Gmail inbox. Instead of triggering for every email, add a **filter** that only allows messages containing specific keywords (e.g., "Urgent" or "Invoice") to proceed.

- This prevents irrelevant emails from consuming tasks.

How to Set Up a Filter:

1. In the Zap editor, add a **Filter** step after the trigger.

2. Set conditions (e.g., "Email subject contains 'Urgent'").

3. The Zap will only proceed if the filter condition is met.

💡 **Tip:** A filter counts as a task only if the Zap triggers, so placing filters earlier in the process reduces overall task usage.

---

2. Leverage Paths Instead of Multiple Zaps

If you have multiple Zaps handling similar actions with minor variations, consider using **Paths** instead. Paths allow a single Zap to handle different scenarios instead of creating separate Zaps, which reduces duplicate triggers.

◆ Example: Assigning Support Tickets Based on Priority

- Instead of creating three separate Zaps for high, medium, and low-priority support tickets, use a **Path** to route each ticket accordingly.

- The Zap triggers **once**, but different actions execute depending on conditions, optimizing task usage.

How to Use Paths:

1. After setting a trigger, add a **Path** step.

2. Define different rules for each path (e.g., if priority = "high", assign to senior support team).

3. Each path executes conditionally, reducing redundant Zaps.

💡 **Tip:** Paths are available on Zapier's **Professional Plan and above**, so assess whether it provides a cost-effective alternative to multiple Zaps.

3. Optimize Multi-Step Zaps to Minimize Steps

Every step in a Zap contributes to task consumption. The more steps, the higher the cost. Consolidating steps can significantly reduce tasks used.

◆ Example: Sending a Consolidated Daily Report Instead of Multiple Notifications

- Instead of triggering an email for each new form submission, store the data in Google Sheets and send **one** daily summary email.

- This reduces email notifications from **many tasks per form entry** to **one task per day**.

Ways to Consolidate Steps:
✓ Use **Formatter** to manipulate data in a single step instead of using multiple apps.
✓ Utilize **Zapier Storage** or Google Sheets to collect multiple data points before sending a notification.
✓ Schedule batch processing using **Zapier Delay** instead of processing each item instantly.

4. Choose the Most Efficient Triggers

Some triggers fire **every time an event occurs**, while others provide **bundled** or **scheduled** updates. Opting for a more efficient trigger can drastically reduce unnecessary executions.

◆ Example: Using "New Spreadsheet Row (Google Sheets)" vs. "New or Updated Row"

- "New or Updated Row" triggers **twice** (once when created and once when edited).

- If you only need to capture new entries, use **"New Spreadsheet Row"**, reducing redundant tasks.

Other Smart Trigger Choices:
✓ Use **"New Email Matching Search"** instead of **"New Email"** in Gmail to avoid

triggering on every email.

✓ Use **"New Event in a View"** in Airtable instead of **"New Record"** to filter specific records.

✓ Use **"Scheduled" triggers** to process tasks in batches rather than individually.

---

5. Optimize API Calls and Webhooks

If you're using **Webhooks by Zapier**, API requests count as tasks. To reduce this:

✓ Request **only necessary fields** from APIs.

✓ Use **one webhook to handle multiple conditions** instead of separate calls.

✓ Store frequently used data in **Zapier Storage** instead of making redundant API requests.

◈ Example: Storing API Authentication Tokens in Zapier Storage

- Instead of requesting a new authentication token every time a Zap runs (which consumes a task), store the token in Zapier Storage and refresh it only when necessary.

---

6. Review and Optimize Existing Zaps Regularly

Even well-optimized Zaps can become inefficient over time. Regularly reviewing task usage helps identify areas for improvement.

◈ Steps to Audit Your Zaps:

1. Go to **Zap History** and identify high-task Zaps.

2. Check logs for **failed tasks**, as retries consume tasks unnecessarily.

3. Analyze **task trends** and disable Zaps that no longer provide value.

💡 **Tip:** Set a monthly reminder to review and optimize your Zaps to keep costs under control.

Final Thoughts on Reducing Task Usage and Costs

By implementing these strategies, you can significantly lower task consumption and reduce Zapier costs while maintaining automation efficiency. Here's a quick recap:

✓ **Use filters** to prevent unnecessary Zap runs.

✓ **Leverage paths** instead of multiple Zaps.

✓ **Optimize multi-step Zaps** to minimize actions.

✓ **Choose efficient triggers** to avoid redundant tasks.

✓ **Optimize API calls and Webhooks** to reduce external task usage.

✓ **Review and audit Zaps regularly** to ensure continued optimization.

Adopting these best practices will help you get the most out of Zapier without overspending on unnecessary tasks. In the next section, we'll explore **how to manage Zap execution speed** to further enhance performance.

6.2.2 Managing Zap Execution Speed

When automating workflows with Zapier, execution speed plays a crucial role in efficiency and productivity. A well-optimized Zap should run quickly and reliably, without unnecessary delays or bottlenecks. In this section, we will explore how Zap execution speed works, common causes of slow execution, and practical steps to improve it.

---

1. Understanding Zap Execution Speed

Zapier processes each Zap in a sequence of steps, from the trigger event to the execution of one or more actions. The speed at which a Zap runs depends on several factors:

- **Trigger Type** – Some triggers run instantly, while others require polling (checking for new data at intervals).

- **App Response Time** – The connected apps must respond to Zapier requests promptly.

- **Number of Steps in a Zap** – More steps can increase processing time.

- **Filters, Conditions, and Paths** – Complex logic can slow down execution.

- **Zapier's Infrastructure and Plan Limitations** – Some Zapier plans prioritize faster execution times.

Before making optimizations, it's important to identify whether a Zap is inherently slow due to the nature of the process or if it can be improved.

2. Common Causes of Slow Zap Execution

There are several reasons why a Zap might take longer than expected to complete:

Using Polling Triggers Instead of Instant Triggers

Zapier offers two types of triggers:

- **Instant Triggers** – These are pushed directly from the app to Zapier, allowing near-instant execution.

- **Polling Triggers** – Zapier checks the connected app for new data at intervals (typically every 1-15 minutes, depending on your plan).

Polling triggers introduce unavoidable delays. For example, if you use a Google Sheets trigger that runs every 15 minutes, there will always be a delay of up to 15 minutes before a Zap starts.

API Rate Limits from Connected Apps

Some apps enforce rate limits on how often Zapier can make requests. If an app restricts API calls, Zap execution may be delayed until the limit resets.

Processing Large Data Sets

Zaps that handle bulk data, such as processing hundreds of rows in a spreadsheet or syncing large datasets, may take longer to complete.

Multiple Steps and Filters

Each step in a Zap introduces processing time. A Zap with multiple filters, conditions, and logic paths can be significantly slower.

Background Processing Delays

Some apps do not process requests immediately, especially CRMs, email marketing tools, and database-related applications. Zapier must wait for the app to process data before continuing the Zap.

3. Strategies to Improve Zap Execution Speed

Use Instant Triggers Whenever Possible

To reduce delays, opt for apps that support **Instant Triggers**. These allow Zapier to execute workflows as soon as an event occurs, rather than waiting for the next polling interval.

To check whether an app supports instant triggers:

1. Open the Zapier **App Directory**.

2. Search for the app you are using as a trigger.

3. Look for a **"Zapier Instant"** label in the triggers list.

If your app only supports polling triggers, consider using **webhooks** (if available) to create an instant trigger.

Reduce Unnecessary Steps

Each step in a Zap requires processing time. To optimize speed:

- Eliminate redundant filters and conditions.

- Consolidate multiple Zaps into one where possible.

- Use Zapier's **Formatter** tool to process data within Zapier instead of relying on external apps.

For example, instead of creating a Zap that fetches data from Google Sheets, processes it in another app, and then sends it to a third app, try doing all transformations within Zapier before sending the data forward.

Optimize API Calls

If an app has strict API limits, consider these workarounds:

- **Batch Requests** – Instead of processing items individually, use tools that support batch processing.

- **Use Delay Steps Wisely** – If an app limits API calls, introduce a **Delay** step to prevent exceeding limits.

- **Minimize Data Lookups** – Reduce the number of times your Zap retrieves data from external sources.

Minimize Data Processing Load

Handling large datasets can slow down Zaps. To improve speed:

- **Use Filters Early** – If a Zap processes a large dataset, use filters at the start to discard unnecessary records.

- **Break Zaps into Smaller Workflows** – Instead of one large Zap that processes hundreds of rows, split it into smaller, task-specific Zaps.

- **Limit Data Sent Between Steps** – Instead of transferring entire database records, only send necessary fields.

Avoid Looping Zaps

A common mistake that slows execution is creating Zaps that trigger themselves in a loop. For example, if a Zap updates a spreadsheet, and another Zap monitors that spreadsheet for changes, they can trigger each other continuously.

To prevent loops:

- Use filters to ensure a Zap doesn't trigger on its own changes.

- Implement **Zapier Storage** or **Zap History Check** to track processed items.

Upgrade to a Faster Zapier Plan

Zapier prioritizes task execution based on the user's plan:

- **Free & Starter Plans** – Zaps execute every 15 minutes.

- **Professional Plan** – Zaps execute every 2 minutes.

- **Team & Company Plans** – Zaps execute every 1 minute.

If execution speed is critical, upgrading to a higher-tier plan can significantly reduce delays.

---

4. Advanced Optimization Techniques

Using Webhooks for Faster Data Transfers

Webhooks allow apps to send data to Zapier in real time instead of waiting for scheduled polling. If an app supports webhooks, you can:

- Create a **Webhook Trigger** in Zapier.

- Configure the external app to send data to Zapier via the webhook URL.

- Use the webhook data in subsequent Zap steps.

This eliminates polling delays and speeds up execution significantly.

Using Paths Instead of Multiple Zaps

Instead of creating multiple Zaps for different conditions, use **Paths** in a single Zap. Paths allow you to define multiple conditional branches, reducing the number of redundant Zaps running separately.

Running Zaps in Parallel

If your Zaps have multiple steps that do not depend on each other, consider splitting them into separate Zaps that run simultaneously. This reduces the total execution time by allowing steps to run in parallel rather than sequentially.

---

5. Monitoring and Testing Zap Performance

To ensure your optimizations are effective, regularly monitor Zap execution speed:

Checking Zap Run History

- Navigate to **Zap History** in Zapier.

- Check execution times and identify slow steps.

- Identify recurring errors or failed actions.

Using Zapier's Performance Metrics

Zapier provides logs that show how long each step takes. If a particular step is consistently slow, investigate ways to optimize it.

Testing and Iterating

- Run test executions after making changes.

- Compare execution times before and after optimizations.

- Continuously refine workflows to maintain efficiency.

---

6. Conclusion

Managing Zap execution speed is essential for creating efficient and reliable workflows. By using instant triggers, minimizing unnecessary steps, optimizing API calls, handling large data efficiently, and leveraging advanced techniques like webhooks and parallel execution, you can significantly improve the speed of your Zaps.

Regularly monitoring performance and making adjustments ensures that your automation remains fast and effective. By following the best practices outlined in this section, you can build high-performance Zaps that save time and enhance productivity.

6.2.3 Avoiding Common Mistakes

Zapier is a powerful automation tool that can save time, reduce manual work, and improve efficiency. However, users—especially beginners—often encounter common mistakes that can lead to inefficiencies, unnecessary errors, or failed automations. This section will guide you through some of the most frequent pitfalls and provide best practices to avoid them.

1. Not Testing Zaps Properly

The Mistake

One of the biggest mistakes new users make is activating a Zap without testing it thoroughly. This can result in unexpected errors, incomplete actions, or even data loss.

How to Avoid It

- **Use the "Test" Feature**: Before turning on your Zap, Zapier allows you to test each step. Always check whether the correct data is being pulled and passed between apps.

- **Run Sample Data**: If possible, create test data in your trigger app to see how it flows through the Zap before using real data.

- **Monitor Zap History**: After enabling a Zap, check the **Zap History** regularly to ensure it's working as expected.

2. Using Too Many Tasks Unnecessarily

The Mistake

Every step in a Zap counts as a task, and overcomplicating workflows can lead to hitting your task limit too quickly, causing unnecessary costs.

How to Avoid It

- **Simplify Your Workflow**: Before creating a Zap, map out your process to identify the most efficient way to automate the task.

- **Use Multi-Step Zaps Wisely**: While multi-step Zaps can be useful, avoid redundant steps that add no real value.

- **Optimize with Filters & Paths**: Instead of running a Zap every time an event happens, use **Filters** to ensure that only relevant data triggers actions.

---

3. Ignoring Task Usage Limits

The Mistake

Many users don't track their task usage and exceed their plan limits unexpectedly, causing their Zaps to stop working.

How to Avoid It

- **Check Your Usage Regularly**: Go to **Settings > Usage** in your Zapier account to see how many tasks you've used.

- **Use Delay and Batch Processing**: Instead of triggering a Zap for every event, use **Delay** actions or **Digest** to process data in batches.

- **Optimize API Calls**: If using webhooks or APIs, ensure you're not making unnecessary calls that consume tasks.

---

4. Not Handling Conditional Logic Properly

The Mistake

Some users expect their Zap to handle different scenarios but fail to implement conditional logic, leading to incorrect outputs.

How to Avoid It

- **Use Paths for Different Outcomes**: Instead of creating multiple separate Zaps, use **Paths** to define different outcomes based on conditions.

- **Implement Filters to Exclude Unwanted Data**: If you only want a Zap to run under certain conditions, use a **Filter** step to prevent unnecessary tasks.

- **Test Conditional Logic**: Always test conditions in real-world scenarios to ensure they behave as expected.

5. Forgetting to Update Zaps When App APIs Change

The Mistake

Zapier integrations depend on app APIs, and if an app updates its API or removes a feature, it can break your Zap.

How to Avoid It

- **Subscribe to App Updates**: Follow Zapier's blog or the app's official announcements for changes to integrations.

- **Regularly Review Your Zaps**: Set a reminder to review your active Zaps every few months to ensure they still work correctly.

- **Check Zapier's Help Center**: If an integration suddenly stops working, check Zapier's support page to see if an update is required.

6. Using Incorrect Data Formatting

The Mistake

Many users assume that data will be passed between apps in the correct format, only to find out that it fails due to missing or incorrect formatting.

How to Avoid It

- **Use the Formatter Tool**: Zapier provides a **Formatter** action that helps convert data (e.g., text, numbers, dates) into the required format.

- **Ensure Date & Time Consistency**: Different apps use different date formats. Use the Formatter to standardize timestamps.

- **Trim Unnecessary Data**: If an app outputs unwanted text, use **Formatter > Text > Extract Pattern** to refine it before passing it to the next step.

7. Forgetting About Zapier's Task Limits Per Zap Run

The Mistake

Some users build complex Zaps with too many steps and exceed Zapier's limit of 100 actions per Zap run.

How to Avoid It

- **Break Large Zaps Into Smaller Zaps**: Instead of a single Zap handling everything, consider using multiple Zaps triggered by the output of the previous Zap.

- **Use Webhooks for Advanced Scenarios**: For complex automations, **webhooks** can sometimes provide a more efficient solution.

- **Check Zap Performance Metrics**: Go to your **Zap History** and review the number of tasks per Zap run to ensure you're staying within limits.

8. Not Using Error Handling Mechanisms

The Mistake

If a Zap fails due to an issue in one of the apps, users often don't have a fallback mechanism, which can disrupt workflows.

How to Avoid It

- **Enable Zapier's Auto-Retry Feature**: Some Zaps can automatically retry if they fail.

- **Set Up Error Notifications**: Use Zapier's built-in notifications or send alerts to Slack/email when an error occurs.

- **Use Webhooks for Advanced Error Handling**: If an action fails, a webhook can log the issue and trigger alternative workflows.

9. Not Taking Security and Privacy Seriously

The Mistake

Many users unknowingly expose sensitive data by using insecure settings, sharing API keys, or not reviewing permissions properly.

How to Avoid It

- **Review App Permissions**: When connecting apps, ensure you grant only the necessary permissions.

- **Use Secure API Keys**: If using webhooks or custom integrations, never share your API keys openly.

- **Monitor Data Flow**: Check your Zap history to ensure that sensitive data isn't being exposed unintentionally.

Conclusion

Avoiding these common mistakes will help you create efficient, reliable, and cost-effective Zaps. Whether you're automating personal tasks, managing a business, or optimizing workflows for a team, following best practices ensures that your Zapier experience is smooth and trouble-free.

Key Takeaways

✓ Always test your Zaps before enabling them.
✓ Optimize task usage to avoid exceeding plan limits.
✓ Use filters, paths, and formatting tools for better automation logic.
✓ Regularly review and update your Zaps to prevent unexpected failures.
✓ Implement error-handling and security measures to protect data.

By keeping these principles in mind, you'll be able to harness the full potential of Zapier while minimizing errors and inefficiencies.

6.3 Security and Data Privacy in Zapier

6.3.1 Understanding Data Flow in Zaps

When working with **Zapier**, understanding how **data flows** between apps is essential for ensuring accuracy, security, and efficiency. Every time you set up an **automation (Zap)**, data is transferred from one app to another based on predefined conditions. In this section, we will break down the **data flow process**, the key components involved, and the potential risks to be aware of when working with Zapier.

1. The Basics of Data Flow in Zapier

At its core, Zapier acts as a **middleman** between two or more apps, allowing them to communicate and exchange information without requiring manual input. This process involves:

1. **A Trigger**: An event in one app that starts the automation.

2. **An Action**: A task Zapier performs in another app based on the trigger.

3. **Optional Steps**: Additional transformations, filters, and conditions applied to the data before reaching the final destination.

For example, consider the following automation:

- **Trigger**: A new lead is added to a Google Sheet.

- **Action**: Zapier sends an automated welcome email via Gmail.

In this case, **data flows** from **Google Sheets** → **Zapier** → **Gmail**, ensuring the right information is used at each step.

2. Key Components Affecting Data Flow

2.1 API Requests and Responses

Zapier interacts with different applications using **APIs (Application Programming Interfaces)**, which allow apps to exchange data securely. Each API call made by Zapier involves:

- **A request**: Zapier asks an app for data (e.g., retrieving a new contact from a CRM).

- **A response**: The app sends back the requested data in a structured format (usually JSON).

Understanding how APIs work helps troubleshoot errors like **"400 Bad Request"** or **"401 Unauthorized"** when setting up Zaps.

2.2 Data Transformation and Formatting

As data flows through Zapier, it may require **formatting** to match the structure expected by the destination app. Zapier provides tools such as:

- **Formatter by Zapier**: Helps modify text, numbers, dates, and more.

- **Code by Zapier**: Allows advanced users to run JavaScript or Python for deeper customizations.

For example, if a **date format** from one app is **MM/DD/YYYY** but another app requires **DD-MM-YYYY**, Zapier can automatically reformat it before sending the data.

2.3 Filters, Paths, and Conditions

Not all data should flow freely between apps. Sometimes, **conditions** need to be applied to determine what happens next. Zapier provides:

- **Filters**: Ensure data moves only if certain conditions are met (e.g., only emails from a specific domain are forwarded).

- **Paths**: Create multiple conditional workflows (e.g., if a lead is from the US, send it to SalesForce; if from Europe, send it to HubSpot).

Using these tools ensures that **only relevant data** is processed and stored.

3. Data Storage and Retention in Zapier

3.1 Temporary Data Storage

Zapier **does not permanently store** the data that flows through your Zaps. However, it does retain temporary logs to help with debugging and troubleshooting.

- **Zap History**: Stores past Zap runs, including the data processed, for up to 30 days.

- **Task History**: Shows each step of the Zap execution, helping users identify potential issues.

3.2 Handling Sensitive Data

While Zapier is designed with security in mind, users should take precautions when handling **sensitive information** such as:

- **Customer data (names, emails, phone numbers, etc.)**

- **Financial information (invoices, payment records, etc.)**

- **Personal health data (if using Zapier in healthcare settings)**

To enhance security, users can:

✓ **Use encryption** when passing sensitive data.

✓ **Avoid storing personal data in Zapier logs** by minimizing unnecessary logging.

✓ **Utilize two-factor authentication (2FA) for added security.**

4. Common Issues with Data Flow in Zapier

Even with a well-structured Zap, **data flow issues** can arise. Below are some common problems and their solutions:

4.1 Data Mismatch Between Apps

- **Problem**: Data from the trigger app is not in the correct format for the action app.

- **Solution**: Use **Formatter by Zapier** to modify data before sending it to the next app.

4.2 Missing or Partial Data in Zaps

- **Problem**: Some fields do not transfer to the destination app.

- **Solution**: Check the **Zap history** to ensure that all required fields are mapped correctly.

4.3 Rate Limits and API Restrictions

- **Problem**: Some apps limit the number of API calls that can be made per hour.

- **Solution**: Upgrade to a premium plan or optimize your Zaps by reducing unnecessary triggers.

5. Best Practices for Secure and Efficient Data Flow

To ensure **smooth and secure data flow**, follow these best practices:

Regularly Monitor Zap Activity

✓ Check **Zap History** to identify errors or failed tasks.
✓ Set up **email notifications** for Zap failures to get alerts in real time.

Keep Zaps Organized

✓ Use **naming conventions** to differentiate between Zaps.
✓ Store Zaps in **folders** based on categories (e.g., "Marketing Zaps," "Finance Zaps").

Limit Data Exposure

✓ Avoid unnecessary **personal data transfers**.
✓ Use **Zapier's built-in security features** like OAuth authentication.

Test Zaps in a Safe Environment

✓ Before running a Zap in production, test it with **dummy data**.
✓ Use the **"Only continue if" filter** to prevent errors in live environments.

6. Conclusion

Understanding how data flows in Zapier is crucial for setting up efficient, secure, and reliable automations. By leveraging Zapier's tools, monitoring Zap history, and following best practices, users can ensure their workflows run smoothly without errors or security risks.

In the next section (6.3.2 Protecting Sensitive Information), we will discuss advanced techniques to enhance data security, including encryption, access controls, and compliance considerations.

6.3.2 Protecting Sensitive Information

In today's digital landscape, data security and privacy are critical concerns for businesses and individuals alike. When using Zapier to automate workflows, sensitive information such as customer data, financial records, and login credentials may be transferred between apps. While Zapier itself follows strong security protocols, it is essential for users to take proactive steps to protect their confidential data.

This section provides a detailed guide on how to safeguard sensitive information while using Zapier, covering best practices, security settings, data encryption, compliance considerations, and risk mitigation strategies.

1. Understanding the Risks of Data Exposure

Before diving into security measures, it is important to understand the risks associated with handling sensitive data in Zapier. These risks include:

Unauthorized Access

If your Zapier account is not properly secured, unauthorized users may gain access to your Zaps and data, leading to potential leaks or misuse.

Data Breaches

If sensitive data such as customer personal information (PII), payment details, or internal documents is not properly encrypted or secured, it may be intercepted during transfers between applications.

API and App Security Flaws

Zapier connects various third-party apps through APIs (Application Programming Interfaces). If an integrated app has security vulnerabilities, your data may be exposed through weak API endpoints.

Misconfigurations in Zaps

Improper setup of Triggers, Actions, and Filters can cause sensitive data to be shared with unintended recipients, leading to data leakage or compliance violations.

2. Enabling Security Features in Zapier

Zapier provides **built-in security features** to help users protect their workflows. Here are some key security measures you should enable:

2.1 Enabling Two-Factor Authentication (2FA)

Two-Factor Authentication adds an extra **layer of security** to your Zapier account by requiring a second form of authentication (such as a code from an authentication app) when logging in.

How to Enable 2FA in Zapier:

1. Log in to your **Zapier account**.

2. Click on your **Profile Icon** (top-right corner) and select **Settings**.

3. Navigate to the **Security** tab.

4. Find **Two-Factor Authentication (2FA)** and click **Enable**.

5. Follow the instructions to set up 2FA using an authentication app like **Google Authenticator or Authy**.

2.2 Managing User Permissions

If you are using Zapier for a **team or business**, ensure that each user has the appropriate **access level**.

Best Practices for Managing User Permissions:

-   Use **Zapier Teams or Zapier for Business** to assign role-based access.

-   Limit **admin-level privileges** to essential users.

-   Regularly review and remove access for users who no longer need it.

2.3 Monitoring Activity Logs

Zapier provides an **Activity Log** that allows you to track all **login attempts, Zap executions, and integrations**.

How to Check Activity Logs in Zapier:

1. Go to **Zapier Dashboard**.

2. Click on **History** (left-side menu).

3. Review logs to identify any suspicious activities.

---

3. Encrypting and Securing Data in Zapier

Data encryption ensures that sensitive information remains protected even if intercepted by **unauthorized parties**.

3.1 End-to-End Encryption (E2EE)

Zapier encrypts data **in transit** using **TLS (Transport Layer Security)**, but users must ensure that **data at rest** is also protected.

Best Practices for Data Encryption:

- Use **built-in encryption features** in connected apps (e.g., encrypting email data in Gmail).

- If handling **highly sensitive data**, use **custom encryption before sending data to Zapier**.

- Store sensitive data in **secure databases** instead of directly passing it through Zaps.

3.2 Masking and Redacting Sensitive Information

If you need to send sensitive data between apps, consider **masking or redacting** parts of the information.

Example of Masking Data in Zapier:

Instead of sending a **full credit card number**, send only the last four digits:

- **Original Data:** 1234-5678-9876-5432

- **Masked Data:** XXXX-XXXX-XXXX-5432

This prevents accidental exposure while still maintaining necessary information.

3.3 Using Secure Webhooks

Zapier allows users to **send and receive data using Webhooks**, which should always be **secured properly**.

How to Secure Webhooks:

- Always use **HTTPS** instead of HTTP.

- Add an **authentication token** to verify Webhook requests.

- Restrict Webhook access to trusted IP addresses.

4. Compliance and Legal Considerations

Businesses handling customer data must comply with **data privacy laws and regulations**, such as:

General Data Protection Regulation (GDPR) (Europe)

If you process data of EU citizens, you must ensure that:

- Customers can request data deletion.

- Data processing is lawful and transparent.

- Sensitive data is encrypted and protected.

California Consumer Privacy Act (CCPA) (United States)

For businesses operating in California, you must:

- Allow users to opt out of data sharing.

- Clearly disclose how data is used.

- Secure personal data from breaches.

HIPAA (Health Insurance Portability and Accountability Act) (US Healthcare Data)

If handling health-related information, ensure Zapier integrations comply with HIPAA regulations by:

- Using HIPAA-compliant apps.

- Avoiding unnecessary data sharing.

- Enabling strong encryption for all health data transfers.

5. Best Practices for Secure Workflows

To ensure **maximum security and privacy**, follow these best practices when designing workflows in Zapier:

Minimize Data Exposure

- Only pass **necessary** data through Zaps.
- Use **filters** to remove **unneeded** sensitive data.

Review and Audit Zaps Regularly

- Check your Zaps every **3-6 months** to identify security risks.
- Disable **unused** or **unnecessary** integrations.

Avoid Storing Sensitive Data in Logs

- Turn off **Zapier logs** for workflows handling confidential data.
- Use **Zapier's Data Retention Policies** to control data storage.

6. Final Thoughts: Staying Secure with Zapier

Using Zapier for automation can increase efficiency, but security should always be a priority. By following best practices for access control, encryption, compliance, and secure data transfers, users can protect their sensitive information while maximizing the benefits of automation.

Remember: Data security is a shared responsibility—while Zapier offers strong protections, you must also take proactive steps to ensure that your workflows remain safe and compliant.

6.3.3 Setting Up Secure Workflows

Zapier is a powerful automation tool, but when handling sensitive data across multiple applications, security should be a top priority. Ensuring your workflows are secure minimizes the risk of data breaches, unauthorized access, and accidental data leaks. This section will guide you through best practices for setting up secure workflows in Zapier, from using strong authentication methods to controlling data flow and monitoring activity logs.

1. Understanding Security Risks in Zapier Workflows

Before diving into security measures, it's essential to understand the potential risks:

- **Unauthorized Access**: If your Zapier account is compromised, an attacker can access all the apps and data connected to it.

- **Data Leakage**: Sensitive data might be exposed if Zaps are not configured properly or if data is stored in unsecured locations.

- **API Vulnerabilities**: If third-party apps used in your workflows have weak security, they could be exploited to gain access to your data.

- **Accidental Data Sharing**: Misconfigured workflows may send sensitive data to unintended recipients.

By recognizing these risks, you can take proactive steps to secure your workflows.

2. Using Strong Authentication and Access Control

Enabling Two-Factor Authentication (2FA)

One of the easiest ways to enhance security in Zapier is enabling **two-factor authentication (2FA)**. This adds an extra layer of protection by requiring a second form of verification, such as a code sent to your phone or an authentication app.

To enable 2FA in Zapier:

1. Go to **My Profile** in your Zapier account.

2. Select **Security** and look for the **Two-Factor Authentication** option.

3. Choose an authentication method (e.g., Google Authenticator, Authy).

4. Follow the prompts to enable 2FA.

Managing User Access with Teams & Folders

If you're using **Zapier for Teams**, you can limit access to sensitive workflows:

- **Assign User Roles**: Set different permissions (e.g., Admin, Editor, Viewer) to restrict access to specific workflows.

- **Use Shared Folders**: Keep sensitive workflows in restricted folders and allow access only to authorized team members.

For personal accounts, avoid sharing login credentials and instead, grant **app-specific permissions** when possible.

3. Controlling Data Flow and Privacy

Minimizing Data Exposure

To reduce security risks, follow these guidelines:

- **Use Only Necessary Data**: When setting up Zaps, ensure only relevant data is transferred between apps.

- **Mask Sensitive Information**: If possible, replace personally identifiable information (PII) with placeholders or anonymized data.

- **Limit Retention of Data**: Some apps store Zap history indefinitely. Regularly delete old logs if they contain sensitive data.

Securing Webhooks and API Integrations

Webhooks are useful for integrating custom applications with Zapier, but they can also be a security risk. Follow these best practices:

- **Use HTTPS for Secure Data Transmission**: Ensure that webhook URLs use https:// to encrypt data.

- **Authenticate Webhook Requests**: Use API keys, OAuth tokens, or HMAC signatures to verify incoming requests.

- **Restrict Webhook Endpoints**: Configure firewalls to accept webhook requests only from trusted sources.

Encrypting Data in Transit and Storage

Zapier itself encrypts data in transit using **TLS (Transport Layer Security)**, but you should also:

- Enable encryption for third-party apps where possible.

- Avoid storing sensitive data in plain text within Zap notes or log files.

4. Monitoring and Auditing Zapier Activity

Regularly Reviewing Zap History

Zapier provides an **Activity Log** where you can track Zap executions. Checking logs can help identify unauthorized or unexpected data flows.

To review Zap history:

1. Go to **Zap History** in your Zapier dashboard.

2. Look for any unusual or failed Zaps.

3. Investigate any activity that seems suspicious.

Setting Up Alerts for Suspicious Activity

You can create a Zap that monitors activity and alerts you if something unusual happens. For example:

- **Slack Notification for Failed Zaps**: If a Zap fails multiple times, trigger an alert in Slack or email.

- **Google Sheet Log for Sensitive Zaps**: Log execution details of Zaps that handle sensitive data in a Google Sheet for audit purposes.

Conducting Periodic Security Audits

Schedule periodic security audits to:

- Review connected apps and remove those you no longer use.

- Check permission settings for third-party integrations.

- Update API keys and passwords periodically.

5. Best Practices for Secure Workflows

To summarize, follow these best practices when setting up secure workflows in Zapier:

✓ **Enable Two-Factor Authentication (2FA)** to prevent unauthorized access.
✓ **Use Zapier Teams** to manage user permissions.
✓ **Minimize Data Exposure** by only transferring necessary information.
✓ **Secure Webhooks and API Integrations** with authentication and encryption.
✓ **Monitor Zap History and Set Up Alerts** for unusual activity.
✓ **Conduct Regular Security Audits** to ensure compliance and security best practices.

By implementing these strategies, you can confidently use Zapier while protecting your data and workflows from potential threats.

Next Steps

Now that you understand how to secure your workflows, the next chapter will explore **real-world Zapier use cases**, demonstrating how businesses and individuals can leverage automation effectively.

CHAPTER VI
Real-World Zapier Use Cases

7.1 Automating a Small Business

7.1.1 Managing Customer Inquiries

In today's fast-paced digital world, small businesses receive customer inquiries through various channels—emails, social media messages, live chat, and contact forms. Responding to these inquiries efficiently can be time-consuming, but with **Zapier**, you can automate much of the process, ensuring quick responses, proper categorization, and improved customer satisfaction.

This section will guide you through how to use **Zapier to automate customer inquiries**, including:

- **Collecting inquiries from different sources**
- **Sending automated responses**
- **Assigning inquiries to the right team members**
- **Tracking and managing inquiries efficiently**

By the end of this chapter, you'll have a fully automated system to handle customer inquiries, reducing response time and improving overall efficiency.

---

1. Collecting Inquiries from Different Sources

Customers may contact your business through various platforms, such as:

- **Emails** (Gmail, Outlook)
- **Live Chat** (Intercom, Drift, Tawk.to)

- **Social Media** (Facebook Messenger, Instagram, Twitter DMs)

- **Website Contact Forms** (Google Forms, Typeform, JotForm)

- **Help Desk Software** (Zendesk, Freshdesk)

Manually monitoring all these channels can be overwhelming. **Zapier can automatically collect inquiries from all sources and centralize them into a single place** (e.g., a Google Sheet, a CRM, or a Slack channel).

Example Workflow: Collecting Inquiries from Multiple Sources into a Google Sheet

◆ **Apps Involved**: Gmail, Facebook Messenger, Google Forms, Google Sheets
◆ **Trigger**: A new inquiry is received from Gmail, Facebook Messenger, or Google Forms
◆ **Action**: Add the inquiry details to a Google Sheet for tracking

Steps to Create This Zap:

1. **Log into Zapier and Click "Create a Zap"**

2. **Select a Trigger App:**

    o Choose **Gmail** (for email inquiries)

    o Choose **Facebook Messenger** (for social media inquiries)

    o Choose **Google Forms** (for website inquiries)

3. **Set Up Trigger Conditions:**

    o For Gmail: Choose "New Email in Inbox" and filter only customer inquiry emails

    o For Facebook Messenger: Choose "New Message Received"

    o For Google Forms: Choose "New Form Response"

4. **Select an Action App: Google Sheets**

5. **Configure Action:**

    o Choose "Create Spreadsheet Row"

    o Map fields (customer name, email, inquiry message, source)

6. **Test and Activate the Zap**

This workflow ensures that **all customer inquiries are logged in a single Google Sheet**, making it easier for your team to track and manage them.

2. Sending Automated Responses

Customers expect **quick responses** when they reach out to a business. Instead of manually replying to every inquiry, you can use **Zapier to send automated email or chat responses**.

Example Workflow: Sending an Automatic Acknowledgment Email

- **Apps Involved**: Gmail, Typeform, Mailchimp
- **Trigger**: A new customer fills out a contact form
- **Action**: Send an automated acknowledgment email

Steps to Create This Zap:

1. **Trigger: New Form Submission (Google Forms, Typeform, or JotForm)**

   o Select your form tool and trigger condition: "New Form Entry"

2. **Action: Send Email with Gmail or Mailchimp**

   o Select **Gmail** (if sending direct emails)

   o Select **Mailchimp** (if using an automated email sequence)

   o Personalize the email (e.g., "Thank you for reaching out! Our team will get back to you soon.")

3. **Test and Activate the Zap**

With this automation, **customers instantly receive confirmation that their inquiry was received**, improving trust and engagement.

3. Assigning Inquiries to the Right Team Members

If you have multiple employees handling customer support, you need a system to **automatically assign inquiries based on category, urgency, or source**.

Example Workflow: Assigning Support Inquiries to Different Team Members in Slack

- ◆ **Apps Involved**: Gmail, Slack, Zendesk
- ◆ **Trigger**: A new inquiry is received
- ◆ **Action**: Assign the inquiry to the correct team member

Steps to Create This Zap:

1. **Trigger: New Email in Gmail with Specific Keywords**

   o Set up filters like "urgent," "billing issue," or "technical support"

2. **Action: Send a Message to a Slack Channel or User**

   o Select **Slack** as the action app

   o Choose "Send Direct Message" or "Post to Channel"

   o Customize the message with inquiry details and assign it to the right person

3. **Test and Activate the Zap**

This ensures **each inquiry is automatically assigned to the appropriate team member** without manual intervention.

---

4. Tracking and Managing Customer Inquiries

To keep track of all customer inquiries, you can integrate **Zapier with a CRM or project management tool** (e.g., Trello, Asana, HubSpot, Salesforce).

Example Workflow: Creating a Trello Card for Each Inquiry

- ◆ **Apps Involved**: Gmail, Trello, Google Sheets
- ◆ **Trigger**: A new email inquiry arrives
- ◆ **Action**: Create a Trello card in the "Customer Support" board

Steps to Create This Zap:

1. **Trigger: New Email Inquiry in Gmail**

2. **Action: Create Trello Card**

   o Set up Trello board "Customer Inquiries"

   o Map fields: **Customer Name, Email, Inquiry Type, Status**

3. **Optional: Update Google Sheets with Inquiry Status**

4. **Test and Activate the Zap**

With this setup, all inquiries are logged into **Trello** or another task management tool, ensuring **no request goes unanswered**.

Final Thoughts: Why Automate Customer Inquiries with Zapier?

✅ **Saves Time:** No need to manually sort, assign, or log inquiries
✅ **Faster Response Times:** Customers receive immediate acknowledgment emails
✅ **Better Organization:** All inquiries are centralized in one system
✅ **Improved Customer Experience:** Inquiries are directed to the right team members quickly

With **Zapier**, even a small business can **build a professional, automated customer support system without coding**. Start automating today and focus on growing your business!

Next Steps

In the next section, we'll explore **how small businesses can automate invoice and payment processes using Zapier**, reducing manual work and improving efficiency.

7.1.2 Automating Invoice and Payment Processes

Managing invoices and payment processes is a critical aspect of running a small business. Manually creating invoices, sending payment reminders, tracking transactions, and updating records can be time-consuming and prone to errors. With Zapier, small business owners can automate these tasks, reducing administrative overhead while ensuring accuracy and efficiency.

This section will provide a step-by-step guide on automating invoice and payment processes using Zapier, covering:

1. **Automatically Generating and Sending Invoices**

2. **Automating Payment Reminders**

3. **Tracking and Recording Payments**

4. **Integrating with Accounting Software**

5. **Handling Failed or Late Payments**

By the end of this section, you will have a fully automated workflow that simplifies your invoicing and payment management.

---

1. Automatically Generating and Sending Invoices

Why Automate Invoice Creation?

Instead of manually creating invoices for every customer or client, Zapier can automatically generate invoices based on trigger events such as:

- A new sale is recorded in an e-commerce store (Shopify, WooCommerce, etc.).

- A new contract or project is approved in a project management tool (Trello, ClickUp, Asana).

- A new customer signs up for a service (Typeform, Google Forms, CRM).

Step-by-Step Guide: Setting Up Automatic Invoice Generation

Step 1: Choose a Trigger

1. Log in to Zapier and click **Create a Zap**.

2. Select a trigger app (e.g., Shopify, Stripe, Google Forms, or any CRM like HubSpot).

3. Choose the event that will trigger invoice generation (e.g., "New Order," "New Form Submission," or "New Customer").

4. Connect the app to Zapier and test the trigger to ensure it pulls the right data.

Step 2: Choose an Invoice Generation App

1. Select an action app such as **QuickBooks, Xero, or Wave**.

2. Choose an action event like **"Create Invoice"**.

3. Map the invoice fields using dynamic data from the trigger app (e.g., customer name, order amount, product details).

4. Configure any additional settings, such as due dates and payment terms.

Step 3: Send the Invoice Automatically

1. Add another action step to **send the invoice via email** using Gmail or Outlook.

2. Personalize the email with customer details and attach the generated invoice.

3. Activate the Zap and test it by creating a new order or client entry.

☞ **Result:** Every time a new sale or customer entry is recorded, an invoice is automatically created and sent to the client.

---

2. Automating Payment Reminders

Why Set Up Automated Payment Reminders?

Many businesses face late payments from clients, which can disrupt cash flow. Instead of manually tracking and reminding customers, Zapier can automate this process by:

- Sending follow-up emails before an invoice due date.

- Sending SMS reminders using Twilio or WhatsApp.

- Creating a task in a project management tool for manual follow-up if needed.

Step-by-Step Guide: Setting Up Payment Reminders

Step 1: Use an Accounting Tool as a Trigger

1. In Zapier, create a new Zap.

2. Select QuickBooks, Xero, or Wave as the **trigger app**.

3. Choose the event **"Invoice Due Date Approaching"** or **"Invoice Overdue"**.

4. Set up filters to trigger reminders for unpaid invoices only.

Step 2: Send Automated Email or SMS Reminders

1. Choose an action app such as **Gmail, Outlook, or Twilio (for SMS reminders)**.

2. Customize the reminder message, including the invoice number, amount due, and payment link.

3. Schedule the Zap to run at specific intervals (e.g., 3 days before due date, on the due date, and 5 days after due date).

4. Test the Zap by marking an invoice as "Unpaid" and checking if the reminder is sent.

☞ **Result:** Clients automatically receive reminders before and after their invoice due date, reducing the chances of late payments.

---

3. Tracking and Recording Payments

Why Automate Payment Tracking?

Keeping track of which invoices are paid and updating records manually can be tedious. With Zapier, you can:

- Update a Google Sheet or Airtable whenever a payment is received.

- Notify your team via Slack or email when a payment is made.

- Sync payment records with your accounting software.

Step-by-Step Guide: Automating Payment Tracking

Step 1: Set a Payment Processor as the Trigger

1. Choose a payment gateway like **Stripe, PayPal, or Square** as the **trigger app**.

2. Select the event **"New Payment Received"**.

3. Test the trigger to ensure it captures payment details correctly.

Step 2: Update a Payment Tracking System

1. Choose **Google Sheets, Airtable, or a CRM (e.g., HubSpot, Salesforce)** as the action app.

2. Set the action event to **"Update Spreadsheet Row"** or **"Create Record"**.

3. Map payment details to the appropriate fields (e.g., customer name, amount, payment method).

Step 3: Notify the Team (Optional)

1. Add another action step to send a notification via **Slack or Email**.

2. Customize the notification with details such as **"Payment received from [Customer Name] for $[Amount]"**.

☞ **Result:** Every time a customer makes a payment, records are automatically updated, and your team is notified instantly.

---

4. Integrating with Accounting Software

Why Sync Payments with Accounting Tools?

To maintain accurate financial records, payments need to be recorded in accounting software. Zapier can automatically:

- Add new payments to **QuickBooks, Xero, or FreshBooks**.

- Generate reports summarizing all transactions.

- Reconcile payments with invoices.

How to Set It Up?

1. Use Stripe or PayPal as the trigger app (event: **"New Payment"**).

2. Select **QuickBooks or Xero** as the action app (event: **"Record Payment"**).

3. Map payment details to the appropriate accounting fields.

4. Activate the Zap and test it with a dummy transaction.

☞ **Result:** All payments are automatically recorded in your accounting software without manual data entry.

---

5. Handling Failed or Late Payments

Automating Failed Payment Handling

If a customer's payment fails (e.g., credit card decline), Zapier can:

- Send an **automatic email notification** asking the customer to update payment details.

- Add the issue to a **customer support ticket system** (e.g., Zendesk).

- Notify the sales or finance team via **Slack or email**.

How to Set It Up?

1. Use Stripe or PayPal as the trigger app (event: **"Payment Failed"**).

2. Select Gmail or Outlook to send a **"Payment Issue"** email to the customer.

3. Create a ticket in Zendesk or add a Trello task for manual follow-up.

☞ **Result:** Customers are notified instantly, and your team can take action to resolve the issue.

Final Thoughts

By automating invoice and payment processes with Zapier, small business owners can save time, reduce errors, and improve cash flow. Implementing these automations ensures that invoices are sent promptly, payments are tracked accurately, and overdue payments are handled efficiently.

7.1.3 Syncing Sales and Marketing Data

In today's fast-paced digital world, small businesses rely on efficient sales and marketing processes to drive revenue and maintain customer relationships. However, keeping sales and marketing data synchronized across different platforms can be a daunting task. Manual data entry between CRMs, email marketing tools, e-commerce platforms, and advertising services can lead to inefficiencies, data discrepancies, and lost opportunities.

With **Zapier**, small businesses can **automate the synchronization of sales and marketing data**, ensuring seamless communication between platforms. In this section, we will explore the importance of syncing sales and marketing data, common integration challenges, and a step-by-step guide to setting up automated workflows using Zapier.

Why Syncing Sales and Marketing Data is Important

Marketing and sales teams often work with different tools, but their efforts should be aligned for maximum efficiency. Proper synchronization helps businesses:

✓ **Ensure Data Accuracy** – Avoid duplicate entries, incorrect customer details, and outdated records.

✓ **Save Time** – Eliminate manual data transfer, reducing administrative workload.

✓ **Improve Lead Nurturing** – Ensure marketing teams have up-to-date sales data to refine campaigns.

✓ **Enhance Customer Experience** – Provide consistent and timely communication with leads and customers.

✓ **Increase Revenue** – A well-integrated system allows businesses to act on opportunities faster.

For example, a business may want to automatically **add new customers from an e-commerce platform** (such as Shopify or WooCommerce) to their **email marketing tool** (like Mailchimp or ActiveCampaign). Without automation, this process requires manual effort, leading to potential delays and lost sales opportunities.

Common Challenges in Syncing Sales and Marketing Data

Before implementing automation, it's important to understand common challenges businesses face:

1. Different Platforms Store Data in Different Formats

CRM platforms (e.g., HubSpot, Salesforce) might structure customer data differently than e-commerce stores (e.g., Shopify, WooCommerce) or marketing tools (e.g., Mailchimp, Klaviyo). Zapier's **Formatter** tool can help standardize these differences.

2. Delays in Data Syncing

Some tools update in real-time, while others have delays. Understanding how often your tools update data helps you set appropriate Zapier triggers.

3. Duplicate or Incomplete Data

If a lead exists in both the CRM and the email marketing system but isn't updated properly, duplicate records may be created. Using **Zapier's filters and search steps** helps prevent duplication.

4. API Limitations and Integration Restrictions

Certain tools have API rate limits that may slow down or restrict automation. Businesses need to optimize their Zaps to prevent exceeding these limits.

Step-by-Step Guide to Syncing Sales and Marketing Data with Zapier

Now, let's walk through the process of syncing sales and marketing data using Zapier. We'll focus on a real-world use case: automatically sending new e-commerce customers to a CRM and email marketing platform.

Scenario: Syncing Shopify Customers to HubSpot and Mailchimp

We will create a **multi-step Zap** that:

✅ **Triggers** when a new customer places an order in Shopify.

✅ **Adds or updates the customer** in HubSpot CRM.

✅ **Subscribes the customer** to an email list in Mailchimp.

Step 1: Setting Up the Trigger (New Order in Shopify)

1. **Log into Zapier** and click **"Create a Zap"**.

2. In the **Trigger** section, choose **Shopify** as the app.

3. Select the **trigger event: "New Paid Order"**.

4. **Connect your Shopify account** and authorize Zapier.

5. Choose **your store** and select **"Any Paid Order"** as the event.

6. Click **"Test Trigger"** to fetch a sample order.

☞ **Why this step is important**: Capturing new customer details as soon as they make a purchase ensures **real-time updates** in both sales and marketing platforms.

Step 2: Adding the Customer to HubSpot CRM

1. Click **"Add a Step"** and select **HubSpot** as the app.

2. Choose the action event: **"Create or Update Contact"**.

3. **Connect your HubSpot account** to Zapier.

4. In the **action settings**, map the Shopify customer fields:

   ○ First Name → HubSpot First Name

   ○ Last Name → HubSpot Last Name

   ○ Email → HubSpot Email

   ○ Phone Number → HubSpot Phone Number (if available)

   ○ Address → HubSpot Address

5. Click **"Test & Continue"** to ensure data is added correctly.

☞ **Why this step is important**: Keeping CRM records up to date helps the sales team track leads and follow up on customer interactions.

Step 3: Adding the Customer to a Mailchimp Email List

1. Click **"Add a Step"** and select **Mailchimp** as the app.

2. Choose the action event: **"Add/Update Subscriber"**.

3. **Connect your Mailchimp account** to Zapier.

4. Select the appropriate **audience list** in Mailchimp.

5. Map the Shopify customer email field to Mailchimp's subscriber email.

6. Click **"Test & Continue"** to verify the customer is added to Mailchimp.

☞ **Why this step is important**: Adding new customers to Mailchimp automatically allows businesses to send **welcome emails, promotional offers**, and **loyalty rewards**.

Step 4: Adding Filters to Avoid Duplicate Entries

To prevent adding the same customer multiple times:

1. Click **"Add a Step"** and select **"Filter by Zapier"**.

2. Set the condition: **"Only continue if email does not already exist in HubSpot"**.

3. Add another filter to ensure **only subscribed customers** are added to Mailchimp.

☞ **Why this step is important**: Filters **prevent redundant data** and ensure only relevant customers are synced.

Additional Automation Ideas for Sales and Marketing Syncing

Beyond syncing e-commerce and CRM data, small businesses can automate other key processes:

✓ **Syncing Facebook Lead Ads with CRMs** – Capture Facebook leads in HubSpot or Salesforce automatically.
✓ **Automating Google Ads Lead Tracking** – Send Google Ads form submissions directly to email marketing platforms.
✓ **Connecting LinkedIn Ads to Email Campaigns** – Automatically add LinkedIn leads to a Mailchimp email list.
✓ **Tracking Website Signups in CRM** – Sync new website signups from WordPress or Wix into HubSpot or Pipedrive.

Final Thoughts: Why Every Small Business Should Use Zapier for Sales & Marketing Automation

Manually managing sales and marketing data can be time-consuming and error-prone. By automating key workflows with **Zapier**, businesses can:

✅ **Save time** by eliminating manual data entry.
✅ **Ensure accuracy** with real-time synchronization.
✅ **Improve marketing ROI** by sending the right message at the right time.
✅ **Scale operations** without hiring additional staff.

By following this guide, small businesses can set up **smart workflows** that keep their sales and marketing data perfectly in sync, ensuring smooth operations and higher revenue.

📌 **Next Steps:**

- Try setting up your first sales-marketing Zap using this guide.

- Explore Zapier's built-in **formatter, filters, and multi-step workflows** to optimize automations.

- Join Zapier's community forums to learn advanced automation tips!

7.2 Productivity Hacks for Individuals

7.2.1 Automating Personal Tasks

Productivity is a major concern for individuals managing both personal and professional responsibilities. Whether you are handling daily routines, tracking habits, managing reminders, or organizing emails, repetitive tasks consume valuable time. This is where Zapier can become a game-changer. By automating personal tasks, you can free up mental space and focus on what truly matters.

In this section, we will explore practical ways to use Zapier to automate various aspects of your personal life. You will learn how to set up workflows (Zaps) to streamline email management, automate reminders, keep track of personal finances, schedule events, and much more.

---

1. Automating Email Management

Email overload is a common issue. Manually sorting through newsletters, archiving important messages, and responding to emails can take up hours every week. Zapier can help you automate several aspects of your email workflow.

1.1 Organizing Your Inbox Automatically

If your inbox is constantly cluttered with promotional emails, invoices, or personal messages, Zapier can help you sort them automatically. Here are a few useful Zaps:

- **Move emails to specific folders:** You can set up a Zap to move emails from a particular sender (e.g., bank statements) to a designated folder in Gmail or Outlook.

- **Auto-tagging emails:** If you use Gmail labels, Zapier can automatically apply labels based on keywords in the email subject.

- **Saving email attachments to the cloud:** A Zap can automatically save email attachments to Google Drive, Dropbox, or OneDrive.

✅ **Example Zap:** Move all emails from your bank to a folder called "Finance."

- **Trigger:** New email in Gmail from a specific sender.

- **Action:** Move the email to the "Finance" folder in Gmail.

1.2 Setting Up Auto-Replies

If you frequently receive similar inquiries, an automatic response can save you time.

- **Trigger:** New email with a specific subject line or keyword.

- **Action:** Send a pre-written response using Gmail or Outlook.

1.3 Forwarding Important Emails

You can use Zapier to automatically forward important emails to another person (such as forwarding work-related emails to your personal inbox).

✅ **Example Zap:** Forward all emails from your child's school to your spouse.

- **Trigger:** New email from the school's domain.

- **Action:** Forward the email to your spouse's email address.

2. Automating Reminders and Task Management

Keeping track of tasks, birthdays, bill payments, and appointments manually can be exhausting. With Zapier, you can create automated workflows to remind you of important events.

2.1 Setting Up Custom Reminders

Instead of manually setting reminders, you can create Zaps that automatically generate alerts.

✅ **Example Zap:** Get a Slack or SMS reminder to pay rent every 1st of the month.

- **Trigger:** Scheduled event on the 1st of each month.

- **Action:** Send a message to your phone via SMS or Slack.

2.2 Adding Tasks to a To-Do List

If you use task management apps like **Todoist, Google Tasks, Microsoft To Do**, or **Trello**, Zapier can help you automate task creation.

✅ **Example Zap:** Automatically create a to-do item when you star an email in Gmail.

- **Trigger:** New starred email in Gmail.

- **Action:** Add a task in Todoist with a due date.

2.3 Automating Calendar Events

Zapier can automatically add events to your Google Calendar or Outlook Calendar based on emails or form submissions.

✅ **Example Zap:** Add a Google Calendar event for every new Zoom meeting scheduled.

- **Trigger:** New Zoom meeting scheduled.

- **Action:** Create a Google Calendar event with meeting details.

---

3. Automating Personal Finance and Expense Tracking

Tracking expenses and managing finances can be tedious. Zapier can connect financial tools to automate record-keeping and notifications.

3.1 Logging Purchases Automatically

If you receive email receipts from online purchases, Zapier can extract the details and log them into Google Sheets, Notion, or Airtable.

✅ **Example Zap:** Save all Amazon purchase receipts in Google Sheets.

- **Trigger:** New email receipt from Amazon.

- **Action:** Extract purchase details and add them to Google Sheets.

3.2 Budgeting and Expense Notifications

If you use apps like **Mint, YNAB, or QuickBooks**, you can automate notifications for overspending.

✅ **Example Zap:** Receive a Slack message when your bank balance drops below a certain amount.

- **Trigger:** Low balance alert email from the bank.
- **Action:** Send a Slack message to remind you to transfer funds.

4. Automating Health and Fitness Tracking

Staying consistent with workouts, diet, and meditation can be easier with automation.

4.1 Logging Workouts Automatically

If you track your workouts in **Strava, Fitbit, or Apple Health**, you can use Zapier to log your activities automatically.

✅ **Example Zap:** Save all Strava workouts to a Google Sheet for progress tracking.

- **Trigger:** New workout logged in Strava.
- **Action:** Add workout details (distance, time, calories burned) to Google Sheets.

4.2 Getting Daily Health Reminders

Set up reminders for hydration, meditation, or stretching.

✅ **Example Zap:** Receive a push notification to drink water every two hours.

- **Trigger:** Scheduled reminder every two hours.
- **Action:** Send a notification via Pushbullet or SMS.

5. Automating Learning and Content Consumption

Zapier can help automate reading, note-taking, and content discovery.

5.1 Automatically Saving Articles for Later

If you come across interesting articles but don't have time to read them, you can save them automatically.

✅ **Example Zap:** Save all bookmarked Twitter threads to Notion.

- **Trigger:** New tweet liked on Twitter.

- **Action:** Save the tweet to a Notion database.

5.2 Transcribing Audio Notes to Text

Use Zapier to automatically transcribe voice notes from **Otter.ai, Rev, or Google Recorder** into written text.

✅ **Example Zap:** Convert voice notes to Google Docs automatically.

- **Trigger:** New audio recording in Otter.ai.

- **Action:** Create a Google Doc with the transcript.

Conclusion

By implementing these Zapier workflows, you can eliminate repetitive personal tasks and improve efficiency. From email automation to personal finance tracking, fitness monitoring, and content curation, automation enables you to focus on what truly matters.

Next Steps:

1. Identify the most time-consuming personal tasks in your daily routine.

2. Explore Zapier's app integrations to find automation opportunities.

3. Start with simple Zaps and gradually incorporate more advanced workflows.

By making small improvements with automation, you'll significantly boost your productivity and free up time for more meaningful activities. 🚀

7.2.2 Setting Up Daily Productivity Workflows

Zapier is a powerful tool that can help individuals streamline their daily tasks by automating repetitive actions and integrating different applications seamlessly. By setting up productivity workflows, you can save time, reduce manual effort, and stay organized. In this section, we'll cover step-by-step methods to set up Zapier workflows for daily productivity, including task management, email automation, calendar scheduling, and information tracking.

1. Why Automate Daily Workflows?

Before diving into specific automation setups, it's important to understand the benefits of using Zapier for daily productivity:

- **Saves time** – Automating repetitive tasks means you can focus on more important work.

- **Reduces errors** – Manual data entry and task switching often lead to mistakes, which automation can minimize.

- **Enhances organization** – Keeping your tasks, notes, and communications in sync ensures nothing falls through the cracks.

- **Boosts efficiency** – Automated reminders and updates help you stay on top of deadlines without extra effort.

Now, let's look at some practical ways to implement daily productivity workflows with Zapier.

2. Automating Task Management

Keeping track of daily tasks is crucial for productivity. Zapier can help by automating task creation, updates, and reminders across different project management tools.

2.1 Automatically Adding Tasks to a To-Do List

One of the best ways to stay productive is by maintaining a to-do list. With Zapier, you can automate task creation from various sources, such as emails, notes, or calendar events.

Example Workflow: Convert Emails into Tasks

⬜ **Trigger:** A new email arrives in Gmail with a specific label (e.g., "To-Do").
⚡ **Action:** Create a new task in a task management app like Todoist, Trello, or Microsoft To-Do.

How to Set It Up:

1. Choose Gmail as the trigger app.

2. Set the trigger to "New Email Matching Search" and define the criteria (e.g., emails labeled "To-Do").

3. Select your task management tool (Todoist, Trello, ClickUp, etc.) as the action app.

4. Configure the task details, such as adding the email subject as the task title.

5. Test and activate your Zap.

Now, every time you label an email as "To-Do," a task is automatically created in your preferred task manager.

2.2 Syncing Tasks Between Apps

Many people use multiple productivity tools, such as Trello for project planning and Google Tasks for personal reminders. Instead of manually copying tasks between apps, use Zapier to keep them in sync.

Example Workflow: Sync Trello Cards with Google Tasks

❏ **Trigger:** A new Trello card is added to a specific list (e.g., "Today's Tasks").
⚡ **Action:** Create a new task in Google Tasks with the same title and due date.

This automation ensures that your important tasks appear in all the tools you use without manual duplication.

3. Automating Calendar Scheduling

Managing meetings, appointments, and reminders can be time-consuming. Zapier can automatically update your calendar, send meeting reminders, and even reschedule events.

3.1 Adding Events to Google Calendar from Other Apps

If you frequently schedule meetings via email or Slack, you can automate event creation in Google Calendar.

Example Workflow: Create Google Calendar Events from Slack Messages

☐ **Trigger:** A specific keyword (e.g., "Schedule Meeting") appears in a Slack message.
⚡ **Action:** Create an event in Google Calendar with the details from the message.

This workflow saves time by eliminating the need to manually add meetings to your calendar.

3.2 Sending Automated Daily Agenda Emails

A daily summary of your tasks and appointments can help you start your day with clarity.

Example Workflow: Email Your Daily Schedule Every Morning

☐ **Trigger:** A scheduled Zap runs every morning at 7:00 AM.
⚡ **Action 1:** Retrieve events from Google Calendar for the day.
⚡ **Action 2:** Format the list of events into a summary.
⚡ **Action 3:** Send an email with your schedule to your inbox.

You'll receive a personalized agenda every morning, ensuring you never miss an important task or meeting.

4. Automating Information Tracking and Note-Taking

Collecting and organizing information is essential for staying productive. Zapier can help by automating note-taking and data collection.

4.1 Saving Important Emails to a Note-Taking App

Instead of manually copying important emails to your note-taking app, you can use Zapier to automate this process.

Example Workflow: Save Starred Emails to Notion or Evernote

☐ **Trigger:** An email is starred in Gmail.
⚡ **Action:** Create a new note in Notion or Evernote with the email content.

This workflow helps you keep track of useful information without extra effort.

4.2 Logging Daily Work Progress Automatically

If you track your daily accomplishments, Zapier can help automate this process.

Example Workflow: Log Daily Work Summary in Google Sheets

☐ **Trigger:** At the end of each workday (scheduled trigger).
⚡ **Action:** Create a new row in Google Sheets with a summary of completed tasks and meetings.

This workflow helps you maintain a record of your productivity without manual effort.

---

5. Automating Personal Productivity Tasks

Zapier isn't just for work—it can also automate personal tasks to improve your daily routine.

5.1 Setting Up Automatic Reminders

If you often forget to drink water, take breaks, or exercise, you can set up automated reminders.

Example Workflow: Send Break Time Reminders via Slack or SMS

☐ **Trigger:** A scheduled Zap runs every two hours.
⚡ **Action:** Send a reminder via Slack, SMS, or email.

This helps you maintain healthy habits without relying on manual reminders.

5.2 Automating Learning and Research

If you regularly read articles or watch educational videos, Zapier can automate content curation.

Example Workflow: Save New Articles to Pocket from RSS Feeds

☐ **Trigger:** A new article is published in an RSS feed (e.g., Medium or a news site).
⚡ **Action:** Save the article to Pocket or Notion for later reading.

This automation ensures that you always have fresh content to read without manually searching for it.

Conclusion

Setting up daily productivity workflows with Zapier can significantly improve efficiency by eliminating repetitive tasks and keeping everything organized. Whether you're managing tasks, scheduling meetings, tracking information, or automating personal habits, Zapier provides countless possibilities to streamline your day.

To get started, pick one or two workflows that match your daily routine, set them up in Zapier, and observe the time and effort you save. As you become more comfortable, you can expand your automation system to create a fully optimized daily workflow.

7.2.3 Automating Learning and Research

In today's fast-paced world, staying updated with the latest knowledge and trends is essential. Whether you're a student, a researcher, or a professional looking to upskill, automating your learning and research process can save time, reduce manual effort, and enhance efficiency. Zapier can help by integrating various tools and platforms, ensuring that you never miss valuable information.

This section will cover how to:
✅ Automatically collect and organize research materials
✅ Stay updated with relevant news and articles
✅ Automate learning through note-taking and summarization
✅ Manage and track learning progress

Let's explore how Zapier can optimize your learning and research workflows step by step.

1. Automating Research Collection and Organization

1.1 Saving Articles and Research Papers Automatically

Manually saving articles from different sources can be tedious. With Zapier, you can create an automation that collects articles from RSS feeds, social media, or email newsletters and saves them in a structured manner.

📌 **Example Workflow: Save Articles from RSS Feeds to Notion or Evernote**

Apps Used:

- **RSS by Zapier** (Trigger)
- **Notion** or **Evernote** (Action)

Zap Steps:

1. Set up an **RSS Feed Trigger** (e.g., from a blog or Google Alerts).
2. Configure Zapier to **extract new articles** from the feed.
3. Automatically **store the article title, link, and summary** in Notion/Evernote for easy access.

Why this is useful?

✓ Saves time by consolidating research in one place.

✓ Ensures you never miss important articles.

✓ Makes retrieval easier when needed.

1.2 Bookmarking Web Pages Efficiently

Instead of manually bookmarking pages, you can use Zapier to automate this process.

Example Workflow: Save Bookmarks from Browser to Google Sheets

Apps Used:

- **Raindrop.io** (Trigger)
- **Google Sheets** (Action)

Zap Steps:

1. Use **Raindrop.io** to save any webpage with one click.
2. Zapier automatically **logs the saved bookmark** into Google Sheets.
3. The sheet stores **URLs, titles, and descriptions** for easy reference.

◆ **Why this is useful?**

✓ Keeps bookmarks organized.

✓ Enables easy filtering and categorization.

✓ Prevents losing important research links.

2. Staying Updated with Relevant News and Articles

2.1 Automating Email Alerts for Research Topics

If you frequently receive research-related emails (e.g., Google Alerts, newsletters), Zapier can help organize them.

📌 **Example Workflow: Forward Research Emails to Evernote**

🔎 **Apps Used**:

- **Gmail** (Trigger)

- **Evernote** (Action)

🔎 **Zap Steps**:

1. Set up a Gmail filter to tag **newsletters or research-related emails**.

2. When a new email with that tag arrives, Zapier **extracts key details**.

3. The extracted information is automatically saved in **Evernote** under the "Research" notebook.

◆ **Why this is useful?**

✓ Keeps research emails in one place.

✓ Reduces inbox clutter.

✓ Ensures quick retrieval of relevant articles.

2.2 Creating a Personal News Digest

Instead of manually checking different websites, Zapier can compile a daily digest of relevant news.

📌 **Example Workflow: Create a Daily Research Digest in Slack or Email**

🔑 **Apps Used**:

- **Google News or Feedly** (Trigger)
- **Slack or Email by Zapier** (Action)

🔑 **Zap Steps**:

1. Select relevant topics in **Google News or Feedly**.
2. Zapier pulls new headlines daily and **formats them into a summary**.
3. The summary is sent via **Slack or Email** as a research digest.

◆ **Why this is useful?**

✅ Saves time by centralizing updates.
✅ Ensures daily knowledge intake.
✅ Filters out irrelevant information.

---

3. Automating Learning Through Note-Taking and Summarization

3.1 Transcribing and Summarizing Podcasts or Lectures

Listening to podcasts or lectures is a great way to learn, but manually taking notes can be tedious.

📌 **Example Workflow: Convert Podcasts to Transcripts and Summaries**

🔑 **Apps Used**:

- **Otter.ai** (Trigger)
- **Google Docs** (Action)

🔑 **Zap Steps**:

1. Upload an audio file to **Otter.ai** for automatic transcription.

2. Zapier extracts the transcript and **saves it in Google Docs**.

3. An AI tool (e.g., ChatGPT API) can **generate a summary** of key points.

◆ **Why this is useful?**

✓ Converts speech into searchable text.

✓ Makes reviewing lectures easier.

✓ Saves time by automating summaries.

3.2 Organizing Notes and Highlights Automatically

Taking notes manually can be inefficient. With Zapier, you can automate the organization of learning materials.

📌 **Example Workflow: Send Kindle Highlights to Notion**

🔎 **Apps Used**:

- **Kindle** (Trigger)

- **Notion** (Action)

🔎 **Zap Steps**:

1. When you highlight text in a Kindle book, Zapier extracts the highlight.

2. The highlight is automatically **stored in Notion** under a specific category.

3. You can later review and use them for research or writing.

◆ **Why this is useful?**

✓ Organizes key insights efficiently.

✓ Reduces manual copy-pasting.

✓ Helps in long-term knowledge retention.

4. Managing and Tracking Learning Progress

4.1 Automating Course Progress Tracking

If you take online courses on platforms like Coursera, Udemy, or LinkedIn Learning, you can automate progress tracking.

📌 **Example Workflow: Track Online Course Progress in Google Sheets**

📍 **Apps Used**:

- **Coursera/Udemy** (Trigger)
- **Google Sheets** (Action)

📍 **Zap Steps**:

1. When you complete a lesson, Zapier **logs progress** in a Google Sheet.
2. The sheet tracks **course name, completed lessons, and pending topics**.
3. You can visualize progress using **Google Sheets charts**.

◆ **Why this is useful?**

✅ Keeps track of learning milestones.

✅ Motivates consistency in learning.

✅ Prevents course abandonment.

Conclusion

By automating learning and research with Zapier, you can:

✓ Save time collecting and organizing research materials.

✓ Stay updated with relevant news and insights effortlessly.

✓ Enhance note-taking and summarization for efficient learning.

✓ Track learning progress automatically.

Try implementing some of these workflows to optimize your learning journey today!

7.3 Zapier for Remote Teams

7.3.1 Streamlining Communication Across Teams

In today's digital workspace, remote teams rely on efficient communication to stay connected and collaborate effectively. However, managing multiple communication channels, ensuring timely responses, and keeping everyone updated can be challenging. This is where **Zapier** comes in, automating communication workflows to improve efficiency, reduce manual work, and enhance team productivity.

This section will guide you through **how to use Zapier to streamline communication across remote teams**, including:

- Automating team notifications and updates

- Keeping track of important messages and deadlines

- Syncing communication between different platforms

---

1. The Challenges of Remote Team Communication

Before we dive into the solutions, let's explore some common communication challenges remote teams face:

- **Message overload:** Remote teams use multiple tools such as Slack, Microsoft Teams, and email, leading to scattered information.

- **Delayed responses:** Important updates might be missed if notifications are not properly managed.

- **Lack of centralization:** Information gets lost when teams work across different platforms without proper integration.

- **Repetitive manual updates:** Manually notifying team members about project changes or meeting schedules can be time-consuming.

Zapier helps solve these issues by **automating communication** and ensuring that the right people get the right information at the right time.

---

2. Setting Up Automated Team Notifications

One of the most useful ways to streamline communication is by automating team notifications. Instead of manually updating your team about new tasks, project changes, or meeting schedules, Zapier can do it for you.

Example 1: Automatically Notify Teams About New Tasks

Imagine you use **Trello, Asana, or ClickUp** to manage your projects. Each time a new task is assigned to a team member, you can set up a **Zap** that automatically sends a notification to a Slack or Microsoft Teams channel.

How to Set It Up

1. **Trigger:** Choose Trello (or Asana, ClickUp) → New Card or New Task Assigned

2. **Action:** Select Slack (or Microsoft Teams) → Send Channel Message

3. **Customize Message:** Include details like task name, deadline, and assignee.

4. **Test & Activate the Zap**

◆ *Result:* Every time a new task is assigned, a message is automatically sent to the team chat, ensuring everyone stays informed.

Example 2: Daily Standup Meeting Reminders

Remote teams often conduct daily or weekly standups. Instead of manually reminding everyone, you can create a **Zap** to send automated reminders.

How to Set It Up

1. **Trigger:** Use Schedule by Zapier → Set Daily or Weekly Reminder Time

2. **Action:** Select Slack or Microsoft Teams → Send Message to a Specific Channel

3. **Customize Message:** "Hey team! It's time for our daily standup. Please update your status!"

4. **Test & Activate the Zap**

◆ *Result:* Your team members receive a daily reminder without anyone having to manually send it.

---

3. Keeping Track of Important Messages and Deadlines

Example 3: Save Important Messages to a Shared Document

When working remotely, important messages in Slack or Microsoft Teams often get lost in conversation threads. With Zapier, you can automatically save key messages to a **Google Docs** or **Notion** file for easy reference.

How to Set It Up

1. **Trigger:** Slack (or Microsoft Teams) → Starred Message in a Channel

2. **Action:** Google Docs (or Notion) → Append Text to a Document

3. **Customize Data:** Save message content, sender, and timestamp.

4. **Test & Activate the Zap**

◆ *Result:* Every time a message is starred, it's automatically logged in a shared document for easy reference.

Example 4: Send Deadline Reminders to the Team

Deadlines are crucial for remote teams, and missing them can lead to project delays. You can use Zapier to automatically remind team members about upcoming deadlines.

How to Set It Up

1. **Trigger:** Google Sheets (or Airtable) → New or Updated Row (Deadline Approaching)

2. **Action:** Slack (or Microsoft Teams) → Send Direct Message to Assigned Person

3. **Customize Message:** "Reminder: Your task '[Task Name]' is due tomorrow!"

4. **Test & Activate the Zap**

◆ *Result:* Team members automatically receive deadline reminders, reducing the risk of missed tasks.

---

4. Syncing Communication Between Different Platforms

Many remote teams use multiple platforms for different purposes. A marketing team might use Slack for quick communication, Gmail for external emails, and Monday.com for project tracking. Manually transferring information between these platforms is inefficient.

Example 5: Sync Slack and Email for Important Updates

If an important message is posted in Slack, Zapier can automatically send it as an email to relevant team members.

How to Set It Up

1. **Trigger:** Slack → New Message in Specific Channel
2. **Action:** Gmail (or Outlook) → Send Email
3. **Customize Email Content:** Include message details and sender information.
4. **Test & Activate the Zap**

◆ *Result:* Important updates from Slack are automatically emailed to key team members, ensuring they don't miss critical information.

Example 6: Automatically Post Meeting Notes to a Project Management Tool

If your team uses Zoom or Google Meet for virtual meetings, Zapier can automatically post meeting notes into a project management tool like Trello or Asana.

How to Set It Up

1. **Trigger:** Google Docs (or Notion) → New Meeting Notes Document Created
2. **Action:** Trello (or Asana) → Create New Card with Meeting Summary
3. **Customize Content:** Add meeting agenda, key takeaways, and action items.
4. **Test & Activate the Zap**

◆ *Result:* Meeting notes are automatically added to the project board, keeping everyone informed.

---

5. Final Thoughts

By leveraging Zapier to **automate communication workflows**, remote teams can:

✓ Reduce manual updates and repetitive messaging

✓ Ensure timely notifications and reminders

✓ Keep track of important information across multiple platforms

✓ Enhance collaboration and productivity

Remote work presents unique challenges, but with **smart automation**, teams can overcome communication barriers and stay connected effortlessly.

💡 *Next Steps:*

- Try setting up a **simple Zap** for your team's most common communication tasks.

- Experiment with **multi-step Zaps** for more advanced automation.

- Explore other integrations to enhance your team's workflow.

7.3.2 Automating Task Assignments

In a remote work environment, ensuring that tasks are assigned to the right team members at the right time is critical for productivity and collaboration. Manual task assignments can be inefficient, leading to delays, miscommunication, or even tasks being overlooked. **Zapier** provides a seamless way to automate task assignments, ensuring that work flows smoothly between team members without the need for manual intervention.

This section will guide you through setting up **automated task assignment workflows** using Zapier. We'll cover:

- How to automatically assign tasks from different sources (emails, forms, messages, project management tools).

- How to distribute tasks based on workload, roles, or predefined rules.

- How to notify team members instantly when they are assigned a new task.

- Real-world use cases of automated task assignments in remote teams.

1. Why Automate Task Assignments?

Before diving into the technical setup, let's understand why automating task assignments is essential for remote teams:

Saves Time and Reduces Manual Work

Instead of managers or team leads spending time manually distributing tasks, Zapier can automate the process based on predefined rules, freeing up valuable time for strategic work.

Minimizes Errors and Oversights

Manually assigning tasks can lead to mistakes—such as missing deadlines or assigning tasks to the wrong person. Automation ensures that tasks are assigned accurately based on predefined rules.

Improves Team Collaboration and Accountability

When tasks are assigned automatically with instant notifications, team members are always aware of their responsibilities, reducing miscommunication and improving overall accountability.

Works Across Multiple Tools

Zapier integrates with hundreds of apps like Trello, Asana, Monday.com, Slack, Gmail, Google Forms, and more, ensuring a seamless workflow no matter what tools your team uses.

2. Setting Up Automated Task Assignments with Zapier

Now, let's walk through how to **set up a Zap** that automates task assignments.

Step 1: Identify Your Task Source

First, determine where tasks are coming from. Common sources include:

- **Emails** (e.g., support tickets from Gmail or Outlook)
- **Forms** (e.g., customer requests from Google Forms, Typeform, or JotForm)
- **Chat Messages** (e.g., Slack or Microsoft Teams)
- **Project Management Tools** (e.g., Trello, Asana, ClickUp, Monday.com)

Step 2: Choose a Trigger in Zapier

A **Trigger** is the event that starts your workflow. Examples include:

- **"New Email in Gmail"** → Trigger when a new email arrives in a specific inbox.
- **"New Response in Google Forms"** → Trigger when a user submits a form.
- **"New Slack Message in Channel"** → Trigger when a message is posted in a specific Slack channel.
- **"New Task in Trello"** → Trigger when a new card is created in a specific board or list.

Step 3: Filter or Process the Data (Optional but Recommended)

Use **Zapier's Filters** to ensure only relevant tasks get assigned. Examples:

- Assign **high-priority** support tickets based on specific keywords.
- Route **marketing-related** tasks to the marketing team.
- Send **technical issues** to developers.

You can also use **Zapier Formatter** to clean or reformat data, such as:

- Extracting the requester's name from an email.
- Converting a message into a structured task description.
- Formatting dates and due times automatically.

Step 4: Choose an Action to Assign the Task

Now, decide where the task should be assigned. Common **Actions** include:

- **"Create a Task in Asana/Trello/Monday.com/ClickUp"** → Assigns a task to a specific person or team.

- **"Create a Ticket in Zendesk/Freshdesk"** → Logs a customer request into a ticketing system.

- **"Create a Calendar Event in Google Calendar"** → Creates a scheduled task with a deadline.

Step 5: Automatically Assign the Task to the Right Team Member

You can assign tasks based on:

- **Round-robin assignment** → Zapier distributes tasks evenly among team members.

- **Skill-based routing** → Assign tasks based on keywords or categories (e.g., "SEO" tasks go to the marketing team).

- **Availability-based assignment** → Zapier checks a spreadsheet or a tracking system to assign tasks to available team members.

---

3. Real-World Task Assignment Workflows

Use Case 1: Automating Task Assignments for Support Tickets

📌 **Scenario:** A remote support team receives customer inquiries via Gmail. Each ticket needs to be assigned automatically based on issue type.

🔧 **Zapier Workflow:**

1. **Trigger:** "New Email in Gmail" (Check the "Support" inbox).

2. **Filter:** Check email subject for keywords like "billing," "technical issue," "feature request."

3. **Action:** "Create a Ticket in Zendesk" and assign it to the appropriate agent based on the issue category.

4. **Action:** "Send a Slack Message" to notify the assigned agent.

Use Case 2: Assigning Marketing Tasks from Google Forms

📌 **Scenario:** A marketing team collects content requests from various departments through a Google Form. Tasks should be assigned to the right person automatically.

🔧 **Zapier Workflow:**

1. **Trigger:** "New Response in Google Forms."

2. **Filter:** Identify the request type (e.g., "Blog Post," "Social Media," "Email Campaign").

3. **Action:** "Create a Task in Asana" and assign it to the appropriate content creator.

4. **Action:** "Send an Email" to the requester confirming the task was assigned.

Use Case 3: Automating Task Assignments in Slack for Remote Teams

📌 **Scenario:** A project manager posts a task in a Slack channel, and it needs to be assigned automatically.

🔧 **Zapier Workflow:**

1. **Trigger:** "New Message in Slack Channel."

2. **Filter:** Identify task-related messages with keywords like "urgent," "deadline," or "@assign."

3. **Action:** "Create a Task in Monday.com" and assign it to the next available team member.

4. **Action:** "Send a Slack DM" to notify the assigned team member.

---

4. Best Practices for Automating Task Assignments

✅ 1. Define Clear Assignment Rules

Clearly document how tasks should be assigned. Who handles what types of tasks? What are the priority levels?

✅ 2. Use Conditional Logic for Smarter Routing

Zapier's **Paths** and **Filters** allow you to route tasks based on content, priority, or other criteria.

✅ 3. Notify Team Members Effectively

Send task notifications via Slack, email, or push notifications to ensure nothing is missed.

✅ 4. Regularly Review and Optimize Workflows

Check Zapier's **Task History** to ensure everything runs smoothly. Make adjustments based on performance.

---

5. Conclusion

Automating task assignments with Zapier can **dramatically improve efficiency** in remote teams by reducing manual work, ensuring quick response times, and improving collaboration. By following this step-by-step guide, you can set up **smart workflows** to assign tasks seamlessly across your team.

💡 **Next Steps:** Try setting up your own task automation workflow with Zapier today! 🚀

7.3.3 Integrating Zapier with Collaboration Tools

In today's remote work environment, collaboration tools play a crucial role in keeping teams connected and productive. Platforms like Slack, Microsoft Teams, Trello, Asana, Google Drive, and Notion help teams communicate, manage tasks, and share documents seamlessly. However, manually managing these tools can become overwhelming.

This is where **Zapier** comes in—it helps **integrate collaboration tools, automate workflows, and eliminate repetitive tasks**, allowing remote teams to **focus on meaningful work** rather than switching between apps.

This chapter will guide you through the process of integrating Zapier with popular collaboration tools, setting up essential automations, and optimizing workflows for a **smooth and efficient** remote work experience.

---

1. Why Integrate Zapier with Collaboration Tools?

Without automation, teams spend **countless hours** switching between apps, updating statuses, notifying colleagues, and keeping track of tasks. Zapier helps by:

- **Automating notifications** (e.g., sending Slack alerts when a new task is assigned in Trello).

- **Syncing data across platforms** (e.g., adding new Google Forms responses to Asana).

- **Reducing manual updates** (e.g., updating Google Sheets automatically when a task is completed in ClickUp).

- **Improving response time** (e.g., receiving instant alerts in Slack for new customer inquiries).

By setting up Zaps (automated workflows), teams can streamline their collaboration, **minimize errors, boost productivity, and enhance communication**.

---

2. Popular Collaboration Tools You Can Integrate with Zapier

Zapier supports over **6,000+ apps**, including various collaboration platforms. Below are some of the most commonly used ones:

Communication & Messaging Apps

- **Slack** – Send automated messages, create reminders, notify teams about important updates.

- **Microsoft Teams** – Post messages in channels when an event happens in another app.

- **Discord** – Notify teams when new files are uploaded or meetings are scheduled.

Task & Project Management Apps

- **Trello** – Automatically create Trello cards from new emails, form responses, or chat messages.

- **Asana** – Assign tasks automatically based on form submissions or CRM updates.

- **Monday.com** – Sync data between Monday.com and other platforms.

- **ClickUp** – Move completed tasks to different folders or update task statuses automatically.

File & Document Collaboration Apps

- **Google Drive** – Automatically upload, organize, and share files across teams.

- **Dropbox** – Save attachments from emails, Slack, or project management tools.

- **Notion** – Create new database entries from form submissions or customer tickets.

---

3. Setting Up Essential Zaps for Remote Team Collaboration

Let's explore some of the **most useful Zapier integrations** for remote teams and how to set them up.

Automating Team Communication

Example 1: Send Slack Messages When a New Task is Assigned in Asana

Why? To notify team members instantly when they are assigned a task.

How to set it up:

1. **Trigger:** Choose **Asana** → Select "New Task Assigned".

2. **Action:** Choose **Slack** → Select "Send Channel Message".

3. **Customize Message:** Include details like task name, due date, and assignee.

4. **Test & Activate Zap:** Ensure notifications work correctly.

◆ **Result:** Every time a task is assigned in Asana, a Slack message is sent automatically.

Example 2: Get a Microsoft Teams Notification for New Google Forms Responses

Why? Helps teams get instant alerts when someone submits a form (e.g., feedback, job applications, support tickets).

How to set it up:

1. **Trigger:** Choose **Google Forms** → Select "New Response in Spreadsheet".

2. **Action:** Choose **Microsoft Teams** → Select "Send Message".

3. **Customize Message:** Include form response details.

4. **Test & Activate Zap:** Verify message delivery in Teams.

◆ **Result:** Every time a Google Form is submitted, the team is notified in Microsoft Teams.

Streamlining Task and Project Management

Example 3: Create Trello Cards from New Emails in Gmail

Why? Automatically turn important emails into actionable tasks.

How to set it up:

1. **Trigger:** Choose **Gmail** → Select "New Email Matching Search".

2. **Action:** Choose **Trello** → Select "Create Card".

3. **Customize Card:** Add details like sender name, email content, and labels.

4. **Test & Activate Zap:** Ensure emails are correctly converted into Trello cards.

◆ **Result:** Important emails are automatically added to Trello as tasks.

Example 4: Move Completed ClickUp Tasks to a Google Sheet

Why? Keeps a record of finished tasks for reporting and tracking.

How to set it up:

1. **Trigger:** Choose **ClickUp** → Select "Task Completed".

2. **Action:** Choose **Google Sheets** → Select "Create Row".

3. **Customize Row:** Include task name, completion date, and assigned team member.

4. **Test & Activate Zap:** Ensure completed tasks appear in Google Sheets.

◆ **Result:** Every completed task in ClickUp is logged in a Google Sheet automatically.

Managing File Sharing and Documentation

Example 5: Save Email Attachments to Google Drive

Why? Automatically store important attachments without manual downloads.

How to set it up:

1. **Trigger:** Choose **Gmail** → Select "New Attachment".

2. **Action:** Choose **Google Drive** → Select "Upload File".

3. **Customize File Path:** Define where to save attachments.

4. **Test & Activate Zap:** Ensure attachments appear in the correct Google Drive folder.

◆ **Result:** Email attachments are automatically saved in Google Drive.

---

4. Best Practices for Zapier Integrations in Remote Teams

To **maximize efficiency and prevent errors**, follow these best practices:

Keep Zaps Organized

- Use **folders** to categorize Zaps by department (e.g., Marketing, Sales, Support).

- **Label** Zaps clearly (e.g., "Slack Notification for New Trello Tasks").

Monitor Zap Performance

- Regularly check **Zap History** to ensure smooth execution.

- Adjust **triggers and actions** as workflows evolve.

Optimize Task Usage

- Combine multiple steps into **one Zap** to reduce task usage.

- Use **filters and paths** to refine automations.

Ensure Data Security

- Limit access to sensitive Zaps.

- Use **two-factor authentication (2FA)** for connected apps.

- Regularly review **app permissions** in Zapier.

Conclusion

Integrating Zapier with collaboration tools **saves time, boosts productivity, and enhances communication** for remote teams. By automating repetitive tasks, teams can focus on **high-value work** rather than manual updates.

This chapter covered:
✓ Why Zapier is essential for remote teams
✓ Popular collaboration tools supported by Zapier
✓ Step-by-step automation guides
✓ Best practices for optimizing workflows

Now that you've learned how to integrate Zapier with collaboration tools, the next step is to **experiment, refine your workflows, and explore more advanced automations**!

Conclusion

8.1 Recap of Key Takeaways

After exploring the vast capabilities of **Zapier**, learning how to create efficient **workflows**, and troubleshooting potential issues, it's time to take a step back and review the most important takeaways from this book. Understanding these concepts will ensure that you can **confidently use Zapier to automate your tasks, optimize productivity, and integrate various applications seamlessly**.

This chapter serves as a **comprehensive summary** of everything covered in the book. Let's go through the most critical lessons one by one.

1. Understanding Zapier and Its Benefits

At its core, **Zapier is a no-code automation tool** that connects thousands of apps, enabling you to create workflows that automate repetitive tasks. Some of the biggest benefits include:

✓ **Saving Time** – Zapier eliminates the need for manual data entry and task switching.
✓ **Boosting Productivity** – Automating processes allows you to focus on higher-value work.
✓ **Improving Accuracy** – Reducing human errors that often occur with manual input.
✓ **Enhancing Integration** – Connecting apps that don't natively integrate.
✓ **Scalability** – Automations grow with your business and adapt to changing needs.

By setting up **Zaps**, you can create automated workflows that move data between your favorite apps seamlessly.

2. The Basics: How Zapier Works

Understanding how Zapier functions is essential to leveraging its full potential. The fundamental concepts include:

◆ **Zaps** – Automated workflows that connect two or more apps.

◆ **Triggers** – Events that start an automation (e.g., receiving an email).

◆ **Actions** – The tasks that follow the trigger (e.g., saving an email attachment to Google Drive).

◆ **Multi-Step Zaps** – Workflows that involve multiple actions.

◆ **Filters & Conditions** – Used to refine automation by specifying when a Zap should run.

◆ **Formatter** – A tool within Zapier that modifies data before passing it to the next step.

◆ **Webhooks** – Advanced functionality for connecting apps that don't have built-in Zapier integrations.

By mastering these building blocks, you can create increasingly complex and efficient automations.

3. Setting Up and Managing Your Zaps

Creating a Zap is a **straightforward process**, but optimizing them requires careful planning. Here's a quick refresher on how to set up a successful Zap:

Step 1: Choose a Trigger App

Pick an app that will start the automation (e.g., receiving a new email in Gmail).

Step 2: Define the Trigger Event

Select the event that will activate the workflow (e.g., a new email with an attachment).

Step 3: Choose an Action App

Select the app where the automated task will take place (e.g., Google Drive).

Step 4: Configure the Action

Determine what the automation should do (e.g., save the attachment to a specific folder).

Step 5: Test & Activate the Zap

Run a test to ensure everything works as expected, then activate the Zap.

4. Optimizing Zapier Performance

To ensure **maximum efficiency**, you need to optimize how you use Zapier. The following best practices can help:

☐ **Reduce Task Usage** – Every step in a Zap counts as a task, so keep workflows efficient to avoid unnecessary usage.
☐ **Use Multi-Step Zaps** – Instead of creating multiple single-step Zaps, consolidate actions into one workflow.
☐ **Apply Filters & Conditions** – Prevent unnecessary Zaps from running by specifying conditions.
☐ **Optimize Zap Execution Speed** – Avoid bottlenecks by minimizing unnecessary delays in workflows.
☐ **Organize Zaps** – Use folders and naming conventions to keep workflows structured.

5. Debugging and Troubleshooting Zaps

Even the best-designed Zaps can sometimes **fail**. When this happens, knowing how to troubleshoot is essential:

✓ **Check Zap History** – Review past executions to identify errors.
✓ **Resolve Connection Issues** – Ensure apps have the necessary permissions and API access.
✓ **Fix Failed Actions** – Modify workflows to handle unexpected data inputs properly.

By systematically debugging issues, you can keep your automations running **smoothly and reliably**.

6. Security and Privacy in Zapier

Since **Zapier handles data between multiple apps**, security is a top priority. Important security measures include:

🔐 **Understanding Data Flow** – Be aware of how data is processed and stored.
🔐 **Using Secure Connections** – Enable **two-factor authentication (2FA)** for added protection.
🔐 **Restricting Access** – Only provide necessary permissions to apps and integrations.
🔐 **Monitoring Data Sharing** – Ensure that sensitive information is handled appropriately.

By following these security practices, you can use Zapier **safely and responsibly**.

---

7. Real-World Applications of Zapier

For Businesses

✦ **Customer Support** – Automatically assign customer inquiries to support teams.
✦ **Invoicing** – Automate billing and payment reminders.
✦ **Sales & Marketing** – Sync leads between CRM tools and marketing platforms.

For Individuals

✦ **Task Management** – Create automatic reminders and to-do lists.
✦ **Daily Productivity** – Automate personal notifications and workflows.
✦ **Content Curation** – Save important articles and resources for later review.

For Remote Teams

✦ **Collaboration** – Keep team members informed through automated Slack updates.
✦ **Task Assignments** – Automatically distribute work to the right people.
✦ **Document Sharing** – Sync files between cloud storage and communication apps.

By exploring **real-world use cases**, you can **apply Zapier to your own needs** and unlock new possibilities.

Final Thoughts: What's Next?

Now that you have a solid understanding of Zapier, you are ready to take automation **to the next level**. Here's what you can do next:

🖊 **Experiment with More Apps** – Explore **Zapier's extensive app directory** to find new integrations.
🖊 **Build More Complex Zaps** – Start using **multi-step Zaps, webhooks, and filters**.
🖊 **Optimize Existing Workflows** – Continuously refine and improve your automation processes.
🖊 **Stay Updated** – Follow **Zapier's blog and community forums** for the latest updates and tips.

Key Takeaways from This Book

✅ Zapier simplifies automation by connecting different apps without coding.

✅ Triggers and Actions form the foundation of any Zap.

✅ Multi-step Zaps and advanced features help create powerful workflows.

✅ Optimizing performance and troubleshooting ensures reliability.

✅ Security best practices protect your data and privacy.

✅ Zapier has real-world applications across businesses, individuals, and remote teams.

Final Encouragement

Automation is not just about saving time—it's about working smarter. By using Zapier effectively, you can streamline your workflow, reduce repetitive tasks, and focus on more important work.

No matter where you started, by now, you have the knowledge and tools to build powerful automations. So go ahead—start experimenting, create smarter workflows, and unlock the full potential of Zapier!

💡 **Next Steps:**

✓ Try building a **new Zap** today.

✓ Join **Zapier's online community** to learn from others.

✓ Continue exploring **advanced integrations** to expand your automation skills.

Happy Automating! 🎉

8.2 Additional Resources and Communities

Zapier is a constantly evolving platform with new integrations, features, and best practices emerging all the time. To stay up-to-date and continue improving your automation skills, it's essential to take advantage of the wealth of resources available online. In this section, we'll explore various resources, including official documentation, learning platforms, blogs, communities, and expert-led courses, that will help you become a Zapier power user.

1. Official Zapier Resources

Zapier provides a comprehensive set of official resources that can help you troubleshoot issues, discover new integrations, and expand your automation knowledge.

1.1 Zapier Help Center

📌 **URL:** https://zapier.com/help

The Zapier Help Center is the best place to start when you have questions about using the platform. It includes:

- **Step-by-step guides** on setting up Zaps and using different features
- **Troubleshooting tips** for resolving errors and optimizing workflows
- **FAQs and solutions** for common problems

If you run into an issue with a Zap, checking the Help Center should be your first step before reaching out for additional support.

1.2 Zapier Learning Center

📌 **URL:** https://zapier.com/learn

Zapier's Learning Center offers structured courses for users of all levels. Some of the most popular courses include:

- **Zapier 101: Basics of Automation**
- **Advanced Zapier Features: Multi-Step Zaps, Paths, and Webhooks**

- **Automating Workflows for Marketing, Sales, and Customer Support**

These courses include video tutorials, quizzes, and interactive lessons to help reinforce learning.

1.3 Zapier Blog and Updates

📌 **URL:** https://zapier.com/blog

The **Zapier Blog** is a great way to stay informed about:

- **New app integrations** and features

- **Productivity hacks and automation strategies**

- **Case studies from real users** who have streamlined their work with Zapier

If you want to learn about the latest trends in automation and how other professionals use Zapier, this blog is an excellent resource.

---

2. Online Communities and Forums

Engaging with the broader Zapier community is a great way to learn from others, get help with complex workflows, and stay inspired. Below are some of the most active forums and online groups where Zapier users gather.

2.1 Zapier Community Forum

📌 **URL:** https://community.zapier.com

The **Zapier Community Forum** is an official discussion board where users can:

- **Ask for help** with troubleshooting issues

- **Share automation ideas** and learn from experts

- **Request new features and integrations**

Many Zapier employees and experienced users regularly participate in discussions, making this a valuable place to get insights and solutions.

2.2 Zapier Subreddit (r/Zapier)

📌 **URL:** https://www.reddit.com/r/Zapier/

The **r/Zapier subreddit** is an informal but active community where users share tips, ask for help, and discuss automation strategies. Some common topics include:

- *"How do I automate X task?"*

- *"What's the best way to integrate Zapier with my CRM?"*

- *"Is there a workaround for this specific Zapier limitation?"*

If you're looking for real-world examples and community-driven solutions, this subreddit is a great place to explore.

2.3 Zapier User Groups on Facebook and LinkedIn

There are several **Facebook and LinkedIn groups** dedicated to automation, where professionals exchange ideas and solutions. Some of the most popular groups include:

- **"Zapier Experts & Enthusiasts" (Facebook Group)**

- **"Automation & No-Code Community" (LinkedIn Group)**

These groups often feature discussions, webinars, and Q&A sessions with automation experts.

---

3. Third-Party Courses and Training

If you want to take your Zapier skills to the next level, there are several third-party platforms that offer in-depth courses on workflow automation.

3.1 Udemy: Zapier Courses

📌 **URL:** https://www.udemy.com

Udemy has multiple courses on Zapier, ranging from beginner to advanced levels. Some of the most popular ones include:

- *"Zapier Masterclass: Automate Your Work Without Coding"*

- *"Zapier for Entrepreneurs: Automate and Scale Your Business"*

Most Udemy courses are **affordable and include lifetime access**, so they're a great investment for long-term learning.

3.2 Coursera & LinkedIn Learning

📌 **Coursera:** https://www.coursera.org
📌 **LinkedIn Learning:** https://www.linkedin.com/learning

Both Coursera and LinkedIn Learning have courses on **automation and no-code tools**, often featuring Zapier as part of the curriculum. These courses are ideal for professionals looking to improve workflow efficiency.

3.3 YouTube Tutorials

📌 **URL:** https://www.youtube.com/results?search_query=zapier+tutorial

YouTube is an excellent free resource for Zapier tutorials. Some recommended channels include:

- *Zapier's Official YouTube Channel*

- *Automate.io (Now Part of Zapier)*

- *NoCode.Tech*

You'll find **step-by-step guides, case studies, and troubleshooting solutions** for various Zapier use cases.

---

4. Expert Zapier Consultants and Freelancers

If you're working on complex automations or need help optimizing existing workflows, hiring a **Zapier expert** might be a good idea.

4.1 Zapier Certified Experts

📌 **URL:** https://zapier.com/experts

Zapier has an official directory of **certified experts** who can help businesses with:

- *Custom workflow setups*

- *Integration with advanced tools (APIs, Webhooks, etc.)*

- *Optimization of existing Zaps*

Hiring a certified expert is recommended for companies that rely heavily on automation and want to maximize efficiency.

4.2 Hiring Freelancers on Upwork and Fiverr

📌 **Upwork:** https://www.upwork.com
📌 **Fiverr:** https://www.fiverr.com

If you need **affordable** Zapier support for small projects, freelancers on Upwork and Fiverr can assist with:

- *Building and optimizing Zaps*

- *Custom integrations and API connections*

- *One-on-one coaching sessions*

These platforms allow you to **hire experts on a per-task basis**, making it cost-effective for small businesses and individuals.

Final Thoughts

Mastering Zapier doesn't stop with this book. The more you explore and experiment, the more opportunities you'll find to automate your tasks and improve productivity. Whether you're learning from **official Zapier resources, online communities, courses, or experts**, staying engaged with the automation world will help you continuously optimize your workflows.

🚀 **Take the next step:**

- **Join a Zapier community today** and share your experiences

- **Experiment with new Zaps** and integrations beyond what you've learned so far

- **Keep learning and exploring** new features as Zapier continues to evolve

The future of work is **automation**, and with the right tools and knowledge, you can **save time, reduce errors, and focus on what truly matters.** Happy automating!

Acknowledgments

First and foremost, I want to express my deepest gratitude to **you**, the reader. Thank you for picking up *Smart Workflows with Zapier: A Step-by-Step Guide for Beginners*. Whether you are new to automation or looking to refine your skills, I hope this book has provided you with valuable insights and practical knowledge to streamline your workflows and boost productivity.

Writing this book has been an incredible journey, and knowing that it might help you save time, reduce repetitive tasks, and unlock new efficiencies in your work makes all the effort worthwhile. Your willingness to embrace automation and explore new tools like Zapier is what drives innovation and efficiency in today's digital world.

I also want to extend my appreciation to the **Zapier team** for creating such a powerful platform that empowers individuals and businesses to automate tasks without needing to write a single line of code. Their dedication to simplifying automation has made it possible for countless users to work smarter, not harder.

To the **Zapier community**, thank you for sharing your insights, tips, and real-world use cases. The collaborative spirit within the automation space is truly inspiring, and I encourage all readers to continue learning and engaging with fellow automation enthusiasts.

Finally, if you found this book helpful, I would greatly appreciate it if you could **leave a review** or share your thoughts. Your feedback not only helps other readers but also encourages me to continue creating content that supports your learning journey.

Remember, automation is a journey, not a destination. Keep experimenting, refining, and expanding your workflows. The possibilities with Zapier are endless, and I can't wait to see how you use automation to transform your work and life.

🚀 **Here's to working smarter and unlocking new efficiencies!**

Thank you, and happy automating! 🎉

www.ingramcontent.com/pod-product-compliance
Lightning Source LLC
LaVergne TN
LVHW062306060326
832902LV00013B/2079